The Modern Scientist–Practitioner

The Modern Scientist–Practitioner argues for a radical rethink of how we understand the science–practice relationship and the notion of the scientist–practitioner model.

Drawing on the latest innovations and research from the fields of anthropology, industry, philosophy, psychology and science, David Lane and Sarah Corrie present a new vision of the scientist–practitioner model that is dynamic, contextualized and synergistic. Subjects covered include:

- innovation and improvization: the unacknowledged world of the creative scientist–practitioner;
- what kind of scientists are we? Re-examining the nature of scientific knowledge;
- acquiring the art of reasoning: straddling the worlds of rigour and meaning;
- arriving at shared psychological narratives: formulation and explanation;
- the scientist–practitioner in applied psychology settings;
- learning for tomorrow: professional survival in an uncertain world.

This timely and thought-provoking book will appeal to professionals at all stages of their careers, including psychologists of all disciplines, researchers, educators, policy-makers, health-care professionals and students.

David A. Lane is Research Director at the International Centre for the Study of Coaching at Middlesex University and Director of the Professional Development Foundation. He chairs the BPS Register of Psychotherapy and is convenor of the EFPA Psychotherapy Group.

Sarah Corrie is an Associate of the Professional Development Foundation and the University of London. She trained as a clinical psychologist and, in addition to running her own practice, is a member of British Actors Equity and the Imperial Society of Teachers of Dancing. She is also a freelance writer, trainer and lecturer.

Guest contributors: Edward de Bono, Dennis Bury, Michael Cavanagh, Norah Frederickson, Anthony Grant, Val Haarbosch, Richard Kwiatkowski, Andy Miller, Ian Newey, Susan Maise Strauss, Barry Winter.

The Modern Scientist-Practitioner

A guide to practice in psychology

David A. Lane and Sarah Corrie

Routledge
Taylor & Francis Group

LONDON AND NEW YORK

First published 2006 by Routledge
27 Church Road, Hove, East Sussex, BN3 2FA

Simultaneously published in the USA and Canada
by Routledge
270 Madison Avenue, New York, NY 10016

Routledge is an imprint of the Taylor & Francis Group

Typeset in Times by Regent Typesetting, London
Printed and bound in Great Britain by MPG Books Ltd, Bodmin, Cornwall
Cover design by Design Deluxe

British Library Cataloguing in Publication Data
A catalogue record for this book is available from the British Library

Library of Congress Cataloging in Publication Data
Lane, David A., 1947-
   The modern scientist–practitioner : a guide to practice in psychology
 / David A. Lane and Sarah Corrie.
      p. cm.
   Includes bibliographical references (p.   ) and index.
   ISBN 1-58391-886-8 (hbk : alk. paper)
   1. Clinical psychology–Practice.   2. Psychology–Practice.   3. Psycho-
therapy–Practice.   4. Counseling–Practice.   I. Corrie, Sarah. II. Title.
   [DNLM: 1. Psychology, Clinical.   2. Psychology, Applied.   3. Psycho-
therapy.   4. Counseling.   WM 105 L265m 2006]
RC467.95.L36 2006
616.89–dc22
                                                    2005023321

ISBN13: 978-1-58391-886-9

ISBN10: 1-58391-886-8

For John R. Corrie,
who would have enjoyed reading this book.

Contents

Figures and Tables

Figures

Tables

Contributors

Andy Miller is Special Professor of Educational Psychology, School of Psychology, University of Nottingham and Senior Educational Psychologist, Derby City LEA. He has published widely and was co-founder of the Behaviour Support Conference which brings practitioners together to share their work and research.

Norah Frederickson is Professor of Educational Psychology, University College London and Senior Educational Psychologist, Buckinghamshire LEA. She has published widely and been actively involved in supporting professional development through her work with the British Psychological Society.

Dennis Bury is a lecturer in psychology at the Syracuse University London Program. Dennis is a Chartered Counselling Psychologist, a registered Cognitive Behavioural Psychotherapist and a registered Personal Construct Therapist, and works in independent practice.

Susan Maise Strauss holds a PhD in Counselling Psychology and is licensed as a psychologist in the state of Texas, and serves as Assistant Director of the Syracuse University London Program.

Val Haarbosch is Manager of the Sexually Appropriate Youngster's Project Norfolk Youth Offending Service.

Ian Newey is a Clinical Psychologist Bethel Child and Family Centre Norfolk and Waveney Mental Health Partnership NHS Trust.

Michael J. Cavanagh is the Deputy Director of the Coaching Psychology Unit, Sydney University, National Convenor of the Australian Psychological Society Interest Group in Coaching Psychology, and a practising coaching psychologist. At Sydney University, Michael teaches post-graduate level courses in coaching practice, coaching theory, systems and group dynamics. Michael's practice and teaching are informed by his background as a clinical psychologist and his research interest in the area of complexity.

Anthony M. Grant is the Director of the Coaching Psychology Unit, in the School of Psychology, University of Sydney. His PhD focused on delineating a psychology of coaching and examined the impact of coaching on mental health and goal attainment. In addition to teaching the Masters program in coaching psychology at the University of Sydney, he writes on coaching-related issues and maintains an executive coaching practice.

Richard Kwiatkowski has been focused on developing people for 20 years in a variety of contexts. He is a Chartered Occupational Psychologist and a Chartered Counselling Psychologist. He has worked within the NHS, as a senior organizational psychologist and manager at BT and as a consultant to many Public Limited Companies and several consultancies. He set up and was the director of the first UK Doctorate in Organizational Psychology. He is a former Chair of the British Psychological Society's Division of Occupational Psychology, member of the BPS Council and the Board of Directors.

Barry Winter is a Chartered Occupational Psychologist and consultant with extensive experience in the applications of psychology to business and people development. He now works in the School of Engineering (Warwick Manufacturing Group) at the University of Warwick.

Edward de Bono, psychologist and pioneer of lateral thinking is the leading authority of thinking skills. His many books, workshops and consultancies have resulted in the widescale acceptance of his approach to the development of thinking. His work has influenced organizations and individuals worldwide.

Foreword

This book provides a welcome addition to the relatively small number of texts that address the complex issue of what it means to be a 'scientist–practitioner'. The authors claim that they aim to explore what this means 'in the twenty-first century'. In the 50 or so years since the term was first applied to the education and practice of professional psychologists in Boulder, Colorado in 1949, the context in which professional psychologists work has changed almost unrecognizably. Most, though not all, countries in the Western world claim that the scientist–practitioner model informs their mode of professional training in psychology. However, how this model is interpreted varies considerably across different countries.

I would like to consider briefly three ways in which the context has changed. First the employment and working contexts of professional psychologists, second the rise of evidence-based practice, and considerations of what is meant by 'evidence', and finally the structural and organizational links between science and practice in psychology at a more international level.

Over the past 50 years, the number of professional psychologists has risen astronomically across the world, and recently particularly in the majority world. In many countries psychologists work in private practice, or private offices, which has led to a rapid increase in legal regulation of the title 'psychologist'. Legal regulation is linked to ethical practice and the enforcement of compliance to ethical codes, yet this raises fundamental questions concerning the scientific 'validity' and competence of much of psychologists' work (see Poortinga and Lunt, 1997). The rise of evidence-based or at least evidence-informed practice has led to demands for 'scientific' evidence to justify social interventions within our so-called 'knowledge-based' society (OECD, 2000). This implies a re-examination of the relationship between science and practice, and the ways in which the two can be linked for the production of knowledge. Internationally, the International Union of Psychological Science (IUPsyS), traditionally the home of fundamental science, has extended its remit to cover psychological practice, acknowledging that the separation makes little sense substantively and is now an anachronistic and artificial distinction. I explored some of these issues ten years ago when it appeared to me that the claim by educational psychologists to be practising as 'scientist–practitioners' was being undermined by the context in which this group found themselves (Lunt, 1996).

For these and many other reasons this volume is timely and we should all welcome it. The authors are well-qualified to write such a book. They have managed to provide a coherent account of a 'modern' scientist–practitioner model, and have attracted additional authors to cover the specific areas within professional psychology. This means that the book has the advantages of presenting a generic model of professional or applied psychology, which may then be applied to the particular context of practice (clinical, counselling, educational, occupational and so on). This fits well with the model currently being developed as a European standard for psychologists' training and practice through the European Diploma in Psychology.

As the authors claim, 'at the turn of the century, our professional lives are being shaped by an increasingly complex array of social, professional and political forces' (p. 9). We are, as it were, at a crucial point in the history of the profession. It is, therefore, timely that we revisit the scientist–practitioner model and consider if this framework continues to serve as a useful basis for professional practice. David Lane and Sarah Corrie make a persuasive and coherent case that it not only continues to serve its purpose, but that it can be reinvigorated to inform and enhance our practice and to support us as we move forward to face the challenges of the twenty-first century.

Professor Ingrid Lunt
London
February, 2005

Acknowledgements

There are many people who have contributed to the development of this book and whose generosity, interest and support we would like to acknowledge.

We begin by thanking Joanne Forshaw, our editor at Routledge, for her faith in this project and her advice along the way. The ideas presented in this book have also benefited greatly from the contributions of those who gave us permission to use, quote and in some cases, reproduce their work. We would particularly like to thank David Berliner, Clare Crellin, Peter Critten, Lucy Edwards, Neil Fleming, Elena Manafi, Willem Kuyken, Ming-cheng Miriam Lo, Ingrid Lunt, Michael Rosenbaum, Keith Waldron and Jill D. Wilkinson. We are also grateful to the British Psychological Society for granting permission to reproduce their policy on continuing professional development and for allowing us to reference the subject benchmarks for psychology.

This book was written using the 'CNFL Authors Team Room', to share ideas and draft. Our thanks to Matt Dower of CNFL for creating and facilitating the team room. (Matt Dower matt@cnfl.co.uk). We also thank Annette Fillery-Travis and Peter Hoy for their help in reviewing the work in progress, and Sarah Raeburn for providing essential management support.

Finally, special thanks go to Diana Osborne for her critique, support and the title, and to Ian Lacey for his enthusiasm for this project, for critical review, and for devoting time and energy to its realization in many different ways.

Introduction

This book has been fuelled by a belief that there are many ways of being a professional psychologist. We celebrate this diversity, believing that it contributes to a rich tapestry of informed, effective and creative practices that can benefit an increasingly wide range of clients. However, such diversity also implies an inherent responsibility to define the psychology we practise and the type of identity we wish to inhabit. This includes defining the skills that underpin our work and identifying substantive frameworks that can help us reflect upon, critique and refine those skills in systematic ways.

We believe that the scientist–practitioner model offers a valuable framework for guiding the processes of critique and refinement and also represents, at least for some psychologists, an identity which informs the ways in which they approach their enquiries. However, in order to address the needs of professional psychologists today, we must think carefully about what exactly we mean when we describe ourselves as scientist–practitioners. The original vision developed in 1949 had key advantages for an embryonic profession, but does not meet the needs of a discipline that is now well-established, actively thriving and rapidly expanding. We need, therefore, to think about being a scientist–practitioner in new ways, to create frameworks that furnish our practice with a strong scientific foundation and which also enable us to innovate and create.

WHY WRITE A BOOK ABOUT BEING A SCIENTIST–PRACTITIONER?

The relationship between science and practice has, over the years, been hotly debated. Indeed, since its inception, the scientist–practitioner model has provoked considerable controversy, raising questions about whether it is possible to train psychologists to operate as both scientists and practitioners and whether applying science to human problems really is the optimum way of advancing professional practice. Every psychologist from undergraduate level upwards will be only too familiar with the debate surrounding the inherent tensions between science and practice where it has often been argued that:

- The discipline of science has proved insufficient to illuminate the muddled and murky realities of problems encountered in the 'real world'.
- Professional psychology practice has, in many ways, developed largely independently of the research literature that was supposed to guide it.

For every argument that has highlighted the advantages of psychologists maintaining their stance as scientist–practitioners equally convincing arguments have demonstrated the inappropriateness of the model in practice. For there is no mistaking the fact that the two disciplines have lived in parallel, but in many ways unconnected, worlds, each driven by different priorities, languages and technologies.

Perhaps, in view of these difficulties, it would be better to consign the scientist–practitioner model to history and begin a search for something that creates a more accurate fit with the realities of professional practice. However, even if that were the ideal scenario, the matter is not that simple.

In recent years, the relationship between science and practice has taken on a new mantle within the context of a broader preoccupation with effectiveness and accountability. For psychology, as well as other professions, the emphasis has shifted increasingly towards the notion of evidence-based, or evidence-informed practices, a requirement that aims to ground our interventions within the latest research findings. If we add to this the concepts of practice-based knowledge, service-planning initiatives, knowledge management and the contribution of so-called 'new science', a cocktail of models and frameworks begins to emerge.

Are these ideas offering something essentially new, or do they merely represent a rehashing of an old idea from a new angle? Whatever the answer, one thing is certain: these developments add another dimension to the question of what is meant by ethical and effective practice and pose new questions and dilemmas that as professional psychologists, we have to learn to navigate.

So why write a book about being a scientist–practitioner? Simply, we are writing this book because we believe it needs to be written. The demands faced by applied psychologists in their day-to-day work are legion and, over the course of this century, promise to become more so. The ability to achieve and sustain effective practice requires a high level of skill in different domains and at multiple levels. Embedded within this is also the expectation that psychologists will make informed choices about their needs for continuing professional development and behave in ways that are consistent with the code of conduct of their professional bodies: all within work settings that are constantly evolving, multi-professional and, arguably, increasingly complex. However, the ways in which psychologists are to respond to these changing circumstances and achieve and maintain the required competencies and standards are seldom clearly articulated. Knowledge of the precise components of practice, what makes one practitioner more effective than another, and frameworks for thinking about how we should develop our skills over the course of our careers are all emerging as areas of concern.

We consider that the skills required of the psychologist today could be understood as falling within four main themes which we propose as a useful framework for exploring what it means to be a modern scientist–practitioner. These themes, which emerge in different forms throughout the chapters of this book, are as follows:

- The ability to think effectively. This encompasses the full range of practitioners' intellectual skills including reasoning, judging, decision-making and problem-solving, as well as understanding the implications of using theoretical and methodological frames of reference that have been drawn from diverse and sometimes conflicting traditions.
- The ability to weave the information we gather into a story (or formulation), grounded in psychological concepts, that has substantive implications for change.
- The ability to act effectively. This refers to the ways in which we intervene, how we translate theoretical constructs into workable intervention strategies and how we design intervention plans according to the needs of individual clients. We would include within this the ability to create, innovate and invent.
- The ability to critique our work in systematic ways. This somewhat broad category encompasses any vehicle we use (officially or unofficially) to evaluate ourselves and our actions. Sources that support this may be as diverse as moments of private reflection, relevant reading, personal audits, use of supervision and choices about continuing professional development. For some, it may also include a commitment to personal development in the form of coaching or personal therapy. Most significantly for scientist–practitioners, however, we would see this as a commitment to the use of scientific enquiry to guide and evaluate their work.

Of course, these skills are intimately connected. Intervening in any meaningful sense relies on an ability to make decisions, problem-solve and think about the arena of an intervention in systematic ways. Similarly, thinking without doing, without translating ideas into specific methodologies to create change would, for the applied psychologist, be a largely pointless exercise. It will be evident that without the capacity to be creative, practice can become formulaic, unrewarding and ultimately unresponsive to the needs of our clients. However, creativity which remains unfettered by the discipline of systematic evaluation will fall victim to individual whim and could, at worst, result in malpractice. The ability to reflect upon and critique one's work is ultimately essential in bringing all these resources together in a meaningful and effective way.

In addressing the question of what it means to be a modern scientist–practitioner we have tried to take account of all of these strands. It is our belief that the scientist–practitioner model is not about trying to 'glue together' science and practice in some counterintuitive way, but about an approach to professional practice that encompasses rigour, science, artistry and ingenuity. It is not our intention to mourn once again the difficulties inherent in uniting science and practice and to pronounce some ultimate verdict on whether the model is viable or untenable. Rather, our intention is to move beyond these well-worn debates, to think about the challenges of being a practitioner and to offer a range of ideas and resources which we hope will illuminate rather than obscure.

Before we begin, we must acknowledge the underlying principle that has guided the development of this project. We believe that the scientist–practitioner model enables us to respond effectively to the demands we face in our current work settings and helps equip psychologists to respond to the challenges of the future. However, it makes no sense to us to argue that there is any single scientist–practitioner model. The realities of our work settings and the complexities of professional practice dictate otherwise, requiring considerable flexibility and diversity in order to achieve consistently effective results.

Contrast, for example, the priorities of an organizational psychologist whose task is to identify the impact of team relationships on organizational success, with the work of a forensic psychologist who is responsible for producing a report to guide risk management in the context of sentencing and future care. Could we really be justified in proposing that these professionals do, or should, act according to the dictates of one model simply because they both share the title of psychologist?

Our position is that they cannot and should not and so differences of perspective are to be welcomed. If we welcome such diversity, it follows that being a scientist–practitioner cannot be encapsulated within any one descriptive or explanatory model. Just as it would be difficult to suggest that one model could adequately capture, let alone guide, the activities of psychologists working in settings as diverse as industry, schools, or secure mental health facilities, so too it would be unwise to present one single model as 'the answer' for which psychologists have been waiting. Despite an authorized version, we are all operating with our own idiosyncratic definitions of the scientist–practitioner model. The question is, are some versions more helpful than others – and which ones do we want to nurture for the future of our profession?

Even closer to home than these hypothetical scenarios, are the differing viewpoints of the authors themselves. In coming together for the purposes of collaborating on this book, we were aware from the first of subtle differences in how we viewed the scientist–practitioner debate. These were reflected in more obvious external influences, such as the clients with whom we work and differences in where and how we offer our services. They were also revealed in less tangible influences such as how we were each inducted into the worlds of science and practice, how we have been influenced by various teachers along the way and how we have responded to opportunities and obstacles presented to us over the course of our careers. Add to this the influence of personal values and idiosyncratic assumptions about what 'really' makes practice effective and it is hardly surprising that differences of perspective emerge. However, our position has been to view these differences as part of the creative tension that has characterized the relationship between science and practice itself. We have not aimed to iron them out, to reach some unified, polished or even definitive suggestion about what the scientist–practitioner model should be. Instead, we have aimed to celebrate the diversity of ideas and approaches to professional practice, some of which are represented in this book.

We would not, of course, want to suggest that psychologists are so diverse in their approach that they have nothing in common. This would eliminate any hope of disciplined enquiry, of informed decision-making and of critiquing and refining our practice. If this were so, then psychology as a discipline would be in chaos and professional practice would be unrecognizable. This, clearly, is not the case.

In trying to identify what it means to be a scientist–practitioner in the twenty-first century, we can be reassured to learn that there is something that connects us all, a fabric of ideas, values and traditions that binds all psychologists to their discipline, however extreme the differences between us might sometimes seem. For embodied within the scientist–practitioner model is something much more fundamental than any single activity or technique. Our task, as authors of this book, is to explore and contribute to a better understanding of the essence of this something so that we can draw upon it more effectively and with greater awareness.

AN OVERVIEW OF THIS BOOK

We hope that each of the chapters will hold something of value to all psychologists, whatever their stage of professional development. For those at an early stage of their careers, who are perhaps encountering the breadth and diversity of psychology for the first time through undergraduate and other higher education programmes, we invite you to familiarize yourselves with some of the fundamental debates concerning the relationship between science and practice that have informed the development of professional psychology. These will be influencing how you are now being taught. We invite you to use each chapter as a way of developing your essential framework for psychology and to think about some of the skills that are deemed crucial to the profession.

For those now committed to a specific professional pathway within psychology, we invite you to use this book to revisit some of the ideas you acquired during your training and to clarify which ideas are still valuable and which now need to be discarded. We also hope to assist you in identifying some new approaches that you can incorporate within the existing framework of values and principles that guide what you do.

For those already very familiar with the debate on the relationship between science and practice, and who are experienced practitioners, we offer this book as one of many possible frameworks for reflecting on your stage of career development, opening up new creative possibilities and examining (or re-examining) ideas with which you might now wish to experiment.

We have tried to reflect different strands of the tension between science and practice in the chapters that follow, with each one addressing what we see as some of the fundamental questions that face us as scientist–practitioners.

We start in Chapter 1 with the original context of the scientist–practitioner model in clinical psychology as a response to the demands of societies emerging from years of war. Science was seen as the source from which practice could be derived. The different versions of this model in the USA and UK are presented as they reflect differing views on the purpose of psychology and the contribution we should offer. The challenges we faced, the evolving forms of practice and the beginnings of doubt about the role of science in practice are discussed.

Chapter 2 examines the effectiveness of our reasoning and decision-making skills. The tension here is that as 'scientists' our decisions should be the product of rational criteria, logically applied. Apparently, however, they are full of inconsistency and bias. How do we make sense of and resolve this discrepancy? What frameworks exist for enabling us to enhance our reasoning skills?

Chapter 3 examines the role of formulation; that is, the way in which we use psychological language to construct coherent stories about the puzzles we encounter in our day-to-day work. By providing us with systematic frameworks against which we can test the validity of our ideas formulation has, arguably, been one way we have attempted to manage the tension that surrounds our ability to make accurate decisions. Yet the concept itself is contentious and raises disputes about what the term 'formulation' actually means, to whom the formulation belongs (psychologists or their clients), what frameworks exist to enable us to formulate more accurately and whether arriving at a useful formulation is more important than arriving at a 'correct' one.

Chapter 4 examines the ways in which psychologists might critique and refine their use of creativity. Arguably the most neglected topic in the scientist–practitioner debate, the art (as opposed to science) of skilled practice involves being able to improvise and invent in response to novel situations. The tension here is how we marry up the demand for rigour and accuracy with the need to be creative and expansive. How can we engineer desired outcomes systematically when the skills we use to do so may involve a realm of knowing that is qualitatively different from our instrumental problem-solving and other reasoning skills, based in rationality?

Chapter 5 leads into a consideration of the ever-present and hotly debated tension between science and practice. It asks the question, what sort of scientist should scientist–practitioners aim to be? Is the tension between science and practice inevitable, or is it the result of allying ourselves too closely with one story about the nature of scientific knowledge? How, if at all, would changing our model of science help us explore our work from new perspectives?

Chapter 6 examines our identity as scientist–practitioners. We pull together our thinking about the role of the scientist–practitioner in the arena of professional practice. We look at the development of professions and the social embeddedness of practice. Our relationship to the state through credentialing raises concerns about the denial of agency to our clients, by dependence on authorized forms of knowledge. We argue that we must examine the skills we need for a more diverse approach to practice. This leads us to a reformulation of the scientist–practitioner model as a distinct form of professional identity.

This is followed by a series of chapters from our guest contributors who share the type of scientist–practitioner identity they inhabit and describe how this identity impacts on their work. Each contributor examines one or more themes outlined in the first six chapters and applies them to their own area of interest. We have not set out to represent all forms of applied practice as there are too many, but rather to identify some of the issues that arise in practice for us as scientist–practitioners and to share ways in which different psychologists, from different disciplines, have responded to these issues.

The future and the role of continuing professional development to our own practice and our credibility as a profession is explored in our final chapter, Chapter 13. Psychology takes its place alongside other offers in the market place, so we need to consider what we bring that adds value and how our position as scientist–practitioners contributes to that value. The implications for public policy in research funding is discussed as part of the question of the type of scientist we seek to be and how different modes of knowledge are prioritized. Issues for the future of our practice are outlined.

Drawing the previous chapters together, we set out in our conclusion to describe what this new vision of the scientist–practitioner model might look like. Avoiding a 'hard line' view that equates the model with any particular method or function, we abandon scientism as the foundation of a modern scientist–practitioner model in favour of a broad approach to enquiry that embraces a multitude of purposes, perspectives and processes. This leads us towards our conclusion: namely that a reformulated scientist–practitioner model is viable, retains rigour and acknowledges the social and the scientific in our work. It will necessitate, however, the promotion of multiple narratives and emergent identities rather than being bound by any set of activities based on a 50-year-old definition of what it is to be a professional.

Throughout this book, you will find references to material from fields as diverse as psychology, philosophy, science, industry and inspirational literature. This diversity is intentional and does not, we believe, in any way detract from the rigour and discipline to which psychology appropriately aspires. The study of human experience and behaviour is a complex endeavour and so we have cast our net more widely than has traditionally been the case when debating the place of the scientist–practitioner model in our work. By including the contribution of different disciplines we recognize that there are multiple ways of making sense of the phenomena we seek to understand. The aim is to broaden the range of options we have available to us, to be open to the insights from diverse sources and to pool these insights for our individual and collective benefit. We encourage you to approach each chapter in a spirit of enquiry and to explore how each of the ideas and frameworks presented might (or might not) relate to your own practice.

More specifically, embedded within each chapter are specific questions which represent signposts for personalizing each of the debates described. These signposts are pulled together in the Conclusion in the form of what we have termed 'a Reflective Tool'. This tool represents one means through which we can each consider our work from different perspectives and which we offer as an aid to reflective practice, supervisory discourses and career development. By engaging with the questions situated in the individual chapters, as well as with the Reflective Tool, we hope you can develop new insights into your philosophy of practice and that as a profession, we can find new ways of strengthening the links between our rhetoric and our reality.

As we begin the process of rethinking what it means to be modern scientist–practitioners, we recall the writer Katherine Paterson who reminds us that books enable us to enter another person's life in an imaginative way (cited in Ban Breathnach, 1999). This book can be seen as an invitation to enter imaginatively into your own life as a professional psychologist. We offer it to you in recognition of the extraordinary work you undertake each day in the service of your profession and the clients whose issues you seek to understand.

Chapter 1

What does it mean to be a scientist–practitioner? Working towards a new vision

I must create a system or be enslaved by another man's.

(William Blake)

Even when all the experts agree, they may well be mistaken.

(Bertrand Russell)

There can be few models of professional practice that have been subjected to such extensive scrutiny, such high levels of endorsement and such severe criticism as the scientist–practitioner model. However, despite the controversy which has surrounded this professional edifice, the last few years have witnessed a renewed interest in what it means to operate as a scientist–practitioner (Corrie and Callanan, 2000, 2001; Kennedy and Llewelyn, 2001; Manafi, 2004; Trierweiler and Stricker, 1998).

This re-emerging interest can be attributed to a number of factors. At the turn of the century, our professional lives are being shaped by an increasingly complex array of social, professional and political forces. These include substantial technological advances, an increased emphasis on consumer rights, the need to revise our theories of human experience in the light of cultural diversity and political issues relating to how (and which) psychological services are funded. We are, as Drabick and Goldfried (2000) observe, at a crucial point in our history, one which requires us to re-examine our identities, roles and activities in the light of those we work alongside. As part of this process of re-examination, we consider it vital to review our allegiance to the scientist–practitioner model and to ascertain if this framework can contribute to a robust future for our profession.

Of course, it is not the first time that psychology has faced such challenges. Over the course of its history, applied psychology has continually grappled with how best to respond to social need, how to define itself in ways that will ensure long-term survival and the extent to which it should aspire to the status of science or art. To address the questions that face us now, and to frame the chapters which follow we will, therefore, begin by revisiting some of the early influences on psychology's dialogues with science, dialogues from which a distinct vision of the scientist–practitioner model ultimately emerged. We also consider some of the opportunities and challenges that have arisen from attempting to forge an integrated relationship between science and practice and how a lack of clarity surrounding definition and function have impacted on psychologists at both an individual and collective level.

Although there have been several historical reviews of the scientist–practitioner model (see Barlow *et al.*, 1984; Trierweiler and Stricker, 1998), we make no apologies for revisiting the origins of the debate once again. Psychology is committed to grounding its knowledge within developmental and contextual frameworks. Given that the scientist–practitioner model emerged within a distinct zeitgeist, revisiting its origins can help us appreciate more fully the enormity of the task that faced our predecessors, thus enabling us to see its strengths and limitations in better perspective.

THE BIRTH OF THE SCIENTIST–PRACTITIONER MODEL: A VERY BRIEF HISTORY

The extent to which psychology should, or could, be scientifically driven is a debate that goes back to the dawn of its history. Both William James (1842–1910), credited with founding psychology in America, and Wilhelm Wundt (1832–1920), the founder of European psychology, had a keen interest in psychology's relationship with science, albeit arriving at different conclusions about what the nature of this relationship should be.

Wilhelm Wundt's vision of the science of psychology favoured experimentation. A physiologist by training, Wundt opened the first psychology laboratory in 1879 at the University of Leipzig in Germany where he and his colleagues inaugurated the scientific study of mental processes. Wundt believed that by identifying stimuli and reactions that could be measured, psychological processes could be open to experimental methods in a way that had formerly been considered impossible. It was this attempt to observe, measure and analyse phenomena such as thoughts and feelings under controlled conditions that marked European psychology's radical departure from philosophy and paved the way for a new era of psychology as a scientific enterprise.

Unlike Wundt, who was concerned with the quest for 'pure' knowledge, James believed that a psychology grounded in science could not advance our understanding of human experience in any definitive sense. Concerned with the more cognitive and teleological conceptions of individuals, James favoured a holistic worldview that embraced philosophical pragmatism: that is, that the truth of an idea needed to be demonstrated in practice. Truth, for James, was always relative and its ultimate test was the extent to which ideas were useful. Leary (1992) highlights two major features of James' perception of human understanding that are relevant to later debates about the scientist–practitioner model. The first is that all knowledge, including that derived from scientific data, is based on finding analogies or metaphors. The second is that analogies in any discipline, including science, should always be changing rather than fixed. Scientific knowledge is simply one of many, inevitably incomplete, explanations of human experience.

Within educational psychology, the role of science had also been debated. In his historical review, Berliner (1993) highlights the contribution of the philosopher and early psychologist Johann Herbart (1776–1841) whose disciples claimed that science had a central role to play in shaping education and that teaching methods should be the subject of formal scientific investigation. Later contributors, such as G. Stanley Hall (1844–1924) de-emphasized science as a laboratory-based activity in favour of a science that took place in naturalistic settings and was open to all, whilst John Dewey (1859–1952) saw psychological knowledge as needing to be filtered through the wisdom of the practitioner. These perspectives differed from the later vision of educational psychology developed by Edward Lee Thorndike (1874–1947) whose faith in experimental science over the practical wisdom of teachers contributed to a dismissive outlook on the knowledge base of the practitioner.

Although these early debates about the relationship between science and practice formed an influential backdrop against which more modern conceptualizations emerged, the official birth of the scientist–practitioner model can be attributed to the now famous conference held at Boulder, Colorado, in 1949, whose delegates were credited with the vision of professional practice that subsequently emerged. Proposed as the most appropriate framework for the training and professional practice of the then emerging profession of clinical psychology (Raimy, 1950), its aim was to train psychologists to work as both practitioners and scientists. Through conducting research and applying the results to practice-related puzzles, the partnership between science and practice would ensure that psychologists achieved a rigour in their clinical work that typified the academic world. This would not only ensure the systematic advancement of the discipline in ways that could be shared with the wider scientific community, but would also enable psychology to respond effectively to matters of social concern.

The relevance of psychological knowledge to societal issues had, of course, been of interest prior to 1949. Both World Wars had played a key role in 'midwifing' applied psychology, involving psychologists in the selection and assignment of personnel to army positions and later, calling on psychologists to act as paid advisors to industry, government and the military (Murphy et al., 1984). Following the Second World War there was a particular demand for practitioners who could assist with the rehabilitation of veterans and their reintegration into society. However, there were significant problems in applying existing psychological knowledge to the treatment of emotional distress and psychological disability. While there had been many contributions in the applied sphere up until the post-war era (including those in industrial, educational, and forensic areas), academic psychology had devoted its efforts principally to animal learning, resulting in a body of knowledge that could not be readily applied to social welfare (John, 1998).

These deficits led to a drive to create a new breed of psychologist who would be better equipped to respond to the health-care needs of the population. The creation of such a practitioner was fuelled further by what Drabick and Goldfried (2000) identify as three pivotal developments:

- The introduction of a training program for clinical psychologists, instituted by the Veterans Administration which provided (1) financial support for those wishing to pursue a career in professional practice and (2) clinical experience through access to the Veterans Administration's treatment centres.
- The establishment, by the American Psychological Association, of a Committee on Training which provided the Veterans Association with information on training schemes that were eligible to participate in Veterans Administration programs.
- The provision of grants by the United States Public Health Service to ensure that professional training programs would become more widespread and accessible.

As Drabick and Goldfried observe, these developments proved to be something of a mixed blessing. Whilst providing an incentive for psychologists to embark upon a clinical career, training programmes began to flourish in an idiosyncratic and unregulated fashion. Psychologists learned their trade through apprenticeships with more experienced practitioners, whose work was seen to be predicated on tradition, precedent or preference, rather than on any rigorous knowledge base. The lack of a collective vision on how psychologists were to be trained and monitored caused professional practice to be viewed with a certain amount of suspicion, which would need to be addressed if professional psychology was to secure its place in the post-war era. (As an aside, it should be noted that this suspicion of clinical practice had been long-standing. The first psychological clinic had in fact been opened in Philadelphia in the US in 1896, under the auspices of Lightner Witmer who pioneered a 'clinical method'. Reisman (1991), however, notes that this method was not greeted favourably by the American Psychological Association, partly because it was deemed to depart too greatly from the model of scientific psychology dominant at that time and also because the science of psychology was considered too embryonic to risk innovating in such an apparently radical manner. It was some time before psychology, as applied to the clinical domain, would be recognized as having a credible knowledge base.)

In the light of these growing concerns about the place of psychology in society, systematic planning for the future of the profession became a necessity. Sponsored by The National Institute of Mental Health and the American Psychological Association, the Boulder Conference drew heavily on the previous work of David Shakow and his colleagues (Shakow *et al.*, 1947) whose report had emphasized the central roles of diagnosis, therapy and research. The delegates at Boulder were assigned the onerous task of assessing existing psychological provision and predicting what would be needed in the future. Spanning an intensive two-week period, the debates examined topics as varied as the core curriculum, the relevance of the curriculum to social issues, relationships with other professions, accreditation of training programmes and funding for students. Faced with such a complex task, and in an attempt to secure the future of the profession, it is perhaps not surprising that the delegates arrived at a model which sought to furnish practice with the trappings of scientific respectability.

THE BRITISH VISION OF THE PARTNERSHIP BETWEEN SCIENCE AND PRACTICE

At the same time as these developments were occurring in the USA, similar challenges were confronting psychologists in Britain. British psychologists also needed a distinct framework for guiding their work that could secure the place of psychology in a changing social climate. However, under the influence of Hans Eysenck, arguably the most influential proponent of the profession during the post-war period, the British vision of the scientist–practitioner model was somewhat different from its American counterpart.

Rather than emphasizing the need to combine research and clinical interventions in the service of social need in the way that had been envisioned by Shakow and his colleagues, the British scientist–practitioner model diminished the role of therapeutic practice. In a statement which personifies this position, Eysenck spoke of therapy as 'essentially alien to the clinical psychologist' (1949: 174). Interpreting the scientist–practitioner model in the light of rigorous empiricism, Eysenck believed that the profession should concern itself solely with research and diagnosis, leaving the delivery of therapeutic interventions to psychiatry. As he argued, 'We must be careful not to let social need interfere with scientific requirements . . . Science must follow its course according to more germane arguments than possibly erroneous conceptions of social need' (1949: 173).

The emphasis on scientism was also endorsed by M.B. Shapiro (1955, 1957), another influential figure during this period. Appointed by Eysenck to run the clinical department at the Institute of Psychiatry, Shapiro developed Eysenck's vision of the clinical psychologist as diagnostician and researcher, emphasizing the study of the single case and the experimental method in the pursuit of empirically driven knowledge. Specifically, Shapiro pioneered a methodology which enabled assessment and conceptualization of psychiatric disorders in their clinical context. Its main assumption was that each client constituted a 'scientific puzzle' in his or her own right. Through applying general methods of experimental psychology in a special framework of learning theory, the psychologist could find ways to solve this puzzle.

Such a stance undoubtedly helped secure this branch of professional psychology as a scientific enterprise and, as in America, there were distinct political advantages from doing so. A direct appeal to the profession's scientific status enabled psychology to justify itself as a social institution and attract the prestige necessary for its survival. The emphasis on expertise in research design and diagnosis ensured that psychology would have a unique role to play in post-war health care (John, 1984), albeit a different one from psychology in the USA.

Eysenck's rejection of therapeutic practice as a legitimate activity for the scientist–practitioner soon became problematic. The close relationship between psychology and developments within the British health-care system meant that the profession evolved more closely in accordance with social welfare priorities than Eysenck had envisaged. As the National Health Service principally required skilled practitioners, psychologists became increasingly involved in providing clinical interventions, rather than assessments and diagnoses. In contrast to the Institute of Psychiatry's model of rigorous empiricism, psychologists began to embrace approaches to intervention that were more traditionally psychotherapeutic in orientation. Eysenck (1952) subsequently ignited the debate on the question of whether psychotherapy worked and concluded that it did not. He actively promoted behaviour therapy as a more appropriate alternative for the scientist–practitioner and insisted that therapy should be based on sound experimental work and theory development (Eysenck and Martin, 1987; see Lane, 1990 for a summary of this argument). As behaviour therapy proved successful in treating a range of problems, this further eased the introduction of a therapeutic component into the British scientist–practitioner model of applied practice.

Despite the ways in which professional practice has subsequently evolved, the scientist–practitioner model undoubtedly presaged the development of a new mindset about the place of psychology in a changing world. To meet social need, psychologists would not only need to deliver effective interventions but also contribute to the development of the knowledge base itself. The relationship between research and practice was reciprocal but the superiority of science was nonetheless assumed (Peterson, 1991). A similar perspective arose within educational psychology, influenced by Thorndike's positive regard for science as providing a foundation for education (Berliner, 1993). As Pilgrim and Treacher (1992) observe, however, this vision of the scientist–practitioner model left a legacy of underlying tension between research and practice which has had implications for psychologists ever since.

A TROUBLED RELATIONSHIP: THE PROBLEM OF INCOMPATIBILITY

It is one thing to espouse an ideal but quite another to implement it. Of all the criticisms levied against the scientist–practitioner model, perhaps the most resounding has been that it represents a vision of professional practice that can rarely, if ever, be fulfilled (Barlow *et al.*, 1984). This led Jones (1998) to argue that the scientific identity of the practitioner is in fact 'fraudulent' and should be abandoned in favour of a more honest account of how psychologists actually function. A similar case has been argued by Williams and Irving (1996) and Rennie (1994) who see the different priorities of scientist and practitioner as leading to an insurmountable rift in both activity and function.

One of the central difficulties in attempting to marry science and practice within a single model of practice, as noted previously by William James, is that scientists and practitioners have fundamentally different priorities. Whilst the scientist is arguably concerned with knowledge that is rigorous, objective and generalizable, the practitioner is more concerned with knowledge that is subjective, holistic and applicable to the individual (Meehl, 1954; Coan, 1979). Indeed, as Trierweiler and Stricker (1998) point out, even the delegates at the Boulder Conference were acutely aware of the inherent difficulties of integrating science and practice within a single framework; it was not assumed that training psychologists in research and practice would be sufficient to ensure involvement in both at a post-qualification level.

The apparent rift between science and practice was addressed in a subsequent conference in 1973. In contrast to that at Boulder, the Vail Conference (Korman, 1974) de-emphasized the scientist–practitioner model in favour of a practitioner-oriented approach to training programmes for clinical psychologists. The central argument proposed was that doctoral dissertations needed to be relevant to the delivery of social welfare. As trainees principally needed to develop an awareness of research and to acquire the ability to evaluate its implications for practice, extensive training in the production of empirical work was deemed unnecessary. The focus needed to be on the application of knowledge rather than the detailed specifics of experimental design.

If the work of scientists and practitioners is underpinned by different assumptions and priorities, it is not surprising that attempts to conjoin them have been beset with difficulties. In the context of applied practice, concerns have been raised about the extent to which the scientist–practitioner model enables psychologists to develop practice-based skills. Pottharst (1973), for example, pointed out that as originally defined, the model paid insufficient attention to how students were to achieve competence in clinical work, a concern echoed by Rachman who warned of the potential danger of the 'scientist . . . squeezing out the practitioner' (1983: p.xiii). This concern has been shared by Sheehan (1994) who argues that the scientist–practitioner model fails to equip trainees with the prerequisite skills for effective professional functioning.

Additional confirmation of the difficulties embedded within the scientist–practitioner model has come from the world of practice itself. In considering what professional psychologists *actually* do (as opposed to what official discourse says they *should* do), it has been pointed out that many psychologists are unlikely to engage in research once qualified (Nathan, 2000; Head and Harmon, 1990), that professional psychologists often rank research as a lower priority than service-related commitments (Allen, 1985) and that they may not even feel a need to read research (Nathan, 2000). This would appear to be endorsed by the oft-quoted finding that, for many years, the modal number of publications for clinical psychologists was zero (Levy, 1962; Norcross *et al.*, 1989).

Nowhere is the hiatus between science and practice more succinctly summarized than by Matarazzo, whose disillusionment with science was captured in a survey of practitioners by Bergin and Strupp (1972) and which feels as heretical today as it did then: 'even after 15 years, few of my research findings affect my practice. Psychological science per se doesn't guide me one bit . . . My clinical practice is the only thing that has helped me in my practice to date' (cited in Bergin and Strupp, 1972: 340).

Each of these critiques suggests the failure of science to inform the realities of practitioners' work. However, Dawes (1994) has argued that the converse is true: namely, that it is practitioners who have failed to pay sufficient heed to the scientific literature and in doing so have fallen short of their obligations to the societies they seek to serve. In his somewhat damning critique of professional practice, Dawes elevates the science–practice schism to the realms of professional responsibility. He argues that psychologists have consistently failed to use the research evidence to inform their work, relying instead on procedures of dubious validity such as professional experience and outdated technical procedures. As scientific knowledge about how to optimally address human needs is incomplete, he further argues that psychologists should restrict their work to areas where knowledge (particularly actuarial information) already exists.

A decade later, it would be difficult to argue convincingly that psychologists do not take account of the research literature in their work, particularly in the current climate which privileges the delivery of interventions that are informed by the available evidence (Department of Health, 1996, 1997). However, Dawes' argument remains persuasive by highlighting how, despite official endorsement of our allegiance to scientific knowledge, we often stray into territory that is far less rigorous.

It would seem, then, that claiming we are scientist–practitioners is not an entirely accurate representation of our roles and skills and that it may be time to replace this model with one that is more practitioner-oriented. However, others have warned of the danger of throwing out the baby with the bathwater and invite us to consider the relationship between science and practice anew. This is considered next.

THE CASE FOR SAVING THE SCIENCE–PRACTICE PARTNERSHIP

Despite its contentious history, the scientist–practitioner model has retained its supporters. Many training programmes in both clinical (O'Sullivan and Quevillon, 1992) and counselling psychology in the USA (Baker and Benjamin, 2000; Vacc and Loesch, 1994) continue to operate along scientist–practitioner lines. Indeed, in their study investigating anticipated developments in clinical training amongst trainers, trainees and regional clinical psychologists in Britain, Kennedy and Llewelyn (2001) found strong support for the prediction that the scientist–practitioner model would continue to be a major framework for training, albeit tempered by models of evidence-based practice, critical analytical skills and generic professional competences. Moreover, as the field of professional psychology continues to grow, it is interesting to note that a number of newer psychological professions such as counselling psychology (Woolfe and Dryden, 1996) and the psychology of coaching (Grant and Cavanagh, 2004) have chosen to embrace the scientist–practitioner model rather than promote an alternative.

These trends appear to be reflected in recent documentation by the British Psychological Society (2005) which, in detailing the subject benchmarks for psychology, identifies the scientist–practitioner model as central to the activity of applied practice. Within this framework, the emphasis is on the appropriate use of psychological knowledge in order to (1) deliver high quality client services; (2) work autonomously in complex settings and (3) draw upon psychological knowledge, skills, and theory to make professional judgements. Priority is given to the core skills of the applied psychologist (assessment, intervention and evaluation) and includes high levels of research skill and scholarship, as manifest in the ability to conduct relevant research and to apply research to practice.

A cynical view of these trends would be that, in the absence of any viable alternative, it would be professional suicide to state publicly that the scientist–practitioner model is unsustainable. However, there may be a more optimistic interpretation. For all its apparent flaws, it may be the case that embodied within the scientist–practitioner model are certain qualities that are deemed important for psychologists to retain.

Drabick and Goldfried (2000) amongst others (see Halgin, 1999; Nathan, 2000) have argued that the current professional climate necessitates our renewed commitment to the scientist–practitioner model so that we might distinguish ourselves from colleagues in medical, educational and social work settings. This echoes the earlier argument of Dosier (1947) who claimed that what makes psychology unique in comparison with medicine is its emphasis on research in conjunction with practitioner-based training.

It has also been proposed that the scientist–practitioner model represents a vehicle through which our knowledge of the human condition can systematically advance. Stoltenberg *et al.* (2000), for example, claim that the model provides a framework through which important scholarly and practice-based advances can continue to occur. In contrast to Matarazzo's dismissal of research as irrelevant to the practitioner's endeavours, Stoltenberg *et al.* argue that psychologists simply cannot be competent in the delivery of their practice unless they know how to evaluate it and that conducting one's own research is an essential precursor to understanding and utilizing the published research literature in an informed way. Thus, the scientist–practitioner model really represents what they term an integrated approach to knowledge.

Hoshmand and Polkinghorne (1992) have also suggested that separating science and practice creates an artificial distinction. However, the relationship between these two disciplines may take the form of more subtle synergies that are easy to overlook. Stricker (1992) argued this point convincingly when he highlighted that the impact of research on practice often occurs through an indirect 'meta-effect' whereby the research questions of one generation influence the professional developments of the next. Using psychotherapy outcome research as an example, he describes how the early research questions about whether therapy 'works' and 'which one works best' subsequently gave rise to distinct new therapeutic techniques, as each therapeutic tradition attempted to display its superiority. Similarly, he argues that the paradoxical status of equivalence amongst the different psychotherapies established in the 1970s led to the development of new types of research questions to overcome uniformity which moved therapeutic practice towards a more prescriptive outlook.

In a similar vein, Belar and Perry (1992) have proposed that the scientist–practitioner model provides an invaluable framework for theory-building whereby, through a systematic approach to enquiry, random observations can be shaped into hypotheses that presage the development of new theories and interventions. The influence of science is not always instantaneous (perhaps that is why we often mistakenly believe it is not occurring) but shapes how psychologists work in more subtle ways.

REDEFINING THE SCIENTIST–PRACTITIONER MODEL IN THE LIGHT OF MORE SUBTLE NUANCES

Recognition of a more complex relationship between our scientist and practitioner roles has given rise to a growth of interest in the different types of activities that might be encompassed under the scientist–practitioner umbrella. Crane and McArthur Hafen (2002) emphasize the scientist–practitioner model as integrating the three complementary roles of practitioner, consumer of research and producer of research. Unlike the evidence-based practitioner whose role is one of implementing specific interventions and consuming research to stay up to date, they propose that the scientist–practitioner is more concerned with integrating the consumption and production of research in practice with a distinct professional identity.

Milne *et al.* (1990) also point out that many of the debates which have discredited the scientist–practitioner model have relied on survey methods, which focus on a limited number of variables such as publishing quantitative studies in refereed journals. However, they argue that when a wider definition of research is adopted – a definition which encompasses publishing in non-refereed journals, preparing service evaluation documents, undertaking small-scale research projects and keeping up to date with scientific studies – a closer approximation to the ideal begins to emerge.

Intuitively, these broader definitions of the scientist–practitioner model make sense. Just as Stricker (1992) proposed that the research of one generation presages the practice-based developments of the next, so we could argue that a similar process occurs for each of us at an individual level. We can all, no doubt, identify some research study that either resonated with our own practice or struck us as completely irrelevant and which shaped our views about science and practice accordingly. Perhaps our choices around post-qualification specialization were also influenced by the current literature on outcome and effectiveness. Similarly, our own experiences of conducting research, on whatever scale, have the power to shape our outlook on the services we provide. In other words, the relationship between science and practice may be alive and well. However, the way in which we have constructed the scientist–practitioner debate may have prevented us from studying the more subtle interplay that takes place between them, including our own individual constructions of what being a scientist–practitioner is all about.

In their qualitative study examining beliefs about research and the scientist–practitioner model in the context of 'real-world' practice, Corrie and Callanan (2001) found marked variations in how the scientist–practitioner model was defined, which could be placed on a continuum of closed to open definitions. The most closed definition related to a model of science that prioritized prediction and control and the use of statistical testing, whilst the most open definition conceptualized the scientist–practitioner model as a spirit of enquiry whereby psychological evidence could be used in a more holistic way, according to the needs of a given enquiry. These definitions played a key role in shaping perceptions of its value and led Corrie and Callanan to conclude that the scientist–practitioner model no longer represents a single way of working but comprises more idiosyncratic definitions, models of practice and systems of values which should become a focus of exploration, investigation and classification in their own right. A similar conclusion was reached by Manafi (2004) who also found that perceptions of the scientist–practitioner model were closely tied to psychologists' epistemological assumptions. Higher levels of endorsement were associated with viewing the approach as an 'integrative tool' that permitted use of a range of methods and outlooks on knowledge which in turn promoted a mutually informative relationship between science and practice.

Of course, adopting a broader vision of the scientist–practitioner model raises further questions. As Milne *et al.* (1990) highlight, a more inclusive definition leads to very different impressions of its characteristics and functions. This leaves applied psychology with important questions including:

- What do practitioners mean when they define themselves as scientists?
- Who is entitled to use the title of scientist–practitioner? Should it be for everyone or reserved for those who have a specific status in relation to research (e.g. those producing data that can influence practice on a wide scale)?
- To what extent is it legitimate for the profession to encompass multiple definitions of the scientist–practitioner model and for each of us to carve out our own definitions according to the nature of our work and the values that underpin it?
- How do we protect our identities, roles and activities if we do not have recourse to one over-arching framework through which we can justify and publicize our work?

It would seem then, that a central task at the current time is to decide whether the scientist–practitioner framework represents a single model or a meta-model.

Each position has strengths and limitations. For example, aiming for one model may be simpler, clearer and potentially more rigorous. However, it may also result in a lack of flexibility and alienate a proportion of the profession in a way that seems to have been characteristic of the debate so far. Alternatively, construing it as a meta-model may offer maximum flexibility but lead to diluted versions that permit a loss of rigour in how we practise or even threaten our unique status among other professions. How we define the scientist–practitioner, and the extent to which it represents a single or meta-model are questions which, we believe, deserve our individual and collective attention as we contemplate the future of the profession.

SOME INITIAL THOUGHTS ON A SCIENTIST–PRACTITIONER MODEL FOR THE TWENTY-FIRST CENTURY

Whatever our individual reactions to the outcome of the Boulder Conference, what is clear is that embedded within the scientist–practitioner model is a certain moral imperative to ensure optimum effectiveness. However, beyond this we can assume little consensus of definition, role or function. At the current time, there seems to be more than one way of being a scientist–practitioner (Kennedy and Llewelyn, 2001).

Different interpretations of the scientist–practitioner model are hardly surprising when we appreciate that the debate has often 'lumped together' myriad functions in a way that tends to confuse mission and method. Thus, the scientist–practitioner model has been described as a vehicle for protecting our unique identity and status; a framework for providing the profession with a clear direction; a way of making training and practice more uniform; a means of making practice socially relevant and protecting the public against poor practice and an approach to enquiry that can inform our practice in systematic ways. The above functions are not necessarily congruent, however. The matter is complicated still further in that the original debate was weighted heavily around clinical psychology. Yet applied psychology has expanded significantly since 1949. What is meant by science and practice in these contexts? Does science equate with scientism or do we need a broader interpretation of both science and practice to reflect the diversity of situation and context in which psychologists now find themselves?

These questions become even more significant when we appreciate that certain branches of professional psychology are starting to define and work towards the creation of a new type of practitioner, one which is based just as much on an individualized career pathway as it is on activity or role. One striking example of this is the introduction of the Register of Psychologists Specialising in Psychotherapy (British Psychological Society, 2003), which emphasizes career development as taking place through the personalization of knowledge. Rather than measuring applicants against a list of pre-established criteria, the process of registration seeks to establish a 'personal ownership' of knowledge demonstrated through the overall coherence of an individual's portfolio of career experiences.

These changes illustrate a growing interest in the development of a cohesive professional identity that capitalizes on personalized approaches to learning rather than criteria that are externally imposed. Within the context of these more individualized career pathways, we must think again about how we can arrive at a suitable and beneficial relationship with science.

The necessity of practice-led enquiry has been endorsed particularly strongly by counselling psychology which has actively promoted alternatives to the narrow definitions of science which have perpetuated the scientist–practitioner divide. Duerzen-Smith (1990), for example, has argued that psychology has traditionally organized itself around discovering objective facts rather than exploring what it means to be human, with all the dilemmas and choices that this entails. For her, psychology needs to embrace more fully its artistic and dialogic dimensions over and above what she sees as its preoccupation with overly narrow scientific principles. As a discipline strongly connected with humanistic values and principles, counselling psychology argues for a scientist–practitioner model that is practice-led, phenomenologically-focused, respectful of diversity and interested in the uncovering of subjective truths (Woolfe and Dryden, 1996).

This sentiment has been echoed within other branches of applied psychology. In clinical psychology, for example, Trierweiler and Stricker (1992) have introduced the concept of 'the local clinical scientist'. As a form of professional identity, the local clinical scientist is construed as a 'critical investigator' who draws upon a range of knowledge (including research, theory, general knowledge of the world and personal experience) to develop hypotheses about clinical problems. The aim is both to facilitate understanding of human phenomena in the context of specific enquiries and also to encourage appreciation of how these phenomena relate to broader notions about the nature of science.

Within educational psychology, Berliner (1992) and Snow (1981) have argued that the task facing the profession is essentially one of 'psychologizing' about the educational issues with which real-world settings present us, rather than applying knowledge to people and situations in a linear fashion. Berliner (1992) argues that this requires us to bring psychological ideas to the problems encountered in the classroom, regardless of what those problems are.

Similarly, from an organizational perspective, Argyris (1999) remarks on the necessity of aiming for 'actionable' or 'usable' knowledge, which can assist practitioners in the process of implementing policies and procedures. The role of science, he argues, is not to provide definitive judgements but rather to make an offering to the practitioner in the form of hypotheses that are relevant to, and testable in, the organizational context in which they occur. Our science, it seems, needs to be increasingly practical.

Thus, despite its chequered history, we are witnessing a renewed allegiance to the scientist–practitioner model, at least in certain sectors of applied psychology practice. Amongst the diverse disciplines which make up the profession, there is a growing awareness of the need to find a mid-point between the purely pragmatic and the experimentally rigorous, suggesting a more liberal, flexible and stakeholder-focused basis for our science. This implies that the scientist–practitioner model is a workable reality, albeit one that first requires a new vision of its aims and functions.

A suitable analogy for this process of 'revisioning' comes from Wheatley (1999) who, in her work on organizations, explains how a structure that is created in response to a profound sense of calling can gradually acquire a rigidity that impedes its effectiveness. When a structure reaches such a stage, it must fall apart in order to reorganize itself. If we apply this outlook to the scientist–practitioner debate we could argue that although developed with sound intentions, the model became a rod for our own backs which is now being deconstructed in order to reconfigure more adaptive versions that create a closer 'fit' with the realities of our work. Our task then changes. We can free ourselves from the notion that being a scientist–practitioner means working according to the dictates of any specific model or activity in favour of developing operational systems that enable us to organize and develop our skills in a systematic way. Through redefining the scientist–practitioner model as an operational system we can perhaps move beyond the problematic legacy of the past, in order to construct a more helpful one for the future. Some of the different ways in which this might be achieved are explored in the chapters which follow.

Chapter 2

Acquiring the art of reasoning: straddling the worlds of rigour and meaning

Doubt may be an uncomfortable position, but certainty is a ridiculous one.

(Voltaire)

We have become obsessed with analysis and spend far too much time on analysis and far too little on design.

(Edward de Bono)

As professional practitioners, we take pride in our skills in judgement and reasoning. In applying ourselves to the puzzles we encounter in our work, we promote ourselves as offering perspectives and solutions that are substantively different from those that our clients can arrive at unaided. Arguably, this is what justifies our claims to a professional status. But how exactly do we make these judgements? Presumably, what separates us from the public we seek to serve is our familiarity with the knowledge base of psychology and our ability to apply it in systematic ways. This implies an approach to decision-making that is rational and logical.

Rationality and logic are greatly esteemed in our society. Enshrined in our cultural preoccupation with murder mysteries and detective stories, these styles of reasoning follow a clear-cut sequence. The problem (the committing of a crime, to continue with the detective analogy) is unambiguous from the outset. The task that must be undertaken (in this case, by the detective) is the systematic process of evidence-gathering from which the facts eventually emerge. This leads predictably towards the resolution of the problem (namely the identification of the perpetrator and thus, the solving of the crime).

Unfortunately, however, the world of applied psychology affords no such luxury. As Noam Chomsky somewhat pessimistically, observed, 'As soon as questions of will or decision or reason or choice of action arise, human science is at a loss' (1978; cited in Knowles, 1999: 12).

If, as Noam Chomsky suggests, human science has largely failed to inform us about the complexities of decision-making, it is perhaps because it has clung too rigidly to the detective style of reasoning. The problems with which psychologists are generally concerned do not come clearly defined and neatly packaged, but have to be assembled, even crafted, from an array of complex and potentially competing demands and priorities. How, then, can we be certain that the decisions we make are the right ones?

In this chapter we consider some of the attempts that have been made to investigate psychologists' decision-making and examine what these approaches can and cannot tell us about our reasoning skills in professional practice. We propose that many of the existing attempts to improve our decision-making have fallen short of what is actually required of applied psychologists and attempt to address this by identifying some tentative frameworks for better understanding, articulating and developing what we term the 'art of reasoning'. We use the term 'art' here, to encompass all aspects of professional thinking, including decision-making, judging and choice-making and also to reflect the fact that psychologists' reasoning abilities depend just as much on creative design as they do on analysis and evaluation.

As our decisions depend, at least in part, on the ways in which we each approach the task of reasoning we invite you first to reflect on how you address the types of puzzles that confront you in your day-to-day practice, including times when effective judgements came easily and occasions when they seemed to elude you. As different ideas are presented, we invite you to consider how each might enable you to structure your investigations differently, with what types of consequences for your enquires, your outcomes and your clients.

THE ART OF REASONING: A NEGLECTED DIMENSION OF THE SCIENTIST–PRACTITIONER DEBATE

It is a curious fact that in the scientist–practitioner debate, very little attention has been paid to how psychologists make decisions. For example, Raimy's (1950) early insistence on the need for 'rigorous thinking' appears to have been couched within the language of science and its methodologies rather than the ways in which psychologists should go about defining problems, discriminating between intervention options and devising novel solutions. As Ivey *et al.* (1999) point out, the importance of making effective judgements is impressed upon practitioners from the earliest stages of their careers, but there has traditionally been a lack of formal guidelines on how to achieve this. This omission has clearly put psychologists at a disadvantage.

Why might the reasoning skills of the practitioner have been neglected? One possible explanation is the tendency in Western culture to privilege certain types of knowledge over others. This is explored further in Chapter 5, but for now it is sufficient to note that the reasoning skills of the individual practitioner have been seen as distinctly inferior to the so-called 'factual evidence' acquired through empirical investigation. Drawing upon Kaminski's (1970) categorial system (cited in Kanfer and Nay, 1982), for example, James (1994) proposes that we can represent different forms of knowledge on a hierarchy of distinction. At the top of the hierarchy lie empirically derived data: the most prestigious and thus the most highly sought-after type of knowledge. However, such data are often unavailable and so, where necessary, James acknowledges that we should look to theory to guide us. Similarly, when theoretical knowledge is lacking, practices established through shared professional beliefs and the common practice of peers represent valid alternatives. The practitioner's individual experiences which stem from being part of a wider social community are also relevant, but really only preferred when other forms of knowledge are absent. We can speculate then that the art of reasoning has been a neglected topic in the scientist–practitioner debate, partly because it has been considered less prestigious (and, therefore, less desirable) than the empirical data afforded by our science.

Categorizing our knowledge hierarchically, according to its origins, can prevent us from becoming overly attached to our own ideas and opinions and encourage us to look to forms of evidence that are free from the influence of our individual predilections. However, organizing information in this way also carries an implicit assumption about the nature of knowledge: namely that the more objective it is, the more credible it becomes. This assumption has proved highly influential and has spawned a tradition of investigating our decision-making abilities that has had significant implications for how our reasoning skills have come to be understood and critiqued.

HOW RATIONAL ARE WE? THE SHORTFALL BETWEEN ACTUARIAL AND PROFESSIONAL PREDICTION

Recent decades have witnessed a growing interest in the decisions made by applied psychologists, with a particular emphasis on information-processing as a conceptual model for investigating them (Ivey et al., 1999). Succinctly, this approach advocates that decisions are made through a series of logical, rational and sequential stages whereby information received from the environment is processed to arrive at a valid representation of the external world. Essentially akin to the detective style of reasoning, this approach focuses on the accuracy of the decision made (Siegert, 1999), in other words, the 'output' of the decision-making process.

The dominance of the information-processing model has resulted in a range of methods that examine how professional judgements compare with the rigorous and objective approach of statistical (or actuarial) prediction (Dowie and Elstein, 1988; Meehl, 1954, 1957).

Unfortunately, however, for a profession which claims to be based on a systematic approach to enquiry, the results have tended to prove far from favourable. In terms of the accuracy of professional judgement in early studies, Goldberg (1959) demonstrated that clinicians were no superior to secretaries, whilst Oskamp (1965) found no relationship between judgement accuracy and training. Comparisons between experienced and inexperienced therapists also found little benefit from experience on a number of measures (Carkhuf and Berenson, 1967). The way in which decision-making appears to have fallen short of statistical methods has led Meehl (1954, 1986) to conclude that the actuarial approach to making predictions has greater reliability and validity than predictions based on the clinical method. Consequently, it is argued that psychologists should restrict their work to actuarial data rather than poorly validated technical procedures based on clinical reasoning (see Dawes, 1994; Dawes *et al.*, 1989).

Studies of decision-making in cognitive case formulation show reasonable levels of agreement between practitioners at a descriptive level but modest agreement at the interpretive level (Bieling and Kuyken, 2003). However, Luborsky and Crits-Cristoph (1990) have shown that interpretations based on a structured process of eliciting core conflictual relationship themes does produce reliable measures. The use of baseline and repeated measures can also improve decision-making as long as the limitations of the data are respected (Turpin, 2001).

Taken as a whole, these findings point to mixed conclusions but do not generate confidence in the general accuracy of our judgements.

One way in which we might understand how we arrive at some (less accurate) judgements over others is to consider the role of heuristics. In their influential work, Tversky and Kahneman (1973, 1974; Kahneman *et al.*, 1982) highlight how the efficient processing of information is dependent upon the use of cognitive strategies or decision-making rules known as heuristics. Heuristics enable us to reduce complex aspects of the decision-making process to more manageable components and so enable us to make inferences in systematic ways.

In their research into the effects of heuristics on the accuracy of clinical judgement Tversky and Kahneman (1973, 1974) identify three specific heuristics that are commonly employed. These are:

- the availability heuristic, whereby estimations of frequency, probability or causality vary according to the extent to which they are 'available' in memory;
- the representative heuristic, whereby objects or people are categorized according to their perceived similarity to a prototype;
- the anchoring heuristic, referring to a tendency to retain our beliefs in the light of new information that disconfirms them.

We should also be aware of two additional decision-making short-cuts:

- The confirmatory bias; that is the tendency to seek out information which confirms our hypotheses. From the perspective of applied psychology, this includes how preconceptions stemming from training or preferred theoretical orientation shape what we actually observe (Lord *et al.*, 1979; Turk and Salovey, 1985).
- The illusory correlation, namely perceiving causal relationships where none exist (Tversky and Kahneman, 1980).

Despite being effective and efficient in many situations, the use of heuristics leads to systematic reasoning biases that often prove problematic. Reliance on a representative heuristic, for example, may lead us to make premature assumptions about the characteristics of people or organizations that result in inaccurate and unhelpful judgements about their situations and needs. Over-use of an anchoring heuristic, in contrast, may prevent us from reformulating our initial hypotheses in the light of new, disconfirmatory data.

Thus, one explanation for the apparent lack of accuracy in our decision-making skills is an over-reliance on heuristics. However, this is not the only explanation. The classic study of Wason and Johnson Laird (1972) looked at the psychology of reasoning and identified the persistent tendency to form a hypothesis and seek data to confirm it when solving tasks, even when the most effective approach would be to seek to disconfirm hypotheses. This was a key feature of failures in reasoning tasks.

Sterman (1994), reviewing a wide range of studies, identifies a number of barriers in decision-making. These include limitations of human cognitive processes, misperceptions of feedback and issues in dealing with ambiguity and confounding variables and the tendency to stop looking after a single causative link has been found. He concludes that neither scientists nor professionals are immune from these influences. The lack of any apparent relationship between professional training, experience and the ability to make accurate judgements raises important questions not just about what we are doing but also about how we investigate what we are doing. As Edwards (2002) observes, whilst essentially descriptive, the heuristic approach to decision analysis has been applied in a way that typically focuses on the difference between how we 'should' make decisions and how we actually do so. This does not, however, necessarily reflect the type of reasoning required in routine practice.

THE LIMITATIONS OF ACTUARIAL APPROACHES: INCORPORATING VARIABILITY AS A FUNCTION OF CONTEXT

Until recently, very little was known about the cognitive processes that enable practitioners to make the varied and often complex decisions required of them (Kassirer *et al.*, 1982). However, it is now recognized that examining the decision-making process outside of the context in which it occurs presents a largely distorted picture of psychologists' decision-making in action. Dowie and Elstein (1988), for example, stressed that professional judgements are not isolated cognitive events and can be understood only in relation to a particular task in a specific context. This had been noted previously by Hogarth (1981) who argued that the task facing practitioners is essentially one of judging situations or objects that are constantly evolving. The actuarial approach cannot, therefore, illuminate those elements that have the most important implications for practice, namely the processes by which psychologists arrive at their decisions.

The fact that there is more to professional judgement than accuracy has led to a burgeoning interest in the ways in which psychologists actually do make decisions. In the domain of clinical practice, Witteman and Kunst (1999) found that therapists' preferred way of working typically represented the starting point of an investigation, rather than a detailed description of the case and that factors such as time constraints, availability of therapists, and preferences for certain types of clients influence the decisions made. It has also been demonstrated that practitioners do not necessarily decide on an approach based on the data available to them but evolve their stance through working with a particular client over time (Seidenstücker and Roth, 1998).

In an elaboration of this literature, Edwards (2002) identified a range of issues which appeared to be central to how clinical psychologists viewed their own decision-making processes during therapy assessments. These were organized around nine main themes relating to (1) the framing of the assessment (comprising psychologists' own needs, the impact of service factors and the preconceived ideas of the client); (2) what the psychologist is likely to do (in terms of typical ways of working and prior openness to treatment decisions) and (3) exploring and responding to the 'fit' (including the fit between the psychologist and the client, assessing clients' issues, the client's ability to work with certain modalities and treatment decisions). Drawing on these themes to develop a framework for exploring the reasoning skills of psychologists across all areas of applied psychology, the questions detailed in Table 1 arise.

The questions in Table 1 can be seen to represent one example of a decision-framing process that can inform professional judgement in useful ways. Specifically, having a decision-framing process provides psychologists with a structure through which they can improve the quality of the decisions made by testing the impact of those decisions regularly. The questions highlight not only the way in which choices are context-dependent and shaped by individual values, but also the need to develop ways of facilitating decision-making in action.

The recognition that our choices are context-dependent has given rise to a number of attempts to improve our reasoning skills. These include the use of computer systems to prevent unhelpful biases in psychotherapists' decisions (Witteman and Kunst, 1999), paper exercises that aim to make decisions more analytical (Maguth Nezu and Nezu, 1995; Ward *et al.*, 1999) and information-processing programmes to help psychologists select relevant questionnaires in their cognitive-behavioural assessments (Bertollotti *et al.*, 1990). Crabtree (1998) has also emphasized the importance of verbalizing the process of decision-making in order to develop a language that better reflects the reasoning process itself and which can help practitioners articulate their reasoning to others. The rationale for this is that voicing the process can enable us to improve our performance, as well as share and teach the process to others (Alnervik and Svidén, 1996).

Of arguably greater significance, however, has been the introduction of manualized treatments and other forms of protocol. Examining their application to health care, Lawton and Parker (1999) highlight how, in a climate increasingly organized

Table 1 A framework for exploring our reasoning skills in action
(Based on Edwards, 2002)

1. In framing the approach to the assessment how do you address:
   - Your own needs as a practitioner? (This includes how the client fits within your caseload and your own preferences for type of client and work.)
   - The impact of organizational factors, including how service restrictions will affect your work?
   - Any preconceived ideas, including the level of confidence you have in the referrer's assessment and any preconceived ideas you have about the client?
2. What are you likely to do?
   - What is your typical way of working and what is your preferred way of working with this client?
   - How open are you to different intervention options before starting the assessment and to what extent do your existing beliefs affect the likelihood that you will take on the client referred?
3. Exploring and responding to the fit
   - How do you see the fit between you and the client? How do you view the influence of the professional relationship and how are your skills and knowledge used in service of the client work?
   - How do you assess the development and severity of the client's issues? How do you assess contextual influences on your own and the client's decision-making and how do you use empathy to establish a coherent narrative with the client?
   - How do you assess client suitability for intervention? What do you believe should be the respective roles of the psychologist and client in relation to conceptualizing the intervention offer? How do you gather data about the practicalities of any intervention for the client?
   - What is your strategy for deciding on treatment? How do you decide on the focus/goals of the intervention? How far is the decision-making process ongoing, or decided and then enacted without change?

around consumer rights and litigation, protocols have been promoted as a means of enhancing efficiency and effectiveness. (We might also add that they represent a response to the growing emphasis on accountability and transparency of professional thought and action; see Miller and Lane, 1993.)

Protocols can take many forms, such as stepped care, decision trees and manualized treatment packages, but share a common aim of standardizing key elements of practice and reducing the decision-making process to component parts. Essentially, they provide a 'map' of options at different stages in any given procedure, with the options available at any stage depending on the answer to those questions asked at the previous stage. Decisions can then be monitored for their results and adjusted where necessary, introducing an important self-monitoring element to the judgement process.

Protocols may have particular benefits for enhancing our reasoning skills when the question of concern is well-defined and uncontentious. They provide a way of uniting professional judgement with research evidence (Robertson *et al.*,

1996) and foster cohesive team working by eliminating the more emotive issues of intervention planning (Intrator *et al.*, 1992). They also standardize elements of practice that enable decisions to be justified and ratified for their adherence (Lawton and Parker, 1999).

However, protocols tell us nothing about the less clear-cut elements of decision-making, such as who defines the issue that the protocol will address. Although providing ways of managing choices in situations where the parameters of a problem are already known, protocols cannot advise practitioners on how to innovate, redesign or even redefine choices as new information comes to light. In fact, as Lawton and Parker (1999) observe, protocols often resort to following the current practice of the team involved, particularly in the frequent absence of research evidence to support the advantages of one direction over another.

Furthermore, articulating choice options does not necessarily mean that any decisions made will translate into action. This is critical because, as noted in Chapter 6, individual practitioners differ in the extent to which they will follow a script that someone else has defined (Rajan *et al.*, 2000). Those who see themselves as innovators may not adhere to the pre-defined choice options at all. This is perhaps consistent with the finding that adherence to protocols can actually have detrimental effects. Mechanizing aspects of intervention delivery may help novice practitioners, but prove constraining and detrimental for effective and experienced ones (Castonguay *et al.*, 1996; Westen *et al.*, 2004).

Part of the problem is that embedded within the actuarial approach is the notion that there is a single, correct answer. Professional judgement is simply compared against this criterion in terms of the extent to which it matches up to or falls short of the correct answer. However, as Bono (1995) points out, eliminating error does not pave the way for developing better ideas. This is evident when we consider the types of choices that psychologists face which often manifest in questions such as:

- What is the nature of the puzzle that needs to be addressed?
- Do all the parties involved agree about what the concern is and what an ideal solution would be, or are there conflicting views? If there are conflicting views, does this matter?
- Where is the puzzle located (within an individual, a family, school, organization or society itself)?
- Who most wants change and what degree of change would be acceptable?
- What kind of change might be achievable given the constraints of context, time, preference, money and expertise?

To engage with these types of questions requires a recognition that there are always multiple decisions to be made and numerous courses of action that may be helpful. As Kwiatkowski and Winter (this volume) observe, we have to exist in several worlds simultaneously. Consequently, all our decisions are relative and need to be interpreted in the light of the most compelling factors facing us, such as crisis intervention, case management issues, organizational and economic constraints and the acceptability of the decision to the client (Sobell and Sobell, 2000). Our task is one of navigating this constant stream of choices and dilemmas (Scaturo and McPeak, 1998). In such situations a decision-making literature that focuses exclusively on accuracy is rendered largely redundant. It is not, therefore, surprising that practitioners continue to rely more on personal experience than on the decision-making literature, of which many do not seem to be aware (Hollon and Kris, 1984; Rock, 1994; Turk and Salovey, 1985).

FRAMEWORKS FOR ENHANCING OUR PROFESSIONAL JUDGEMENTS IN THE CONTEXT OF THE REASONING SKILLS WE USE

If psychologists are not solely, or even primarily, concerned with the issue of accuracy, with what other types of reasoning might they be concerned? Exploring the issue from a philosophical perspective, Crellin (1998) remarks how influential figures such as Husserl, Heidegger and Jung drew a distinction between rational, technologized information which enables us to arrive at an intellectual understanding of a phenomenon and a more holistic type of knowing that involves deriving meanings of personal significance. Interestingly, in recent years a similar distinction has emerged from within cognitive psychology. Teasdale and Barnard (1993), for example, have differentiated propositional from implicational levels of meaning. Whilst the propositional level refers to knowing that can be expressed linguistically and can be evaluated as true or false, the implicational level refers to the more holistic type of knowing to which Jung and others seemed to allude.

Bono (1995) differentiates analytical and holistic categories of reasoning through use of a hunting metaphor. Specifically, he describes our rational, analytical skills as akin to 'shooting'. Shooting questions refer to those we ask when we have a distinct target; like the murder mystery, we know what we are aiming for and have our outcome (a single, correct answer) clearly in sight. Fishing questions, in contrast, are those which entail searching, exploring and uncovering. This is akin to the design aspect of our work, where decisions have to be crafted and chosen from a range of possibilities.

Allingham (2002) develops this idea in the context of choice theory, describing how choice under conditions of certainty involves selecting from a 'menu' of pre-established options (an obvious example here might be identifying the correct diagnosis to assign from a range of pre-established categories). In contrast, choice theory advocates that choosing under conditions of uncertainty involves selecting from a range of gambles where preferences are inevitable. Reliance on preferences does not preclude rationality but choosing under conditions of uncertainty will always require a degree of risk-taking.

Of course, these types of reasoning are not mutually exclusive. Hammond (1996), for example, has focused on how we might oscillate between the two poles of analysis and design, by developing the concept of a cognitive continuum. When tasks are perceived to be structured and goal-oriented (what choice theory might refer to as conditions of certainty), we tend to engage in conscious deliberations, employing analytical modes of thinking. In contrast, when confronted by relatively unstructured tasks with limited resources and time pressures (conditions of uncertainty) then swifter, less conscious modes of deliberation will be employed. This includes use of our intuition.

The implications of these models for the scientist–practitioner debate are that the decision-making skills we require for our work involve two broad categories of reasoning skills: (1) those based on accuracy and requiring rigour, reliability and validity; and (2) those implicated in developing holistic understandings that are based on an ability to design potential solutions through a process of exploration and discovery. Some of the ways in which this distinction might help us develop useful frameworks for enhancing our reasoning abilities in practice are considered next.

PUTTING OUR JUDGEMENTS TO THE TEST BY COMBINING PROTOCOLS WITH CASE FORMULATION

Although stand-alone protocols may be restricted to advancing our reasoning abilities in the domain of accuracy, integrating them with individualized case formulations might enable us to synthesize protocol and clinical judgement in ways that create more of a partnership between our analytical and design-based reasoning skills. This may be particularly advantageous for working with complex cases.

A number of practitioners (see Bruch and Bond, 1998) have made explicit their model of working and decision-making allowing others to follow and question the basis of their judgement. The example of the work of the Islington Educational Guidance Centre (Lane, 1998) provides a detailed protocol, not of treatment but of how to arrive at a joint formulation of a concern with the client and then to devise and evaluate intervention options based on the data obtained. The practice at the Guidance Centre was to provide a detailed framework for decision-making and a series of questions that each practitioner was required to answer in order to justify the intervention proposed. Each case was regarded as unique, but specific questions were regularly asked based on different phases of the process that included:

- defining the encounter;
- exploring factors of influence;
- formulating agreed models of explanation;
- intervening in ways specific to the client and context;
- evaluating progress, the validity of the formulation, the impacts of different elements of the intervention and future maintenance and objectives (see Chapter 3 for a more detailed overview of this model).

The questions themselves were derived from detailed research studies which indicated which factors of influence were likely to be present for clients referred to the Centre. Practitioners had a starting point for their exploration. Each case consisted of a joint exploration with the client. The client was encouraged and enabled to be their own scientist–practitioner developing and testing hypotheses. Thus, a number of tests of the validity of any formulation were introduced. The client(s), practitioner and other significant players all contributed data. Hypotheses were selected and tested. All parties were encouraged to seek data to confirm and disconfirm any conclusions reached. In this way the confirmatory bias was addressed. An agreed formulation was then subjected to detailed questioning by other practitioners (in both a group presentation and in individual supervision) not involved with the client in which the practitioner had to justify the data collected (and why other data were not collected), the interpretation reached (and what alternative interpretations might have been reached) and the evidence that would be used to support and falsify the formulation. Only when those tests were passed was an intervention developed and then it too was subjected to a series of tests. Thus, a protocol provided a framework but actively encouraged individually tailored intervention options. This forced practitioners to confront the thorny issue of consistency and validity of professional judgement (Lane, 1974, 1975, 1978, 1990) without losing sight of the design skills upon which a suitable action plan must inevitably depend.

In this way, we may become scientist–practitioner designers, not just assessors. We can use each idea to craft possible solutions in a kind of parallel process which allows for alternatives, until we arrive at an agreed design. This is akin to an approach which Bono (1995) labels parallel thinking, where ideas are presented in parallel to aid a rich, full exploration of a puzzle (see also Chapter 12, this volume). Decisions can then be reached through a process of design. This approach has proved to have remarkable appeal because it embraces pluralism over the quest for right answers. Contradictory views can co-exist (such as in team meetings where different theoretical ideas can be brought into play to enrich rather than detract from a single explanation of a given psychological puzzle). As there is no primary claim for truth, no answer can be right or wrong but can be appropriate or inappropriate within the design and can be tested for elegance, desirability and feasibility. Incorporating Bono's ideas within a scientist–practitioner framework at the Guidance Centre, for example, permitted multiple perspectives and possibilities; each parallel contributed to the overall picture and from it various solutions were crafted. The children who took part in Bono 'thinking lessons' found that they could use such processes both to challenge professionals and design solutions to their own issues.

As frameworks to assist decision-making have begun to emerge, the disputes over the superiority of actuarial, clinical, and information-processing models have given way to systematic attempts to combine them, giving rise to multiple models of decision-making.

Decisions made on the basis of actuarial risk-prediction employ mathematical formulae to quantify level of risk based upon empirically-established predictive relationships. As Hickey (2004) observes, it is possible to obtain accurate decisions as long as (1) the participants are comparable to those on whom the predictive measure was originally developed; (2) they predict the type of risk that needs to be understood; (3) the prediction is time-limited and (4) the psychometric properties of the measure have been fully ascertained.

However, the difference between a static judgement (i.e. one that is unlikely to change over time) and a dynamic judgement (one that is liable to alter over time) has been emphasized. Hickey (2004) particularly points to the value of using both approaches so that clinicians are able to assess an individual's relative risk on any particular day, given a knowledge of the environment while knowing the individual's absolute level of risk. Where there is a high absolute risk, there is little option but to restrict actions whereas a relative risk can be judged according to the circumstance.

In working with perpetrators of sexual abuse and other violent crimes (see Macpherson and Jones, 2004) it is also recognized that decisions made have important consequences not just for those immediately involved. Consequently, a more sophisticated choice strategy has begun to emerge. For example, Logan (2004) has argued that actuarial approaches have limited professional discretion and they have typically emphasized risk prediction. Professional judgements have allowed for discretion and have been used to structure risk formulation and management, ultimately for the purpose of harm prevention. Different perspectives suit different purposes.

One example of this broader approach is the Multiaxial Risk Appraisal (MARA) (Craig, 2004). The MARA model combines actuarial and psychometric assessments with empirically guided clinical assessments and dynamic changes in risk. Its use in assessing risk for sexual offenders has been discussed by Craig *et al.*, (2004). They argue that its advantage over other approaches is that it investigates risk of recidivism from different trajectories. A single decision-enabling measure may increase consistency but it has reduced applicability to any specific individual about whom the risk decision has to be made. Given the established validity of some actuarial approaches to decision-making it does not make sense to abandon them in favour of clinical judgements. Nonetheless, incorporating ways of viewing decisions on risk from different perspectives, fit for purpose and using a variety of processes, does hold out hope for enhancing decision-making in the future.

THE LEARNING JOURNEY AS A MODEL TO STRUCTURE DECISION-MAKING

In the health-care system, there has been much work in recent years on the notion of a 'Patient Journey'. The concept is designed to focus attention to how clients interrelate with each professional and in doing so restructure the service offer to ease that journey (see Conner *et al.*, 2003). At best, this enables decisions about quality of intervention to be assessed. However, it is still expert led, tracking a client's journey through the hoops of health care. At its worst it is about what makes sense for us as professionals as we move the client between our respective activities.

An additional, and perhaps more satisfactory process is to structure our decision-making around the individual and what makes sense for them. Arguably, in practice, clients faced with a psychological issue embrace change when they learn they have options and come to prefer and enact one or other of those options. They are on a learning journey.

If we think of the client (whether an individual or organization) as being engaged upon a learning journey we can begin to use in interesting ways the literature on adult learning, reflection and action research cycles to map that journey. Our place as professionals becomes one of assisting the thinking and decision-making processes within that journey. In a number of recent projects conducted between the Professional Development Foundation and the National Centre for Work Based Learning Partnerships, for example, such an approach has been used with professionals as diverse as Behaviour Support Teachers, Business Psychologists, Executive Coaches, Emerging Leaders in Government Departments, Management Consultants, and Veterinary General Practitioners (Fillery-Travis *et al.*, 2005). These clients have been asked to shape their own emerging practice through a learning journey that creates a personal framework of practice which they can present to others, including clients, and then demonstrate in practice how their framework adapts to difficulties encountered on their own journey. A not dissimilar process has recently been adopted by The BPS Register of Psychologists Specialising in Psychotherapy (2003). To gain admission psychologists make a case for their identity as 'psychologists specialising in psychotherapy' tracing their journey and lineage and showing how that is reflected in their practice (see Chapter 1).

The concept of the learning journey changes the role of the psychologist entirely. Our task is to assist our clients to recognize, release and enhance their own talent to address their own issues. We assume they are competent (even if that competence is in limited areas) and our task begins to mirror that of a coach. However, when we accompany our clients on their journeys we too are involved in our own new learning for we are in the presence of the client as expert.

Similarly, for us as professionals engaged in the art of reasoning in all its forms, the constructing and assigning of meaning through a journey creates the possibility of looking at our experience from others' points of view. This embodies the idea that our reasoning abilities are both critical and evaluative. Kolb's (1984) influential experiential learning cycle forms one useful way of understanding such a journey. The cycle models his experiential learning theory in which he argues that learning is indeed experiential – a lifelong process in which personal development and work play as much a part as formal education. He argues that, ideally, experiential learning occurs when individuals involve themselves in new experiences in an open-minded way (that is, have 'concrete experiences') and then reflect on their experiences from a range of perspectives (by 'reflective observation'). By integrating their observations into theories ('abstract conceptualizations') they give these observations meanings, which are then tested out in real-world problem-solving situations (by 'active experimentation'). This provides the concrete experience for the next cycle of learning.

Effective learning requires contrasting abilities, which Kolb models as polar opposites on two dimensions of learning. Abstract conceptualization and concrete experience are contrasting ways of what he describes as 'grasping' experience. Reflective observation and active experimentation are contrasting ways of what he describes as 'transforming' experiences that you have grasped in either or both of the ways described above. For example, the 'internal process of reflecting' on your thoughts and feelings about a particular concrete work experience (say, a new administrative procedure you implemented two weeks ago), operates on that experience to transform it through the attribution of particular meanings to it ('it doesn't seem to be working as well as it should'). The 'external process of acting on' the concrete experience is also a way of transforming it, by extending the existing experience in some way ('I'll see if it works better this way instead'). As this example shows, it is often necessary to utilize both reflective and active abilities in order to transform or elaborate or develop existing experience. We can then relate this to our own journey in our work with a client or indeed the client's journey through:

- reflecting on concrete experience: we/our client starts with a review of the current experiences which leads to the request for an intervention;
- developing concepts: we work together to conceptualize, to give form and meaning to existing learning and consider what new learning might be necessary to generate any agreed change;
- active experimentation: we create a coherent 'theory' about our own learning involving designing the future learning experiences that will extend our learning from where it is now to what we intend it to be at the end of the change programme;
- our experimentation in turn provides us with new concrete experience which can be subjected to further reflective observation and so on.

Represented diagrammatically, the process would look as depicted in Figure 1.

In conceptualizing decision-making within a learning journey we recognize that our professional practice forms part of a complex and dynamic system. There is not a series of simple linear relationships leading from problem statement through classification to intervention. Cycling round, within and across various parts of this journey will be common. We can use various tools to structure our decision-making as seems appropriate to the moment within that journey. This structuring applies as much to organizational issues as it does to individual client issues as we recognize that all actions are part of a learning system. For example, in a joint project a group of teachers, psychologists, other professionals and parents came together to create dynamic models of factors influencing disruptive behaviour in school. By introducing increasing numbers of parameters, creating models of practice that appeared to represent a shared understanding of what worked, and

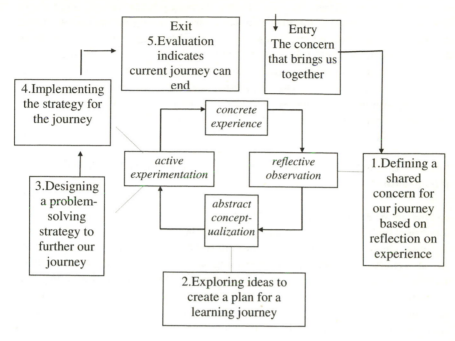

Figure I The learning journey and its relationship to experiential learning

eliminating or adding variables as needed, this group was able to create a set of principles and competencies underpinning their own successful practice. These could then be used to test and inform their own practice and share results with others. A series of simulations of a behaviour system gave rise to frameworks to create more effective systems (Windsor Behaviour Support Group, 1997).

In a review of decision-making in general populations, scientists and various professionals, Sterman (1994) reminds us that people tend to assume each effect has a single cause and often cease their search for explanations when a cause is found, ignoring base rates and situational factors. The use of heuristics (as discussed previously) leads to difficulty when cause and effect are distant as in complex systems where actions have multiple effects. Scientists are subject to the same cognitive limitations and biases as lay people. Psychologists cannot expect to be immune from them. However, Sterman argues that this strengthens the case for the disciplined application of scientific method, in particular the use of disconfirmation of the hypothesis generated.

Complex systems such as the journeys we encounter in our work with clients present multiple barriers to learning. Overcoming them requires the use of many methods and disciplines and attempts at synthesis between them. This includes, as Sterman argues, theoretical work, real-world interventions, rigorous follow-up and evaluation, simulations including virtual experiments, multiple feedback loops and mathematical, psychological and organizational modelling. In particular, as we seek to understand and act within complex policy areas we can make use of simulations and both qualitative and quantitative modelling scenarios. These enable us to test ideas in areas where experimentation is not feasible or ethical so that as we come to apply our work, we do so with a better understanding of the hidden assumptions and biases that influence our actions (Sterman, 2002). Each of these has a place within the learning journey and the more we question ourselves and apply rigour to the process the more we operate as scientists–practitioners even when dealing with worlds of uncertainty (Lane, 1983).

SOME CONCLUSIONS ON HOW TO DEVELOP OUR REASONING SKILLS

In this chapter we have argued that we need a range of reasoning skills, both analytical and design-based, to address the psychological puzzles we encounter in our practice. Much of the decision-making research has traditionally focused on the analytical components of our reasoning skills, relying on actuarial methods which investigate the accuracy of decision-making. The value of this approach is limited to those problems that are easily defined and where a correct solution is (at least theoretically) to be found. The task that faces us, however, is not solely to do with arriving at increasingly accurate judgements, but also constructing stories that have substantive implications for change.

The decision-making research may have come a long way from the early disappointing studies. However, the way in which we approach the art of reasoning remains a relatively under-researched area of the scientist–practitioner debate. There has tended to be a polarization between those areas of psychology (such as forensic) where actuarial and psychometric models have found more favour and areas (such as counselling psychology) which have traditionally rejected psychometrics as representing too narrow a view. That a special edition of the *Counselling Psychology Review* could be devoted to the role of testing in counselling psychology is a sign of an increasingly respectful challenge to conventional thinking (Kanellakis, 2004).

Increasingly, practitioners are drawing on a broader base of academic psychology to inform practice. For example, social psychology has been influential in generating ideas for practice in relation to group behaviour, identity formation and beliefs. This is evident in Ajzen's (1991) theory of planned behaviour which has been extensively used to look at health beliefs and response to interventions (see Steadman and Rutter, 2004, who have used this approach to predicting attendance at breast screening) and in the field of sports and exercise psychology (see Jones *et al.*, 2004, who have used the model in looking at promoting exercise behaviour). The willingness to reach out to multiple theoretical ideas and experimental findings, to find what is fit for purpose points to the increasing sophistication of our skills in the art of reasoning.

We would agree with Swain (2000) that professional judgement must always, to an extent, remain an autonomous domain of activity, However, such autonomy carries inherent responsibilities. Specifically, Mahrer (2000) argues that applied psychology has become 'change immune' by creating a series of foundational beliefs (that is, basic propositions and fundamental assumptions that are taken for granted) that do not lend themselves well to critical analysis. Mahrer suggests that in developing our reasoning skills we should be prepared to articulate our foundational beliefs more explicitly, eliminate selected beliefs and observe the consequences, creating alternative models where necessary. This would lead to greater transparency of thought and action that could be more systematically investigated and which, we would argue, is of critical importance to ourselves and our clients.

What emerges from the different approaches outlined in this chapter is that psychologists need frameworks of reasoning that can help them structure their decision-making in a systematic way. In considering the role of protocols, protocol-based case formulation and learning journeys, amongst others, we have identified some frameworks which might help us engage in a debate about which styles of reasoning we use, when and why. No single reasoning style can be superior to any other; there can be no simplistic hierarchy through which we can categorize our knowledge. However, there are differences in the extent to which different styles are contractive or expansive, analytical or design-based according to how an enquiry is framed. At one end of the continuum, we have the deductive reasoning skills of the detective-style enquiry. These skills are likely to be most useful when:

- the problem is uncontentious;
- the priority task is to make a decision and take action;
- the aim is to achieve uniformity of decision and action to minimize risk to our clients and/or protect ourselves against litigation;
- further exploration is likely to confuse rather than clarify.

At the other end of the continuum are the more expansive and design-based approaches to reasoning which will be most useful when the primary task is to:

- gain a better understanding of how different stakeholders in a psychological enquiry might have different views about the way forward;
- find new ways of thinking about a particular puzzle;
- engineer new possibilities for action;
- engage curiosity, interest and hope.

This suggests that we need to select our questions with an awareness of where they have come from, including individual, organizational and epistemological influences. However, this is only the beginning. In our view, much more attention needs to be given to the circumstances in which applied psychologists use one type of reasoning style over another, as well as the appropriateness of different investigative techniques to explore this. Similarly, there is an urgent need to examine how we instil these reasoning abilities in novice practitioners and monitor their development over time. This implies that greater emphasis should be placed on training scientist–practitioners in different modes of reasoning, not only so they know how to employ each of them but also so they know how to choose between them. Questions, embedded within particular pieces of work, that might represent a starting point include the following:

- Given the demands of this particular psychological puzzle, and the context in which it is presenting, what would be a good question?
- Who has had an influence in determining what is the key question?
- Are all stakeholders agreed on the key question, or are there conflicting views?
- What is the most helpful reasoning style for engaging this particular enquiry, and why?
- What short-cuts might I be tempted to make, with what implications for the enquiry and my client?
- How will I ensure that my decision-making is not unduly biased by errors of thinking (heuristics) or personal influences (such as fatigue, time pressures, organizational pressures and personal feelings towards the client) that could hamper the development of a useful intervention?

By interpreting decision-making as predicated on a menu of options from which we can select in an informed way, we and our clients can be seen as engaged on a journey together and the psychologist is enabled to bring diverse tools and concepts into play as appropriate to the phases of the journey and the specific experiences uncovered.

However, we must take note of Sterman's (2002) reminder that all models are wrong and to learn some humility about the limitations of our knowledge. We need to seek to partner with those in other disciplines such as system dynamics who share our commitment to the disciplined use of scientific enquiry skills and a willingness to work in complex messy areas.

Ultimately, of course, knowing how we make decisions is not enough. The purpose of the reasoning skills used by applied psychologists is principally to bring about desired changes. As Bono points out, 'It is not enough just to judge, criticise, refute and search. You actually have to do something' (1995: 160). In the next two chapters we consider, more explicitly, the fruits of our reasoning labours in terms of what we actually 'do'. Specifically, we consider (1) the psychological stories we create with our clients, often defined as formulation, and (2) the ways in which we innovate and implement creative solutions.

Chapter 3

Arriving at shared psychological narratives: formulation and explanation

> The key to success lies in the creative activity of making new maps, not in the imitative following and refining of existing ones.
>
> (Ralph Stacey)
>
> One world, many ways of knowing.
>
> (Stephen Rose)

Formulation is deemed to be a cornerstone of skilled psychological practice. It has been identified as central to the work of the professional psychologist (British Psychological Society, 2005) and is a pivotal skill of the scientist–practitioner. Yet the use of and process by which formulations are created is contentious. For example, the concept is problematic for many practitioners operating within existential and phenomenological frameworks who see their work with clients as reflecting an unfolding process rather than the imposition of the psychologist's worldview upon the client. For others (e.g. Lane, 1974, 1978, 1990) the term has always included the client's construction of the world and a partnership process in which both client and psychologist create a shared model which forms an agreed process for experiments with behaviour.

This chapter considers what we mean by formulation and how this skill relates to our emerging understanding of what it means to be a scientist–practitioner. Following on from the previous chapter in which we examined some of the challenges we face when engaged in the art of reasoning, we now turn to the way in which we use our reasoning skills to construct coherent and useful psychological explanations about the puzzles we encounter in our work. Specifically, in reviewing some of the debates about what formulation is and to whom it belongs, we hope to encourage reflection and debate on formulation in psychology practice, in whatever context that practice happens. We also outline a generic framework for approaching the task of formulation which we offer as one means of refining our capacity for co-constructing psychological stories with our clients.

As with the previous chapter, we start by inviting you to consider your own assumptions about the function and process of formulation including:

- In what ways is the concept of formulation helpful in your work?
- In what ways might it be problematic?
- What frameworks of decision-making and reasoning enable you to formulate at an optimum level?
- Where does the boundary lie, in your own work, between arriving at an accurate formulation and constructing a helpful one?

THE ROLE OF FORMULATION IN APPLIED PSYCHOLOGY PRACTICE

Formulation is one of the skills that we believe makes psychologists distinct from other professions. Considerable time and effort are devoted to acquiring the ability to formulate during training and over the course of our careers much time will be spent engaged in the process of making sense of the psychological puzzles that confront us.

The importance of formulation to psychological practice is illustrated in a recent document produced by the British Psychological Society (2005) which outlines the basis of different forms of applied psychology. In each of the five areas of psychology presented (clinical, forensic, counselling, educational and health), the centrality of the scientist–practitioner model is endorsed and linked to the importance of reflective practice. For clinical, forensic and counselling psychology, formulation is also identified as a key competence. The extent to which formulation has a scientific basis and is drawn directly from psychological theory varies between disciplines. For example, its assessment pedigree is emphasized for clinical and forensic specialities, whilst counselling psychology emphasizes formulation as a more collaborative unfolding process. Within educational psychology priority is given to the knowledge building process and the structuring of interventions with individuals and systems. The formulation of policy and practice is seen as a key part of the psychologist's role. For health psychologists the application of research to formulation of health policy and health promotion is core.

Although there may be different ways of conceptualizing the essence of this task, the notion of formulation within a scientist–practitioner framework originated within clinical practice. In her review of the use of the term formulation in clinical work, Crellin (1998) traces the historical and social contexts in which the term emerged and evolved, highlighting how formulation came to represent a form of political leverage through which psychology established its autonomy from psychiatry. Yet for many years, psychology remained within the grip of psychiatric description through the use of symptom matching and diagnostic labelling.

As Bruch and Bond (1998) have pointed out, clinicians were traditionally expected to define their clinical work in terms of psychiatric categorization systems, with treatment determined by these criteria. However, psychologists working within behavioural models found little that was helpful in a classification system aimed at order and communication (at times with dubious validity and reliability), when trying to explain or treat the difficulties with which their clients presented.

Following his early rejection of therapeutic practice as a legitimate activity for the clinical psychologist, Hans Eysenck (1990) later argued for a scientist–practitioner approach which emphasized clinical–experimental work centred on learning principles (see Chapter 1). This was elaborated by M.B. Shapiro (1955, 1957; Shapiro and Nelson, 1955). However, in practice clinicians found it difficult to use the approach. Meyer (see Meyer and Liddell, 1975) subsequently tried to adapt the scientist–practitioner approach to the realities of the clinical setting and summed up the problems from the clinician's point of view by pointing out that (1) not all clients sharing the same complaint respond to the procedural requirements of techniques and (2) psychologists are rarely presented with clients with isolated complaints, particularly in mental health settings.

Meyer developed an alternative approach based on an individualized formulation of the client's issues, shared with the client rather than imposed on them, which became highly influential for psychologists seeking more individually-tailored approaches to clinical practice (see examples in Bruch and Bond, 1998). Further key contributions were made by Turkat (1985) and other reformulations have followed (see Kinderman and Lobban 2000; Mumma and Smith, 2001; Young, 1990/1994).

More recently, Tarrier and Calam have adopted an approach which is consistent with the hypothesis-testing framework proposed by Shapiro and Meyer and which endorses a broad range of evidence as relevant to a case formulation framework. As they explain, their approach:

> involves the elicitation of appropriate information and the application and integration of a body of theoretical psychological knowledge to a specific clinical problem in order to understand the origins, development and maintenance of that problem. Its purpose is both to provide an accurate overview and explanation of the patient's problems that is open to verification through hypothesis-testing, and to arrive collaboratively with the patient at a useful understanding of their problem that is meaningful to them.
>
> (2002: 311–2)

THE CHALLENGE OF FORMULATING COLLABORATIVELY: WHO OWNS THE STORY?

Collectively, the models outlined in the previous section favour an approach which provides a rationale for choosing between interventions and through which psychologists are able (at least in principle) to demonstrate that strategies based upon their formulations bring about change. They are also well-elaborated in the way in which they integrate various aspects of functioning and indeed, it could be said that they represent a greater interest in the individual thought processes than are accommodated by earlier behavioural formulations. Quite often, for example, the more advanced cognitive-behavioural models have used explanatory over-arching systemic functions which has prevented the tendency to treat emotions as pathological entities (Bruch and Bond, 1998).

Individualized case formulations, it is argued, form the basis of effective psychological practice. They provide a framework that guides choice of interven-tion strategy and can be understood to be derived from an essentially scientific worldview. For example, Bruch and Bond highlight the aim of case formulation as 'conducting hypothesis-driven interventions that are constantly monitored for effectiveness' (1998: xviii). However, Crellin (1998) has expressed reservations about framing clients' problems as testable hypotheses. Specifically, she warns against the dangers of translating clients' experiences of themselves into empirical constructs because although hypotheses can distil complex material into a man-ageable form, they also fall prey to a reductionism that prevents understanding. By translating human experiences into something we can readily investigate, we lose the essence of the phenomena we seek to understand. As noted already, this may be particularly problematic for practitioners committed to existential and phenomenological approaches who see their work with clients as reflecting an unfolding process.

Jill D. Wilkinson (2004) is also mindful of this issue. She describes some of the challenges of teaching the concept of formulation to doctoral level counsell-ing psychology trainees where humanistic and existential values are paramount but where trainees are also expected to work within different models, including psychodynamic and cognitive-behavioural approaches. In approaching the topic of formulation, she encourages trainees to draw upon their own 'psychological mindedness' to make sense of clients' difficulties. Use of psychological mindedness enables trainees to identify, reflect upon and apply their implicit theories about why a client may be experiencing a particular difficulty in a specific way at a given time in their lives. By trying to make sense of clients' presenting issues from an initial position of psychological mindedness, trainees can then consider how dif-ferent psychological theories might add to, or challenge, their implicit models. At an early stage of the formulation process, therefore, critical questions include: 'What information do I need to reach an initial understanding of what has con-tributed to this person struggling with this issue?' and 'Does this narrative make sense, to me, my client, and to others involved?'

It is, of course, important to recognize that phenomenology is not discounted by those operating within those models of practice which are more wedded to a scientific worldview. For example, the necessity of attending to phenomenology is noted by Salkovskis who, in describing the relationship between theory, prac-tice, experimental psychology and outcome research, explains how professional practice is 'both the target of our work and a source of information and inspiration that drives other aspects of the process of empirically grounded interventions' (2002: 4). In order to ensure ongoing refinement of cognitive therapy theory and practice, he argues that it is essential to have a thorough grasp of the phenomenology that underlies the psychological material we seek to understand.

Salkovskis' outlook on phenomenology would be very different from that adopted by humanistic or existential psychologists but the importance of allowing understanding to emerge gradually from clients' stories is still incorporated. This is because, according to Salkovskis, it is these stories that inspire research questions and that represent the ultimate validating criterion against which the research data must be compared.

However, Crellin's argument remains compelling. Specifically, she alerts us to how we could, when formulating, arrive at premature foreclosure, terminating avenues of exploration before the presenting issue has had sufficient opportunity to emerge. Thus, while formulation aids technical problem-solving in domains where issues can be framed as problems, the process may change if the task is one of arriving at a coherent and meaningful narrative or is organized around enhancing individual or organizational potential. In such cases, as Crellin contends 'no formulation is possible until the end of therapy, and logically, it would be the client and not the therapist who would need to be satisfied with the formulation' (1998: 19). This echoes the earlier concerns of Davison (1991; cited in Davison and Gann, 1998) who argued that psychological problems are for the most part the constructions of practitioners which are then assigned to clients, rather than conjointly developed.

FORMULATION AND THE ISSUE OF ACCURACY

Wilson (1996) amongst others has expressed doubts about the relative merits of case formulation on the grounds of accuracy. Bieling and Kuyken (2003) argue that while psychologists can agree at the descriptive level about key features of a case, their interpretations of the more explanatory components vary widely. They make the useful distinction between top down and bottom up approaches. The former works from inferences from theory or research applied to the single case. Bottom up approaches, in contrast, work from an attempt to map a reliable and valid case formulation onto the client's presenting problems. The practitioner works back to theory as necessary. Given what is known about some of the biases in professional decision-making (see Chapter 2), and that case formulation is predicated on the ability to employ sound judgements, it is not easy to have confidence in the formulations arrived at, even when the task is undertaken by highly experienced practitioners. Perhaps this is why Crellin favours a formulation that emerges at the end of therapy, and one that is essentially owned by the client rather than the psychologist.

For those anxious about the potential pitfalls of formulation, there is always the appeal of using manualized interventions. Here, one of the central aims is to circumvent some of the biases in professional decision-making and defer to methods that have been empirically validated, or at least appear to have some empirical support. However, this also is far from straightforward. As Bond (1998) observes, even manualized approaches cannot protect us from having to make decisions about which type of method to employ, when to introduce it and how to explain it in a way that opens up new avenues for exploration. Similarly, even when allowing a client's issue to unfold in the way that Crellin describes, we are still involved in the process of testing hypotheses and are thus always influenced by implicit frameworks that guide our perceptions of how the world works. Embedded within these frameworks will be the mediating influence of the policies of our professional bodies and employing organizations, as well as the assumption that the skills of a psychologist might be useful in a particular instance.

Seen in this light, the question that concerns us is no longer whether we engage in hypothesis-testing and problem-solving, but rather the types of hypothesis-testing and problem-solving activities in which we do engage. For example, is the task of formulating inevitably wedded to an empirical model of hypothesis-testing or might there be other ways of forming hypotheses? Whose hypotheses are being tested and whose needs is the testing of hypotheses principally designed to serve? Who, therefore, has the right to change the formulation as new ideas or forms of understanding emerge?

ESTABLISHING THE PURPOSE FOR WHICH AN EXPLANATION IS REQUIRED

It is hardly contentious to suggest that psychological theories will never be sufficient to capture clients' experiences in their entirety. Indeed, it may not always be the case that we have to formulate everything in order to identify a helpful avenue for intervention. There may be times when formulating a discrete part of a problem is sufficient to create change and other times when a much fuller understanding of the problem in context is vital (Lane, 1978).

If a case formulation is essentially a broad narrative around 'psychological sense-making' then we need to consider how much information we need to start working with our clients in a meaningful way. Rather than concerning ourselves exclusively with the content of our formulations (including issues of accuracy), we should perhaps aim to combine content with closer attention to process; that is, how we arrive at one particular formulation over another, and the skills we need to construct it. This is important because if we are too wedded to any particular theory too early on in the process, or confuse it with reality as experienced by another, we can easily mistake the map for the territory. Over-attachment to any particular theoretical idea or model of formulation, however holistic its intention, would seem to be problematic. After all, it may have to be discarded a few weeks down the line, when new information or narratives begin to emerge.

Perhaps then, we can most helpfully conceptualize case formulation as a device which helps us organize our thinking about what might be helpful and when. An integral part of this process is being able to articulate these frameworks so they can be reflected upon, examined and where necessary, revised. Seen from this broader perspective, formulation is less concerned with attempting to 'explain' a presenting issue from one theoretical perspective or another, and more organized around encouraging a capacity for creative thinking that is largely atheoretical (although certainly not antitheoretical) in the early stages. Theory is then combined with creative and reflective thinking rather than imposed upon it, with the formulation representing a story that is elaborated through gradually adding layers of theoretical constructs and ideas that can be examined for their implications. Important questions then become: What is the value of locating a given problem within an individual as opposed to locating it within a social or political model of explanation? Does this formulation move us closer or farther away from where the client wants to be? By avoiding the temptation to formulate within a specific model from the outset we may be protected, to a degree, from the kind of exploratory foreclosure that Crellin warns against.

It may be acceptable for the nature of the problem to emerge over time providing certain foundations are in place (e.g. a decision is made that a psychological intervention is preferable to a social intervention or that the client is willing and able to explore their issue within a psychological framework). Being able to articulate these choice points and to recognize the advantages and disadvantages of choosing one approach over another is perhaps, the critical issue. Moreover, as we move from work with single clients to work with groups or organizations these narratives may become broader still. Yet the process of creating a 'shared concern' which can form the basis of a journey of exploration enables the possibility of a cooperative enterprise between psychologist and client in which each party contributes their own worldviews as 'expertise'.

Interpreted in this light, the context and the client are more evident as influencing processes than the 'assessment cycle' notion of formulation suggests. As we argued in Chapter 2, shared decision-making is happening in practice all the time and needs to be acknowledged and incorporated within a new vision of the scientist–practitioner model. Such an approach has formed a key part of the practice of many in occupational, community and educational psychology where systems thinking has been highly influential (Lane and Miller, 1992). Probably as a result of the more explicitly dominant position of the client in decision-making it has also been prevalent in emerging areas of applied psychology such as coaching (Grant and Cavanagh, 2004) and business psychology (Grant, 2005). Moreover, it seems likely that within Health Service provision the idea of shared decision-making to ensure the client understands the range of treatment options and can explore how these match their personal situation and values will feature more strongly in future. Indeed, it has been noted to be providing an impetus for the work of the National Institute for Clinical Excellence (Salkovskis, 2004).

A FRAMEWORK FOR IDENTIFYING PURPOSE, PERSPECTIVE AND PROCESS

The definition of scientist–practitioner to which you subscribe, its strengths and limitations and how it guides your approach to formulation, will be informed by how you construe the purpose of your work. In thinking about formulation, we have found it helpful to organize our reasoning skills around three domains which we would see as relevant to psychological practice across all areas of application. These are: (1) Purpose; (2) Perspective and (3) Process. As a framework for guiding enquiry generally, and case formulation specifically, the Purpose, Perspectives, Process model can be understood as follows:

I Purpose

In undertaking any psychological enquiry, it is vital to be clear about its fundamental purpose. The shape that your enquiry subsequently takes and the stories you tell about that enquiry will follow on from here. Therefore, the starting point on the shared learning journey between you and your client begins as you define the purpose of your work together. This gives rise to the following questions:

- What are you setting out to achieve (you might call it outputs, results, processes of change, relationship, or journey)? How do you explain this; what is your story?
- What is your client defining as their purpose in engaging in this encounter with you, here and now? What do you do to make it possible for the client to tell their story, to feel heard?
- What type of client purpose is best served by your offer or your service context?
- What boundaries do you place on the purpose of the work that would require you to refer the client elsewhere? With whom would you not work and where is the margin of that boundary?
- What definitions of scientist–practitioner model inform your approach to formulation and why are they appropriate to the purpose of your enquiry?

2 Perspective

As part of an agreed purpose it is important to be able to define what you bring to the encounter. This includes an awareness of your values, beliefs and knowledge as well as your sense of what you do well and the limits to your competence. Such an awareness also includes the range of personal, interpersonal and systemic models (official and unofficial) that inform your work. Similarly, the underpinning philosophies within the context of your service form a key part of this perspective. However, your clients also bring perspectives of their own which will inform your work together and which must, therefore, be given equal consideration in the enquiry that follows. Engaging with these perspectives gives rise to questions such as:

- On what sort of journey are you and your client engaged?
- Some journeys proscribe certain routes (perspectives or methodologies). How do you ensure coherence between your and your client's journey?
- What are the values, beliefs, knowledge and competences that you each bring to the encounter?
- What do you do to ensure that the client is able to explore their values, beliefs, knowledge and competence within the encounter?

3 Process

Once you have been able to define the purpose of your work and the perspectives that underpin it, then it is possible to structure a process for the work that you and your client intend to undertake. Without the purpose and perspective defined, the process becomes a technical application uninformed by psychology. Manualized interventions carried out by non-psychologists can be effective and have provided substantial benefit to many clients but we would argue that they are not psychology. Recent years have seen a considerable increase in this type of intervention in both clinical and occupational work where a product, skills training or 360 degree feedback is offered without understanding the features of the learning journey of the client (Lane, 1993). In such cases, a given procedure is applied to a client based on a minimal definition of some aspect of their behaviour (e.g. the 'social phobia = social skills training = send to a social skills group'-type formula). The client as a person is absent, as is the psychological investigation necessary to determine what in fact is happening in the client's life that leads them to the point of change. In this context, the key question becomes: What process (including any method or tool) is necessary to ensure that the purpose is met within the constraints of the perspectives available to us?

WHAT MIGHT A CASE FORMULATION PROCESS LOOK LIKE? A BRIEF ILLUSTRATION

The concept of the encounter is critical to the Purpose, Perspective, Process framework. How you define the purpose of the relationship in the context of your meeting structures the perspectives and processes that can be applied to the encounter which follows. So what might this framework look like in action? We offer a description of how this model can be applied in ways that are consistent with the notion of encounter and partnership, and also congruent with the scientist–practitioner model, drawing on original work by Lane (1974, 1978, 1990, 1998).

In terms of background, Lane's studies incorporated both individual and organizational analysis within the context of working with children and the school system. Cooperation with the Institute of Education (London) and Manchester Metropolitan University (Didsbury), The Behaviour Support Conference (Nottingham University) together with various colleagues (Edward De Bono's Cognitive Research Trust, Stott, Sarason, Krasner, and members of the ILEA Schools Psychological Service) extended this to wider educational settings (see Miller and Lane, 1993). In 1976, at the suggestion of Hans and Sybil Eysenck a 20-year-partnership with Vic Meyer, Ted Chesser and colleagues at Middlesex Hospital/University College London led to an adaptation of both Meyer's and Lane's work into an evolving clinical model of formulation (see Bruch and Bond, 1998). Subsequent work with a wide range of colleagues in forensic (Lane, 1992, Ross and Hilborn, 2005) and occupational psychology led to development of the framework for organizational work (Lane, 1993), and more recent applications in coaching (Lane, 2002; Lane et al., 2005) and business psychology (Lane and Rajan, 2005) have led to further refinements. Thus, numerous colleagues (including Corrie in the co-construction of this book) have contributed to the development of the framework outlined here.

I Purpose

The 1970s saw an increasing concern with the problem of disruption in schools and rising levels of delinquency in our communities. Numerous schemes began to appear to work with disruptive children. Many of these had as their origin existing theoretical models that had influenced adult psychotherapy. Specifically, children and adolescents were identified, diagnosed (as maladjusted) and consigned to special schools, often many miles away from their homes. Pathology was seen as rooted in the child, their history, and in malfunctioning families. The notion that environments might be disabling, that behaviour might be a function of context or that professionals might be part of the problem rarely surfaced. A number of professionals were becoming increasingly unhappy with this emphasis on a pathological model of psychology. Critiques of this deficit-focused psychology from a critical and behavioural psychology perspective (Tizard, 1973) led to the view that in starting a new service the underlying purpose needed to be different.

Lane and colleagues (see Lane, 1975) began by stating their alternative purpose: namely to create a service that enabled each participant (child, teacher, parent, psychologist, social worker, etc.) to address issues that prevented children participating in the school system. They aimed to provide teachers and other professionals with ways of working directly with children by modifying practices to generate benefits for themselves, other children and the referred child. Thus, the purpose was to enable children to benefit from mainstream education as a means to transform the life chances of the child and the effectiveness of the school. Given the nature of the purpose underpinning the enquiry, certain perspectives became relevant. (Historically, it is important to remember that this service emerged before the debate around the effectiveness of schools began.)

2 Perspective

The perspective was derived from four principal sources of knowledge:

1   Detailed therapeutic work drawing on the ideas of several thousand children, their families and their schools, as well as professional colleagues in Islington and elsewhere. Thus, evidence from practice and peer and client experiences were used to inform the knowledge base. Practice explicitly informed theory development.
2   Detailed experimental work that was carried out over 15 years. The research literature was used to generate hypotheses about causes likely to be relevant to the groups of children being studied. The experimental work was used to evaluate factors that generated and maintained problematic behaviours and situations. This was based on research studies of both referred and non-referred comparative samples of participants and drew on a strong commitment to the idea that there are pragmatic ways to apply the concept of the scientist–practitioner even in complex applications. The research generated a series of perspectives that were used to inform hypothesis creation. Experimental work both informed practice and generated theory.
3   Theoretical models (drawn from personal, interpersonal and systemic frames) that had some basis of support in the research literature. These were primarily behavioural, symbolic interactionist (later social constructionist) and subsequently cognitive models as well as a variety of systemic frameworks from sociology, organizational theory and learning. In other contexts different theoretical models might be more appropriate (depending on the purpose). Theory informed the process of creating hypotheses.
4   Networked meetings between Lane and colleagues and other parties, which enabled a lively exchange of ideas between practitioners, and joint training events between the students and other centres. Reflection on practice and the development of a community of practice to share and refine ideas provided both creativity and rigour. Reflection informed practice and theory development.

The underlying value system which permeated this work was one that was committed to inclusion, which recognized that professional systems can be disabling and which retained a belief in the expertise of the child, parent and other professionals. This included the assumption that all parties were doing the best they could with the resources available to them. The perspectives used were thus founded upon a distinct set of values which fuelled the enquiry and formed the basis of subsequent experimentation, theory and practice.

The four sources of knowledge outlined above, as well as the values which underpinned the enquiry, led the project members to the conclusion that there was potential to work for change with both the environment and the individual by selecting the tools for the job rather than being constrained by one theoretical position or diagnostic system. The point at which the analysis started depended upon the purpose of the intervention and the tools used, which varied according to the context. However, in each case the intervention was based around three simple perspectives:

- The focus of the analysis was to seek to understand the context in which one rather than an alternative behaviour occurred (hence it was named 'context focused analysis').
- Each of the participants (child, parent and professionals) was identified as a joint partner (co-researcher) in generating that understanding.
- The focus for change was based on the agreed formulation (the contextual understanding of why the behaviour occurred) and potentially included any of the constituent parts of that understanding. Thus, the child's school was equally likely to be asked to change its practice, as was the child or parent likely to be asked to change theirs.

3 Process

An adult who self-refers to a psychologist is in a different position from that of a child. A child is referred by a parent, teacher, or some other agent. The question of how the referral happens, the label used and the point at which this label is removed, is not a neutral issue. As the issue of diagnostic labelling is critical for the child and will impact on their long-term future, it is not enough to argue that the label might be a good fit or assist communication between professionals. Any label will have very real consequences, and if it is to be used, any justification for its use must outweigh the harm that it can do. In the context of the project described here, a core value was ensuring that no harm was done to the child through diagnostic labelling. This was achieved through the following process:

- *Definition*. Lane and colleagues started with a process to define the encounter, rather than starting with the concept of assessment. A number of issues were apparent in the way the process of defining problems emerged. The idea that a number of agents had the power to impact on the decision was recognized and taken into account. The child was seen as one of those agents and therefore their view had to be incorporated. Thus, the process by which definitions emerged was one of negotiation between the parties involved. In order to deal with power inequalities, an 'open file' system was instituted. This drew on work by Lane and Green (1990, originated in 1973) and was at the time a rare practice (Cohen, 1982). Hence the initial process became one of defining the encounter based on a shared concern between the parties. They created frameworks so that each party (including the psychologist) was able to define their areas of concern, the objectives they wanted to meet and the role they expected to play. Once these areas were defined, it was possible to identify shared areas that could form an initial basis for exploration. This process of negotiated realities was critical to the success of the process.
- *Exploration*. Lane and colleagues had committed themselves to defining problems in a way that would be shared and agreed between all parties;

therefore exploration had to follow the same principles. Increasingly, the idea that this was an assessment-led process caused concern and this led to the development of a more exploration-led process. Assessment built on expert models formed part of the exploration. However, clients were taught how to engage with such assessments and to build their own models to challenge the expert process. The task was to generate models of analysis that were sensitive to the variety of factors that inhibited, generated and maintained behaviours, that were contextually relevant, which addressed power inequalities, and which fostered a partnership for change.

- *Formulation.* This was the foundation of the entire process. Given that this work began in the early 1970s, the concept of formulation embraced was radically different to the dominant theories of the day, being neither assessment- nor diagnostically-led. Instead, it was built around a joint understanding that had been informed by professional and client experience, joint hypothesis-testing, and emerging narratives. It evolved and was subject to further testing and evolution. The decision to use an exploration rather than assessment-dominated process led directly to a concept of a joint understanding, a model of the world, a formulation of the controlling factors and a use of that understanding to create a detailed intervention.
- *Intervention.* The choice of the term intervention (rather than the then much more commonly used 'treatment') to describe the change activities arose from the data and value base. Lane and colleagues were not treating pathology but seeking to assist change wherever in the system it was most desirable or feasible. Thus, changing the policy and practice of professionals was just as likely to be the area of activity as specific work with the child. The child could also become the change agent working to assist the professional to adopt new practices. Intervention described this activity better than treatment.
- *Evaluation.* Given the purpose was to bring about change in the life chances of the child and practice of the school, the aim was to ensure effective evaluation based on the agreed purpose. A wide variety of evaluation processes were adopted and included client-led data gathering as well as long-term follow-up (up to 20 years in some cases). The concern was not simply to be effective but also to understand which elements of a programme had contributed to change, how future programmes might benefit from the learning on the current one and what might be needed to optimize future gains for the client system.

Drawing upon these frameworks a particular process for formulation was constructed which met the overall purpose and drew upon experience and research-generated perspectives. Similar processes were developed by other practitioners which replicated and elaborated on these approaches (see Coulby and Harper, 1983; Gosling, 2001; Gray *et al.*, 1994). We argue from this that case formulation can be undertaken in a way that encompasses personal, interpersonal and systems perspectives with a scientific framework, yet remain a shared journey with the client.

SOME FINAL THOUGHTS

It should be noted that the case example provided in this chapter is presented as just one approach to formulation, not an exemplar. In arguing for a broader base for the scientist–practitioner model, we believe that each of the processes we use at each stage of a psychological enquiry needs to be defined, or at least be capable of definition. Given that the journeys we create with our clients represent a partially unknown destination, these processes are not linear steps but rather a meander through the woods, creating new pathways as we go. It follows then that case formulation within a scientist–practitioner framework can and must be consistent with a client partnership framework into which it is possible to incorporate a variety of theoretical positions. As Rose reminds us:

> For any living phenomenon we observe and wish to interpret, there are many possible legitimate descriptions. There are within-level causal explanations; descriptions that locate the organism as part of a more complex ecosystem; molecular, developmental and evolutionary accounts. These accounts cannot be collapsed into the one 'true' explanation in which the living phenomenon becomes 'nothing but' a molecular assemblage, a genetic imperative, or whatever. It all depends on the purposes for which the explanation is required. To put it formally, we live in a material world that is an ontological unity, but which we approach with epistemological diversity. Every aspect of our human existence is simultaneously biological, personal, social and historical.
>
> (2001: S6)

If there is any value in this argument we cannot claim that there is only one correct way to formulate or that issues of accuracy can always be prioritized over engagement, encounter and utility.

Of course, this is not to suggest that there are not, on occasions, good grounds for specializing in offering a service from the perspective of one particular model. As research evidence highlights the contribution of specific ways of working to particular kinds of difficulties, it makes sense that certain models will be used in preference to others and that the process of exploration may be shortened for very good reasons. However, from the standpoint of the styles of reasoning skill that we believe are integral to operating as a scientist–practitioner, the critical issue is do we know when and why we are foreshortening exploration? Are we aware of what we are not attending to as a result of framing an enquiry in one way rather than another, and the implications of this for our clients?

In essence then, we see formulation as the construction of a joint narrative as part of a learning journey that takes us from where we are now to where we want to be. Nonetheless, like any journey we can always decide to go somewhere else instead. We construct, deconstruct and reconstruct the narrative as we go along and our clients do the same. We, just like our clients, may retrace our steps, stop, start, restart, give up, recommit and arrive somewhere, before starting all over again.

The 'Purpose (where are we going and why?), Perspective (what will inform our journey?) and Process (how will we get there?)' framework has been outlined as one of many possible approaches that might enable us to co-construct more elegant, thought-provoking and empowering psychological explanations. Engaging with this framework will inevitably lead us towards other questions which we offer in the hope that they might facilitate greater reflection on your own approach to formulation. These are:

- How do you attempt to make sense of the issues which your client is presenting? What are the purposes and perspectives you and the client bring to this task?
- How might the way you attempt the task of formulation enable and constrain, empower and disempower your client?
- When you and your client have very different explanations for a presenting issue, how do you attempt to work with this difference?
- Whose needs is the formulation designed to serve? To whom does it belong?
- Where does the boundary lie in your work between arriving at an accurate formulation and constructing a helpful one?
- What frameworks of decision-making and reasoning enable you to formulate optimally?
- What are the processes through which your formulation determines:
  - The method, intervention or model of change offered, including how it is offered?
  - How outcome is measured?
  - How new information is integrated into an existing intervention plan?
  - Who is included in the intervention (individual, group, wider system)?

It is our view that however we approach the task of making sense of psychological puzzles, we should be able to answer the above questions for ourselves and not be afraid to enter into a dialogue about them with our clients. Being able to articulate these choice points and to recognize the advantages and disadvantages of choosing one approach to formulation over another is surely what ultimately enables us to tailor psychological theory to the needs of those who seek out our services.

Chapter 4

The unacknowledged world of the creative scientist–practitioner

Imagination is more important than knowledge.

(Albert Einstein)

The world of reality has limits: the world of imagination is boundless.

(Jean-Jacques Rousseau)

How do we provide transformational interventions? What are the skills we need to help us find novel solutions to seemingly intractable problems, and how do we acquire them? Questions such as these lie close to the heart of all applied psychologists, transcending notions of effectiveness to engage us with a deeper quest: namely one of excavating, understanding and harnessing the artistry behind what we do, which enables our technical knowledge to come to life.

As Wheatley (1999) observes, the ability to facilitate transformational experiences may require not only a willingness to break free from the beliefs and traditions of our prevailing culture, but also an ability to improvise and invent – in other words, an ability to create.

This chapter is concerned with the role of creativity in professional practice and how psychologists manifest their creative abilities through the interventions they provide. Specifically, we consider some of the factors that may have traditionally prevented us from including creativity within the 'official' scientist–practitioner discourse, and propose ways in which this might now be addressed in order to realign our scientific identities with our practitioner skills.

It is our position that each psychologist's capacity to create will always and inevitably be personalized according to individual values, work setting and perceptions of professional role. Consequently, as for previous chapters, we invite you to contemplate the ideas presented in the context of your own work and values. In particular, whilst reading this chapter we invite you to hold in mind the occasions on which you have provided 'transformational' (not merely effective) interventions and what these examples might tell you about your use of and capacity for creativity in your work.

CREATIVITY IN PROFESSIONAL PRACTICE: THE CINDERELLA OF THE SCIENTIST–PRACTITIONER DEBATE

The study of creativity is of critical importance to a science concerned with the study of human behaviour. Creativity is an ability that has potentially profound implications for our lives at individual, organizational and societal levels (Feist, 1999; Simonton, 2002). As individuals, for example, the ability to think and act creatively adds scope and dimension to our decision-making skills. Similarly, organizations capitalize on creative ideas to enhance their products and rise above their competitors (Sternberg and Lubart, 1999). Even at a societal level, the ability to be creative facilitates new discoveries that have potentially life-changing results. A classic and oft-quoted example here would be Einstein, whose capacity for creativity enabled him to undertake an imaginary ride on a sunbeam – a journey which led him to conclude that the universe was finite and curved, which in turn had revolutionary implications both for science and society.

Creativity then, is essential for productive action and the advancement of knowledge. Some have also argued that finding appropriate vehicles for its expression is essential for any sustained quality of life, representing a primary means of fostering the personal authenticity that brings meaning to our lives (Cameron, 1995).

Although the case for a psychology of creativity is compelling, the subject has been curiously neglected within the discipline of psychology generally, and the scientist–practitioner debate specifically. As long ago as 1950, Guilford emphasized the importance of the profession directing its energies towards a study of this human capability. However, despite early interests from Gestalt and humanistic psychologists, mainstream psychology has, in the main, proved slow to respond to this call (Simonton, 2002).

Why might this be the case? In their review of how creativity has been conceptualized within psychology, Sternberg and Lubart (1999) identify a number of factors which mitigated against the developments that Guilford proposed. Among other factors, they highlight that traditionally, the study of creativity took place largely within spiritual and mystical domains which were seen as incompatible, theoretically and methodologically, with the scientific aspirations of psychology. Furthermore, creativity has tended to be viewed as an epiphenomenon of other mental processes, such as intellectual development, which were believed to be of greater relevance to the study of human behaviour.

A further difficulty that Sternberg and Lubart (1999) identify has been the lack of multidisciplinary approaches to investigating the phenomenon which has hampered a clear definition and understanding. Thus, what psychologists term creativity the corporate world may term innovation, causing confusion about terminology and its use in different domains (Wehner et al., 1991). Although for the purposes of this chapter these terms are used interchangeably, it is not difficult to appreciate how differences in the way that creativity has been operationalized may have obscured potentially fruitful multidisciplinary exchanges of theory and methodology.

Despite difficulties with locating its role within mainstream psychological research, there does appear to be fairly universal agreement about the fundamental properties of the creative endeavour (Simonton, 2002). Creativity can be defined as that which is (1) original and (2) adaptive for society. Originality here would include that which is novel, unexpected or even at odds with prevailing social or professional thinking but which is also productive in some way. For the psychologist, this might translate into an intervention that is surprising, relative to the specific model of practice in which the work is grounded, but which nonetheless opens up possibilities for change that enhance well-being or functioning in significant ways.

Whilst this definition of creativity may represent a broadly consensual view, its application to professional practice poses something of a paradox. That the most transformational aspects of our work comprise more than instrumental problem-solving would probably be uncontroversial. However, if an act is truly original, we must accept that we cannot predict the exact form it will take, or indeed have any advance knowledge of its impact. For the scientist–practitioner this poses a significant dilemma. How can we legitimately lay claim to the status of scientist if a substantial component of our 'artistry' entails being unable to predict which ideas will emerge and how we will implement them?

The tension inherent in having to marry up technical knowledge with its more artistic expression has been explored in depth by Donald Schön in his seminal work on the reflective practitioner (1987). Using the analogy of the professional as designer, he highlights how applied practice is a holistic skill that can never be captured through description. Mastery occurs through 'action in the field', not its operationalization into distinct variables that can be taught in component parts. The art of practice is learned and refined through experimenting (and inventing) in context and it is in these contexts that understandings and misunderstandings are revealed. There will always be a gap between 'knowing about' and 'knowing how'.

Another way of understanding this distinction is through Suchman's (1987) notion of 'situated action'; that is, action which takes place in concrete, context-specific circumstances. In her analysis of how we engineer actions in our lives, Suchman highlights how the Western preoccupation with rationality which pervades the behavioural and cognitive sciences rest on an assumption that if a plan (intervention) is developed and implemented with sufficient care and skill, then it will unfold in a predictable and desirable fashion. However, drawing on models of anthropology and sociology, Suchman argues that this assumption is flawed. Specifically, she uses Gladwin's (1964) description of how the methods of navigation differ between Europeans and the Trukese (the inhabitants of an island in the Pacific Ocean) to illustrate this point.

Gladwin described how the European navigator charts a course from a set of general navigational principles. Each stage of the journey is related to those principles which enable the navigator to measure, co-ordinate and control each aspect of the journey. This results in a predictable course and time of arrival. The Trukese, however, approach their voyages with an overall objective rather than a detailed plan. In the service of their objective, they take account of the prevailing conditions (such as the wind, tide, clouds and stars) and the implications of their responses to those conditions. Consequently, the nature of the journey is never entirely predictable or possible to plan.

Suchman argues that our day-to-day actions are more akin to the Trukese method of navigation rather than the European model because 'the circumstances of our actions are never fully anticipated and are continuously changing around us . . . our actions, while systematic, are never planned in the strong sense that cognitive science would have it' (1987: viii–ix). Baillie and Corrie (1996) suggest that this idea of having to be responsive to evolving external contingencies represents a useful analogy for making sense of the twists and turns of engaging in therapy: a journey which requires clients to monitor and adjust their course as they traverse unfamiliar psychological terrain. We would suggest that this is equally true of all spheres of applied psychology and maps on to the essence of what Schön is describing when he refers to a wisdom in practice that can never be fully articulated or planned in advance.

The analogies of design and navigation highlight that there is a fundamental difference between the world of instrumental problem-solving and the type of thinking and action required in professional practice. Guilford's (1967) differentiation of convergent and divergent thinking and Maslow's (1971) description of primary and secondary creativity help us understand this more clearly. For Guilford, convergent thinking is concerned with consensus around a particular decision or action (that is, arriving at a single, correct response), whereas divergent thinking is concerned with the capacity to identify multiple, varied and original responses to a situation (see also Chapter 2, in which we differentiated contractive and expansive reasoning styles and began to explore which skills might be needed for which type of enquiry).

Maslow couches convergent and divergent thinking styles within two distinct types of creativity. Secondary creativity is that which relies primarily upon technical competence for its delivery. It is likely to occur within the existing frameworks of knowledge and although requiring skill, is unlikely to be novel in a way that has transformational implications. Primary creativity, in contrast, is that which evokes inspiration and can lead to transformation. In describing this as 'a diluted, more secular, more frequent version of the mystical experience', Maslow (1971: 62) seems to hint at the vaguely spiritual quality that primary creativity can contain. This quality has been endorsed particularly by those working in the therapeutic field (for example, Harris Williams (1998) talks of engaging the imagination to create a space for knowledge of an altogether different kind from technical reasoning).

Arguably, as scientist–practitioners, we have traditionally felt more comfortable about publicly acknowledging secondary creativity than we do its primary counterpart. The latter seems more mysterious and unknowable than the traditional scientist–practitioner discourse might lead us to believe is acceptable. Similarly, we could argue that the scientist–practitioner model has, by and large, been grounded in a model of convergent thinking which captures only one aspect of professional practice. The result has been, however, that some of the most influential skills psychologists bring to their work (that is, the resources we need to apply our knowledge 'in action') remain poorly understood.

SOURCES OF INSIGHT FOR DEVELOPING OUR PRIMARY CREATIVITY

Despite the historical neglect of creativity as a research topic within psychology, the 1980s and 1990s witnessed a growth of interest in this area (see Glover *et al.*, 1989; Simonton, 1999; Sternberg, 1999). In the context of professional practice specifically, there has been a gradual move towards acknowledging how creativity can provide contexts for transformation as well as more explicit consideration of the sources of inspiration it might be useful and appropriate to draw upon.

Newnes (2001) proposes that we should be more open to and declarative of the highly diverse sources that inform our work, in addition to the technical knowledge base with which our psychology training equips us. If we are to maximize our professional skills in the service of change, he argues that we need to be open to insights from resources as wide-ranging as 'literature, our senses and personal experience' (2001: 6). This sentiment was echoed by Milton and Corrie (2002) who advocate the value of enhancing professional effectiveness and development through searching out contact with the natural world, literature, art, music, drama, dance and spirituality which they propose can help equip psychologists to access the sense of curiosity and playfulness that are essential for transformational practices.

Responses to this call are emerging in myriad ways. They include (but are by no means restricted to) a growing interest in the use of literature to advance our understanding of psychological phenomena (see Symington's (1993) use of the novel *Anna Karenin* to explore the nature and manifestations of narcissism), the introduction of the principles of Zen Buddhism and mindfulness training in mental health care (Linehan, 1993; Segal *et al.*, 2002) and the introduction of spiritual frameworks to understand organizational processes and change (Critten, 2002).

Other examples have been reported, both in the literature and at international conferences. Milton and Corrie (2002) describe how drawing on a client's passion for writing fiction, and in particular, using the 'expertise' and advice of the characters the client had created, proved to be a transformational tool for unlocking alternative possibilities in the context of a critical life dilemma. Christie *et al.* (1992) have used models from developmental psychology to inform the use of music for non-speaking children. Newsom (1992) has adopted a similar approach in her use of play with children. Ross and Hilborn (2005) have applied models for creative thinking to work with antisocial children (as well as in areas such as driver behaviour). Their work has covered several countries and tens of thousands of children and includes follow-up data.

The role of creativity in practice was also explored at the 34th Annual Congress of the European Association for Behavioural and Cognitive Therapies (2004). During a symposium dedicated to this topic, Rosenbaum defined creativity as a psychological skill relevant to skill-directed models such as cognitive-behaviour therapy. Specifically, the task of the practitioner was conceptualized as one of training clients in creative problem-solving by being creative themselves; all psychological interventions, Rosenbaum proposed, should be viewed as a uniquely creative process. In a similar spirit of enquiry, participants at the European Mentoring and Coaching Conference (2004) looked at the use of music and drama to generate individual and organizational change.

Developments at an organizational level also hint at a change in belief about the resources it is acceptable for psychologists to draw upon. Within the British Psychological Society, recent years have witnessed the inauguration of Sections on transpersonal psychology, consciousness and experiential psychology and the recent creation of a Special Interest Group in Holistic Psychology. Grants provided by the Wellcome Trust as part of their 'sciart' programme (2001) have also aimed to create partnerships between the worlds of science and art for mutual collaboration and inspiration. Taken in combination, these developments suggest an official move towards embracing domains of knowledge that might once have been judged as inappropriate subject matter for a respectable science.

Examples of creativity in practice are no doubt legion, but rarely given the public consideration they deserve. It is not difficult to appreciate why this might be the case. Incorporating traditionally non-psychological and non-scientific practices into our work has fundamental implications for what we regard as legitimate knowledge. For example, are these developments tantamount to saying that pretty much 'anything goes'? Are we in danger of endorsing Feyerabend's (1975) argument that in the absence of any single method that can lead us consistently towards the truth, there can be no logical basis for assuming that science is superior to mythology or astrology?

We are not, in fact, advocating that anything goes. However, we are proposing that, as a profession, we need to start thinking about the role of creativity (particularly primary creativity) in our work in more sophisticated ways. We must elevate this aspect of professional practice to the heart of scientist–practitioner enquiry.

If we are to follow Schön's analogy of the professional as designer, then it follows that our creative endeavours will be highly individualized and become more so over the course of our careers. Moreover, as Gruber and Wallace (1999) observe, unlike many of the models of development within psychology theory which suggest linear and predictable progression, the manifestations of our creativity are unpredictable, multicausal in nature and constantly evolving in the light of ongoing interactions with the world around us. (In fact, this may not be as antagonistic to the scientific status of psychology as initially appears to be the case, particularly when considered in the light of new science; see Chapter 5.)

Thus, we would argue that if we are to understand and harness our creative skills, the question becomes not whether it is legitimate to look to other sources of evidence to guide our innovations, but rather the ways in which we do so. Artists as well as scientists we may well be. However, unlike artists, scientist–practitioners must underpin their creativity with frameworks that enable them to make discerning choices about what constitutes 'acceptable' improvisation, how they monitor its impact and how they differentiate adaptive creativity from practices that are simply 'off the wall'. The practitioner who uses poetry, literature, music or dance but can articulate what has led to the choice of a given method in a particular context, as well as the vision of practice from which it originated, is innovating in a way that we would see as entirely compatible with a contemporary vision of the scientist–practitioner framework. However, the practitioner who resorts to the use of any method (including, in our view, a scientific method) in a way that is unquestioning and which is not grounded in the context of any specific vision of practice, we would see as violating a central ethic of the profession.

The central issue then, is one of obligation. The artistry of our practice needs to be predicated upon a distinct vision and sense of purpose and it is this, we believe, that helps us differentiate the skilled use of creativity from a directionless and potentially detrimental eclecticism. As Holdsworth reminds us, the quintessential task is one of 'applying appropriate frameworks to experience in order to guide our actions' (1993: 143). It is, therefore, to potentially appropriate frameworks we must now turn.

IN SEARCH OF FRAMEWORKS FOR ENHANCING THE DEVELOPMENT OF SKILLED ACTION

In the absence of any clear consensual frameworks that might guide the development of our creativity in systematic ways, it may be beneficial to follow the advice of Gruber and Wallace (1999) who encourage us to embark upon an open-minded search for pathways into our creative selves. If, as identified at the start of this chapter, creativity is important at an individual, organizational and social level, it makes sense to begin with an exposition of creativity as occurring within these domains.

In this section we will, therefore, consider the potential contribution to our creative practice of two frameworks: (1) the influence of idiosyncratic learning styles in the context of individual factors and (2) wider influences at the micro-, meso- and macro-level. Given that creativity is idiosyncratic and multicausally determined, it should be noted that these frameworks will, by definition, be partial. In the absence of a sound phenomenology of creativity in practice, and holding true to the need for divergent thinking, our aim here is to be exploratory rather than prescriptive, enabling us to embark upon a search for ideas that might aid the development of creativity in the workplace, rather than any consensual or definitive statement about 'how to do it'.

INDIVIDUAL PATHWAYS INTO PRIMARY CREATIVITY

There are potentially many ways of conceptualizing our individual role as agents of transformation. However, we can anticipate that the ways in which we improvise and create are likely to be heavily influenced by our individual approaches to learning. As learning preferences determine much of how we best absorb information, it follows that they are likely to influence how we improvise and invent both in our lives and in the workplace.

In recent decades, there has been growing interest in how people learn. This literature addresses how we absorb new material (e.g. the so-called 'deep' vs. 'surface' approaches to learning; see Entwistle and Ramsden, 1983; Gibbs 1992), learning as an experiential process (e.g. Kolb, 1984) and as conversational science (Thomas and Harri-Augstein, 1985) as well as models of adult learning (Knowles, 1990) and transformational education (Wang and Sarbo, 2004).

Other approaches have focused on the unique styles of intelligence we each bring to new information and emphasize the importance of identifying and working skilfully with learning preferences. For example, Multiple Intelligence Theory (Lazear, 1991) identifies at least seven distinct forms of intelligence, incorporating body/kinaesthetic, interpersonal, intrapersonal, logical/mathematical, musical/rhythmic, verbal/linguistic and visual/spatial styles of learning. The VARK (Visual, Aural, Read/Write and Kinaesthetic) model developed by Fleming (2002), in contrast, explores our individual tendencies to favour different sensory modalities to help us engage with and integrate new ideas into our pre-existing knowledge and experience.

Incorporating an assessment of our clients' learning preferences may help us organize our use of primary creativity around those sensory modalities intuitively favoured by our clients, whether that client be an individual or an organization. Fleming, for example, proposes ways of maximizing learning within each modality preference which span (1) the use of diagrams, maps, illustrations and pictures for those with a visual preference; (2) use of discussion, debate, verbal exploration, listening to audiotape recordings, stories and joke for aural learners; (3) written formats for read/writers such as the use of Pepys' style diaries, story books, handouts or manuals and (4) practice, role-play, and putting knowledge into action for kinaesthetic learners.

In reality, Fleming points out that many people are multimodal and, of course, developmental theory would suggest that different sources of learning are predominant at different stages, as well as influenced by cognitive ability. Corrie and Supple (2004) have also pointed out how VARK can be used to support the learning and practice of cognitive therapists in the context of visual impairment, emphasizing the need to be flexible and creative in finding ways to explore techniques that take account of physical impairment and disability.

As a broad framework, models of individual learning preferences provide a useful way of thinking about the style and impact of our own creativity in practice, as well as how we engage our clients. For example, consider the potential impact on your future improvisations of routinely asking your clients the following questions during the early stages of your encounter:

- How do you best absorb new ideas?
- What types of learning environment most often enable you to generate good ideas?
- When you need inspiration, to which sources do you typically turn?
- What are the kinds of activities from which you derive a sense of enjoyment or fun?

If clients' responses to these questions hint at a strong visual learning preference then this presents an opportunity to innovate in visually creative ways through, for example, capitalizing on the use of colour, pictures or contact with visually-inspiring scenes provided by the natural environment. Aural learners might value interventions that capitalize on poetry, music or other forms of expression that are grounded in rhythm. Read/writers might be the clients who lead you to consider types of innovation involving story-telling and use of metaphors and literature, whilst those with a kinaesthetic preference may need the chance to act: to play, to make, to paint, to dance or to engage with the natural world through a specific activity. The point is clearly not to be beholden to any individual learning style, but rather to be attuned to channels of improvisation that might resonate with clients' preferences, with potentially transformational results.

Creativity that is grounded within a framework of learning preferences (and not solely couched within ideas of intellectual capabilities or developmental needs) would be concerned from the outset, then, with questions such as:

- Which style of intelligence/learning does a client intuitively favour?
- How do these preferences manifest themselves in the client's day-to-day existence and functioning?
- To what types of creativity is this client most likely to respond at a deep (holistic) level and how might you use this knowledge to shape any future improvisations?
- How will you monitor the impact of your creativity on this sensory modality?
- How will you know if you need to change direction?

Effective use of creativity will also require some cross-comparisons. If your own learning preference is very similar to that of your client, it will be important to consider how this might enable or constrain your ability to invent pathways that lead to transformational experiences. Similarly, if you and the client have different learning preferences, it will be important to consider the opportunities and challenges that this diversity affords.

As part of the development of our professional practitioner selves it is not helpful, therefore, to assess our clients' capacities for creativity without having an awareness of our own. In our view, each of us as modern scientist–practitioners should be able to provide answers to the above questions and engage in a direct consideration of the following:

*   The form our creativity most often takes in our practice.
*   The ways in which we monitor and evaluate the impact of our creativity.
*   The most interesting pieces of work we have participated in over the course of our careers, and what this tells us about our creative skills and learning preferences.
*   The novel solutions we have created to overcome obstacles, and what this tells us about our creative skills and learning preferences.
*   Those types of improvisation we feel comfortable about using in the name of creative professional practice and those we do not, and what each might tell us about the hidden assumptions and frameworks that guide our work.

If you consider these issues even for a moment, we anticipate that certain themes will begin to emerge. These themes can give you an important clue about your unique approach to creativity and help you monitor its impact more effectively: whether in the context of your own reflective journey or in the context of supervision. However, the ways in which our creativity manifests itself will also depend on the specific environments (personal and professional) in which we find ourselves. Individual learning occurs within a context and will be shaped by contact with teachers, mentors and peers, as well as larger social, political and cultural factors. Indeed, as Fleming (2002) argues, natural preferences may be masked by experiences and so we must develop an awareness of those experiences which impact on how we exhibit our creativity, for better or worse.

HOW MICRO-, MESO- AND MACRO-LEVEL INFLUENCES SHAPE OUR CREATIVITY: THE IMPACT OF EXTERNAL CONTINGENCIES

In their qualitative analysis of practitioners' perceptions of the scientist–practitioner model, Corrie and Callanan (2001) found that beliefs about its value and merits were mediated by a range of external influences that ranged from the impact of individual trainers and supervisors, to specific working environments. These external contingencies created either enabling or constraining conditions that had to be reconciled with individualized codes of practice in order for a sense of professional integrity to be maintained.

One framework that can help us consider the impact of social context on our work is that proposed by Mohan (1996), who differentiated three levels of inter-related influence: (1) the micro-level (that is, processes operating internally to any single organization or corporate structure); (2) the meso-level (the ideology of the political party in power that informs the policies subsequently implemented at service level) and the macro-level (international trends in welfare or the delivery of health and social care).

Mohan's model was concerned with an analysis of interpretations of the NHS reforms during the 1990s. Nonetheless, it is possible to identify how our creativity might be bounded by these three levels of influence. For example, at the micro-level we could consider how our improvisations and inventions may have been enhanced or inhibited by the values of the training schemes through which we acquired our qualifications, our post-qualification training and our current employment settings. This might lead us to contemplate questions such as:

- What assumptions (explicit and implicit) held by the organization in which I work or to whom I am in some other way accountable, govern my use of creativity?
- What forms of improvisation would be considered acceptable by these organizations? What would be considered unacceptably radical?
- What types of creativity are central to my practice that I would feel comfortable revealing to my colleagues in this organization? What does this tell me about the values of the organization?
- What types of creativity are central to my practice but which I would not feel comfortable revealing to my colleagues in this organization? What might this tell me about the values of the organization?
- How is my learning enabled or constrained by the culture in which I am working?

Exploring these types of questions would present opportunities for meaningful discussions about creativity in practice at both a pre- and post-qualification level. At the pre-qualification level, for example, we would need to consider the point at which we encouraged and taught creativity and whether this would lead to radical changes in training procedure. Similarly if, prior to qualifying, trainees were given vivas specifically on their use of improvisation and creativity, what might we learn about their talents, needs and shortfalls in the training experiences we provide? Discovering their individual learning preferences might also provide trainees with information that could guide decisions about post-qualification employment: both in terms of the kind of work they will find most rewarding and in terms of the organizational settings to which they might be best suited.

The above issues might be equally relevant to continuing professional development. For example, appraisals might look very different, and help shape professional identity and individual performance in new ways, if they routinely explored the steps that individuals had taken (or needed to take) to enhance their skills in improvisation and creativity. If opportunities for further training were organized not solely around skill acquisition but also around learning preference, continuing professional development could encompass a whole new dimension of self-knowledge. How we equip ourselves for the challenges of tomorrow is the subject of Chapter 13. For now, however, we might anticipate that taking account of individuals' learning preferences might empower all psychologists, at whatever stage of their professional development, to become more proactive in their learning journeys and to experience greater fulfilment in their work. This could have implications for the prevention of stress and burn out and possibly also for staff retention.

At the meso-level, use of creativity is likely to be influenced in more subtle ways by government policy and the larger debate about what constitutes the 'legitimate' sources of evidence upon which psychologists are expected to draw. Questions that might uncover the impact of meso-level influences on our ideas about suitable creative acts in psychological practice might include those that pay attention to the impact of legislation. One key example here is the current emphasis on 'evidence-based practice' or 'empirically-supported interventions' which may lead us to prioritize certain types of data over others. Another example would be the influence of legislation on the need to promote inclusive practices in the context of diversity (see for example, the Disability Discrimination Act (Department of Social Security, 1995), and the Special Educational Needs and Disability Act (Department for Education and Employment, 2001)), which has caused psychologists to reconsider how to work meaningfully and creatively with clients whose backgrounds, learning styles and needs are different from their own.

Finally, at the macro-level, we would need to consider international trends that impact on what we do. These influences might be harder to access directly, as we may only become substantively aware of their impact as they filter down into the meso- and micro-levels. However, if we consider psychology as responding to these influences at some level, we may be able to identify numerous trends that are worthy of our attention. For example, at an international level, the emerging discipline of positive psychology (see Carr, 2004; Seligman, 2002) highlights the importance of understanding the role of love, optimism and personal authenticity over and above the management of problems, as well as the need to develop a science of human strengths. Could it be that this reflects, at least on some level, the growing public demand for knowledge about how to enhance personal and spiritual development? Certainly, a cursory glance at the wider media culture, with its emphasis on self-help and pathways to emotional and spiritual fulfilment would appear to support this.

EMBRACING CREATIVITY WITHIN A SCIENTIST–PRACTITIONER DISCOURSE: SOME CONCLUSIONS

In this chapter, we have argued that creativity, including, in particular, primary creativity has been a neglected aspect of the scientist–practitioner debate. As this activity is central to the transformational interventions we aim to offer our clients, the lack of attention to the ways in which we create and improvise in our work is a serious omission and one which we believe has, over the years, widened the science–practice schism.

We have presented, for illustrative purposes, two frameworks that could be used to open up a fuller discussion about the ways in which creativity manifests itself in our work. One of these frameworks focuses on how learning preferences may motivate our use of creativity at an individual level; the other emphasizes the social and cultural factors that shape its expression. These frameworks are neither exclusive nor definitive. However, they represent starting points for revisioning the scientist–practitioner model as one that is concerned not solely with the art of effectiveness but also with what Zander and Zander (2000) term 'the art of possibility'.

Arguably, psychology does not yet have an effective language for talking about primary creativity in professional practice. In the absence of such a language, we would agree with Gruber and Wallace (1999) who suggest that rather than aiming for uniformity of definition, we should be prepared to grapple with idiosyncratic expressions of creativity in our lives and work; that is, what creative people actually 'do'. This suggests that a useful starting point would be to examine the modern scientist–practitioners' use of creativity 'in action'. Gathering examples of this skill across the psychological disciplines would enable us to achieve a phenomenology of creativity that can enable us to develop frameworks for guiding the development of this resource in practice. Similarly, it would be of interest to learn whether there are any trends in improvisation or creativity that differ as a function of work context. For example, do those working in public sector services differ systematically from those working in academic institutions or the private sector? Do those working exclusively in one setting differ from those whose practice occurs in multiple settings?

The effects of micro- meso- and macro-level influences highlight that creativity is not solely a personal matter. More public debate about the impact of wider organizational influences on our inventive endeavours might encourage a fuller dialogue. It might also help us avoid premature conclusions about what is and is not acceptable simply because certain aspects of our artistry appear fraught with conceptual difficulty or because a particular professional climate appears to dictate that some things cannot be questioned. Such an approach to enquiry would surely, and helpfully, lead to an exposition of what creativity actually means in the context of skilled practice, the stage in a psychologist's career in which skills in improvisation are explicitly introduced, how we combine invention with technical knowledge and how creativity evolves over the course of an individual's career.

The idiographic focus of professional practice means that as scientist–practitioners, we will always have to invent ways of bridging the subjective and the objective. We hope, therefore, that you, the reader might be encouraged to personalize the quest for creativity, both for yourself and your clients, by being open to appropriate frameworks, in whatever form they emerge.

Nonetheless, for those readers who feel that the ideas outlined in this chapter represent an overly-radical departure from our scientific selves, it may be reassuring to learn that notions of creativity, innovation and spontaneity are also consistent with models of contemporary science. For example, catastrophe theory describes how spontaneous actions promote growth and change, as in the case of spontaneous particle creation. Thus, models of new science describe not so much a steady state which we can plan our way around (akin to the Western approach to navigation outlined earlier) but rather a dance back and forth, spontaneous action and reaction, inventing and creating. This suggests the need to consider the nature of our science afresh and is the subject of the next chapter.

Chapter 5

What kind of scientists are we? Re-examining the nature of scientific knowledge

There is the world of ideas and the world of practice.

(Matthew Arnold)

Who owns the knowledge, and thus who can define the reality?

(Peter Reason)

What exactly do we mean when we say that psychology is a science? What constitutes 'scientific knowledge' and how can we be certain that it should be the foundation of our practice? These questions should be close to the heart of all scientist–practitioners, requiring us to define a form of enquiry that is purported to lie at the heart of our professional identities, roles and activities.

In this chapter, we consider questions relating to what is or what could be meant by science in the context of professional practice. By drawing on philosophical debates, we highlight how science is an evolving landscape of stories about how knowledge accumulates and that, as a result, there are potentially many ways of engaging with science. The task facing psychologists as we conceive it, is deciding how to draw selectively upon these different stories to help us critique, refine and communicate about our practice in systematic ways.

Drawing upon philosophical debate to refine our practice may seem like a good idea in principle, but the task poses some fundamental challenges. By definition, questions about the nature of science are philosophically rather than professionally driven which gives the literature a complex and abstract feel. We must begin, therefore, by stating explicitly that we are not aiming to provide a comprehensive overview of the philosophy of science or any philosophical position within it. Instead, our task is to extract the essence of different stories, to help us identify how each one might contribute to practitioner-led enquiry.

We should also point out that this chapter is concerned with the concept of scientific knowledge rather than the methods used to attain it. Methodology, however important, is not the destination but simply the route taken to get there. It is the way we frame the destination that is critical when it comes to thinking about our relationship with science and upon which a robust and meaningful interpretation of the scientist–practitioner model must ultimately depend. We hope, therefore, that this chapter will provide ideas on how to investigate the puzzles that confront you in your work and encourage you to personalize the debate by reflecting on your own definition of science and how it has shaped your approach to enquiry. Specifically, we invite you to consider the following questions:

- What is the model of science that guides your work (however tightly or loosely defined)?
- How have your perceptions of science been influenced by your practice?
- How has your practice been influenced by your model of science?
- What have been the key influences on your personal definition of science?

Similarly, as new stories about science are introduced, we invite you to consider their implications for the ways in which you critique your practice, including the types of results they lead you to seek.

CREATING A FRAMEWORK FOR EXPLORING DIFFERENT SCIENTIFIC STORIES

In the previous chapters, a central idea was the necessity of having an over-arching narrative framework that can systematically guide our decision-making in the context of any given enquiry. When it comes to thinking about the nature of science, there are a range from which to choose, including those that focus on the competing narratives of discovery and invention (Follette, *et al.*, 1992); those that identify the different 'trajectories' in which scientific enquiry unfolds (Trierweiler and Stricker, 1998) and those that emphasize the ways in which science oppresses or liberates as part of a broader political agenda (e.g. Ussher, 1991).

Although each of these offers something of value, we have found it helpful to adopt the 'Purpose, Perspective and Process' framework that was outlined in Chapter 3. To summarize, this framework proposes that how you and the client define the *purpose* of your work together is shaped by your *perspective* (namely, what you each bring to the encounter including values, beliefs and prior experience) which enables you to structure a *process* for the work to follow. Similarly, the model of science that underpins our practice will be informed by the sense of purpose that guides a particular enquiry which in turn is shaped by the perspectives that we, our clients and other stakeholders bring to the investigation (including various parties' beliefs about what knowledge is and how it accumulates). This in turn informs the way in which the enquiry is carried out, including the types of questions that are deemed legitimate to ask and the methods used to answer them.

Using this framework can help us re-examine our relationship with science in two ways. Firstly, it enables us to navigate this philosophical terrain with greater ease by identifying specific themes and questions for our work. Secondly, it can widen our appreciation of different scientific stories by preventing us from becoming overly enmeshed in our own ideas about what science is, or should be. Our personal definition of science is simply one story about how we can better understand the world.

THE PURSUIT OF TRUTH AND THE EMPIRICIST WORLDVIEW

It is a truism to state that science occupies a privileged position in our society. Filtered through government policy, the media or advertising campaigns, we have all participated in conversations about the latest scientific developments, whether the subject under review is information on the latest way to lose weight or 'proof' of the carcinogenic properties of some household product formerly regarded as harmless.

Why do we esteem science so greatly? In his seminal work *Conjectures and Refutations*, Karl Popper (1963) proposed that Western society tends to equate science with the pursuit of truth. As truth is (arguably) the ultimate goal of knowledge and science (allegedly) brings us closer to it, we regard it as a gateway to wisdom.

When we frame the purpose of science as one of discovering truth, we also buy into a set of related beliefs. These include an assumption that there is such a thing as 'truth'; that truth is the most important type of knowledge to acquire and that, with the aid of the right (scientific) methods, truth has no option but to reveal itself to us. Thus, according to popular wisdom, facts are essentially unambiguous; the role of science is to simply reveal and report them.

The notion that science is a gateway to the truth has its origins in empiricism, a story that originated in seventeenth-century thinking. Empiricist science, of which logical positivism (a movement which emerged in early twentieth-century Europe) was the ultimate refinement, claimed that science should be concerned with validating ideas by examining how they fared when tested against reality.

In emphasizing the need to uncover facts, empiricists were dubious about the contribution of theory and metaphysics as a basis for knowledge, which they regarded as the intellectual playground of society's elite. The belief was that, through recourse to objective data, knowledge would progress in systematic ways and would have substantive implications for social welfare (see, for example, the work of David Hume who was a social reformer and advocate of women's rights). Thus, to apply our original framework, we see that the purpose of empiricist science is to discover truth, and in doing so, to contribute to a moral and just cause. This purpose is underpinned by a perspective that states that reality (truth) exists independently of us. Consequently, its discovery is seen to be philosophically unproblematic; all scientists have to do is apply the correct method and knowledge of the world is assured.

If this is the central purpose and perspective of empiricism, what then is its fundamental process? Empiricist science is based on an assumption that information about the world is directly available to us through sensory experience, in particular observation. It should be noted here, that observation does not refer to the random perceptual experiences of each individual but rather to those observations shared amongst the scientific collective. In other words, through achieving consensus, scientists can be certain that they are achieving ever-closer approximations of an objective reality.

Embedded within this process we can see that there are two additional assumptions. The first is that scientific observation is neutral. The second is that knowledge of the world becomes more robust according to the extent to which scientists agree and are able to generalize their findings. This, in turn, depends upon attaining multiple observations that can be consistently reproduced across a diverse range of situations and ensuring that no single observation conflicts with the universal law that has already been established through prior observations.

Empiricist science tells a story about the need for caution. It warns against attaching too much significance to any single finding because in order to have scientific credibility, we must be able to replicate that finding across time and place. The underlying perspective here is obvious: our interventions will always be contaminated by prior theorizing, preferences or hunches and need to be curbed by the more rigorous evidence which scientific consensus affords.

There can be little doubt that psychology has maintained a definite commitment to this story about science. At the time when psychology was emerging as an applied profession the principal task was to ensure survival. Given that the knowledge base and practices of psychologists were viewed with a certain amount of scepticism (see Chapter 1), there were very good reasons for allying the profession with an empiricist model of science. This story subsequently reasserted itself in the debate about whether psychotherapy 'works' (see Rachman, 1971) and more recently, the need to ensure that our interventions are informed by the latest evidence (e.g. Department of Health, 1996, 1997).

There may, therefore, be distinct advantages of aligning ourselves with this model of science. In a political and economic climate that shapes our practice in increasingly complex ways, presenting ourselves as empiricist scientist–practitioners will serve us well when we want to tell a story to demonstrate our credibility and expertise or to justify aspects of what we do (whether to ourselves, our employers, our funding bodies or society at large). Obvious examples of where an empiricist story has, or might usefully, be told would include the following:

- developing a broad knowledge base that is (hypothetically) universal and generalizable;
- optimizing effective practice through 'standardizing' aspects of technical delivery (such as developing treatment manuals);
- justifying use of a particular practice by demonstrating its effectiveness;
- protecting the public by making us accountable to something more than our own predilections;
- enhancing our professional status by demonstrating our allegiance to know-

ledge that is more powerful than our implicit theories about how the world works.

THE PROBLEM WITH EMPIRICISM

The empiricist worldview is a dominant scientific narrative within psychology but it is only one story about what science is and does. Moreover, it is a story that has proved problematic. One of the difficulties of defining psychological science exclusively in these terms is that it creates a very limited view of human beings and their capabilities. As it frames human experience in the light of what can be observed our scientific knowledge ultimately becomes reduced to anatomy, the only parts of ourselves that can be objectively studied. As Grof explains:

> Everything we thought and felt and knew was based on information that we collected with the aid of our sensory organs. Following the logic of this materialistic model, human consciousness, ethics, intelligence, art, religion and science itself were seen as by-products of material processes that occur within the brain.
>
> (1993: 4)

For psychologists, defining the scientist–practitioner model exclusively in the light of the empiricist story is problematic because the phenomena of interest to us are frequently dilemmas, values, choices and relationships which cannot usefully be understood as epiphenomena of material processes. Moreover, focusing on an objective world that can (at least theoretically) be objectively known fails to take account of the realities of practice, where innovations and improvisations are the order of the day (see Chapter 4). For the professional, the pursuit of truth is ultimately less informative than the pursuit of knowledge that is practical.

It was not just psychologists for whom the empiricist story became problematic. Recognition that observation is always theory-dependent led to the realization that scientists cannot use observation to establish which theories are true and which are false. Observation, as every psychologist knows, is filtered through prior knowledge and assumptions. We observe according to what we believe we already know. An additional difficulty is that no amount of observation can prove something to be true because the future could always contain examples that contradict the universal law. Bertrand Russell's example of the turkey who, based on previous multiple observations, expects to be fed on the morning of Christmas Eve but instead has its throat cut illustrates this flaw all too starkly.

Defenders of the empiricist story will point out that contemporary interpretations favour observational statements that are probabilistically, rather than factually, true and acknowledge that science always involves innovations that lie beyond scientific consensus (Chalmers, 1982). However, the flaw in its central purpose remains. The quest for generalizable findings that lead us progressively towards an objective and universal reality is an incomplete and ultimately inadequate account of how knowledge develops. The scientist–practitioner needs scientific narratives that can accommodate novel ideas and creative inventions as well as ones that can police effectiveness.

THE CRISIS OF RATIONALITY AND THE RESPONSE OF FALSIFICATIONIST SCIENCE

The problems with empiricism presaged a radical change in ideas about the nature of science leading to what has been termed a 'crisis of rationality' (see Chalmers, 1982; Hacking 1983; Manicas and Secord, 1983, for an overview). For psychologists, the crisis of rationality represents an ongoing opportunity to consider how different philosophical responses might open up ways of uniting science with decision-making, formulating, divergent thinking and creativity – the qualities identified as prerequisites of effective practice in the previous chapters. For example, if we want a story about science that can help us devise increasingly sophisticated and useful theories what options are there? Similarly, if we want to speak publicly about our creative acts but still do so within a scientific 'frame' what type of story would we need to tell? One option is to turn to falsification.

Karl Popper (1963, 1968) argued that instead of focusing on uncovering universal laws, scientists should direct their attention towards ensuring that the theories they follow are the best that are available. Essentially, he claimed that all scientific theories are just conjectures and if science deals in conjecture rather than facts, then scientists should not feel constrained by the prevailing theoretical position when developing solutions to scientific puzzles. Progress depends on the ability to engage with the proverbial 'thinking outside the box', which requires a flair for the imaginative.

However, whilst no constraints should be imposed during the early stages of theory construction, a conjecture can only be afforded the status of a scientific theory if it survives rigorous testing based on the criterion of falsification. Put simply, falsification refers to the existence of an observation or observations which, if upheld through scientific investigation, would demonstrate that the original theory was wrong (in other words, that the theory was 'falsified').

According to Popper then, the hallmark of a sophisticated science is the extent to which its theories are framed in falsifiable terms. This requires generating falsifiable hypotheses which can be tested through the processes of observation and experimentation. However, unlike empiricism, falsificationist science argues that these processes enable us to rout out the weaker theories when they fail to withstand the rigours of testing. Only the most robust theories survive for further testing, and in this way, we can have confidence in the theories we devise.

As a story about science, falsification is not without its limitations. As Chalmers (1982) highlights, even a cursory review of the history of science illustrates that falsification is not the way in which major scientific advancements have occurred.

Most theories make observational claims that are inconsistent with the theory to some degree. It is only with time (sometimes years) that the meaning of inconsistent observations becomes clear. However, this does not mean the theory is wrong and applying the criteria of falsification could lead to valuable ideas being abandoned prematurely.

A further obstacle from a professional point of view is that psychologists are unlikely to adopt the ruthlessness that falsificationist science requires. Practitioners are generally reluctant to relinquish their assumptions about how the world works, preferring instead to look for explanations that circumvent the problem of conflicting findings (Mahrer, 2000). Moreover, professional practitioners will always prioritize the search for effective solutions over eliminating ineffective ones, despite taking account of what has not worked when generating ideas on how to solve new problems.

A more sophisticated outlook on falsification may help us overcome some of these difficulties. One possibility is to seek advancement of knowledge through confirmation of speculative hypotheses and the falsification of well-established ones. This position has been developed by Lakatos (e.g. 1970, 1976) who, in attempting to overcome the limits of Popper's theory, argued that the task of science is really to provide structures (or 'research programmes') upon which the development of future research can occur. Scientific theories contain basic assumptions which must be accepted by those operating within them. These represent a core of hypotheses (perspectives) which are 'protected from falsification by a protective belt of auxiliary hypotheses' (Chalmers, 1982: 80). The theory also contains guidelines about how the research programme might develop which may mean adding new assumptions and hypotheses to the 'hard core'. Research programmes are progressing or degenerating according to the extent to which they are able to predict novel phenomena, with modifications being acceptable providing they are testable. However, if scientists violate a 'hard core' assumption, then a new research programme is needed.

The more sophisticated falsificationist position advocated by Lakatos provides a story about science that arguably fits well with certain elements of professional practice. For example, it can be argued that when we develop an allegiance to one particular theory or model of practice, we commit ourselves to the 'hard core', and bring that theory to new practice-based dilemmas. We operate according to the purposes and perspectives dictated by the 'hard core'. We may also adapt or even reject those assumptions which are peripheral. One example of this would be the tendency of many psychologists to work integratively, whereby a set of 'hard core' assumptions inform approaches to formulation and intervention, but into which ideas from other models are incorporated.

Applied psychologists are not typically trained to critique their work in the light of falsificationist science, but there may be some distinct merits in doing so. What is appealing about this story for the modern scientist–practitioner is that it creates a place in science for intuition, creativity and improvisation and provides a framework for their systematic use. Any theory can be admitted to scientific conjecturing, as long as the circumstances in which we would be prepared to relinquish it are clearly specified. Anecdotal support for the advantages of this scientific story comes from Corrie and Callanan whilst interviewing practitioners about their perceptions of the scientist–practitioner model. Specifically, one participant spoke of the use of evidence in a changing professional and political climate in ways that seemed to support the purpose underpinning falsification:

> the danger is that (research) could be used to cut things when people are on the edge of something new . . . [Research] should be used so that when you have the evidence that an intervention isn't effective, that's when it shouldn't be used, not to say you shouldn't develop something new.
>
> (2001: 140)

Stringency, this participant seemed to suggest, should not be imposed in the early stages of an enquiry when novel ideas should be actively developed, but at the stage at which a given practice has been demonstrably unsuccessful.

If we pull together some of the central ideas embedded within Popper's and Lakatos' responses to the crisis of rationality, we can see that defining our science in the context of falsification would lead to a purpose that prioritizes: (1) working with the best theories available (rather than aiming to uncover universal or generalizable findings); (2) ensuring best practice by working towards continual refinement of existing theories and (3) continually refining theory through generating conjectures that can be shaped into falsifiable hypotheses for rigorous testing. Questions for the scientist–practitioner which flow from this position would include:

- What are the relative merits of each competing theory in the context of a given enquiry (in terms of the extent to which they are falsifiable)?
- What are my own criteria of falsifiability (that is, what are my own individual theoretical preferences and at what point would I be prepared to reject them)?
- What are the criteria against which I assess the validity of my hunches, intuition and spontaneous actions?
- What are the factors (personal assumptions, people, situations and work contexts) that have led me to reject certain ideas in favour of others?

Embracing falsification in a climate that is very concerned with grounding practices within the available evidence would mean devoting more attention to searching out practices that are ineffective or developing guidelines for when we can conclude that something is not working. At a collective level, defining ourselves as falsificationists would also enable us to reflect on the history of our thinking as a discipline and how our ideas have developed over time. For example, at what points have particular theories fallen from favour, or even been abandoned? How do we collectively decide when certain theories or techniques should be rejected as ineffective? As scientist–practitioners, this story of science would lead us to articulate our criteria for falsification and subject these criteria to public scrutiny.

NORMAL AND REVOLUTIONARY SCIENCE: KUHN'S CONCEPT OF THE PARADIGM

Both empiricism and falsification share a belief that knowledge is accrued through the activities of a collective body of scientists working in specific contexts. As appreciation of the context in which certain meanings are ascribed over others is undoubtedly critical to psychologists' work, any philosophical position which enables us to better understand how scientific knowledge develops is likely to have important implications for how we relate to that knowledge and communicate with the world about our scientific status.

One philosopher who has been particularly concerned with how science and scientists function (rather than the nature of the discoveries they make) is Thomas Kuhn (1970). Kuhn disagreed with Popper's belief that scientists should look for evidence that falsifies their theories because he argued that scientists, just like practitioners, look for evidence which confirms them. This presents scientists with a range of theories from which to choose rather than any that have been shown to be false. A brief glance at the psychological literature would appear to confirm this, in that any psychological phenomenon will be interpreted differently by different theories. It is difficult, on theoretical grounds, to conclude that one interpretation is right and the other wrong.

For Kuhn, a more helpful response to the crisis of rationality was to examine the contexts in which decisions about the merits of different theories are made. Unlike the empiricist story which suggests that science progresses systematically through an ever-increasing number of observations, Kuhn argued that the development of knowledge is far less logical than this. Therefore, in order to understand how science advances, our purpose should be one of examining the role played by the conceptual or ideological frameworks (the 'paradigms') in which scientists operate. As these paradigms, or perspectives, guide both observation and experimentation, they play a critical role in shaping the pursuits of scientific communities and are vital to our understanding of how scientific discoveries are made.

Kuhn made an important distinction between 'normal' and 'revolutionary' science. Essentially, normal science occurs in the context of a well-established paradigm in which assumptions about the nature of puzzles and how to investigate them are, in the main, universally shared. The function of normal science is to exploit the purpose, perspectives and processes of the existing paradigm to the full, creating an ever-closer fit between the dominant scientific concepts and the data accrued. However, there comes a stage where the issues being investigated no longer fit the solutions presented by the existing ideology. Although there will always be some incongruent data, anomalous findings accumulate to such an extent that ideas central to the existing worldview are challenged. Even advocates of the existing paradigm begin to doubt it, causing scientists to seek solutions from elsewhere. It is then that a state of crisis occurs.

Revolutions occur when opposing sides come together to initiate a radically new era of understanding about the puzzle and how it is to be investigated. Radical here implies a sense that there is no going back (perhaps the obvious example of this was the discovery that the world was round rather than flat, which, once accepted, meant that our view of the universe would never be the same again). The function of revolutionary science thus is to allow scientists to free themselves from inadequate frameworks and discover more helpful ones. Scientists can then return to the established problem-solving procedures of normal science, albeit working within the parameters dictated by the new paradigm.

Given the diversity of contemporary practice, it is unlikely that the whole profession of psychology will undergo the type of revolution that Kuhn describes. Nonetheless, the concept of paradigm has been usefully applied to complex human systems including organizational culture and change (Johnson, 1992; Capra, 1997). If we take as Kuhn's underlying purpose a desire to know how science and scientists function, then some important insights into our own relationship with science also emerge.

Firstly, Kuhn's theory of science warns us against becoming over-attached to any particular scientific story, because all scientific theories are essentially transient explanations which will eventually be overthrown in favour of others. Secondly, it highlights the somewhat haphazard way in which science progresses. Paradigmatic allegiance is not a process which relies on incremental advances in knowledge, but one which is influenced by many factors including social issues, economic factors or political pressures. Additionally, as knowledge of a paradigm can only occur through educating scientists within distinct communities, much of the knowledge of the 'normal scientist' is tacit (there are clear parallels here with Polyani's (1967) argument that scientists always know more than they can say and Schön's (1987) later notion of professional artistry).

Thirdly, Kuhn's story about how scientists function helps us consider the purposes, perspectives and processes of relevance to different generations of psychologists and how they have influenced the practice and evolution of science within our discipline. What might have been the pressing concerns facing psychologists in 1949 are not entirely the same issues confronting us now. Kuhn's model helps us reconsider how we are affected by the prevailing zeitgeist – both in terms of the communities in which we practice and society at large – and paves the way for contemplating how different types of influence may affect the development of our knowledge base.

As Trierweiler and Stricker (1998) observe, there are many paradigms that shape our work, both as scientists and as practitioners, and it is important that we develop our awareness of all of them. Thus, if we were to interpret the scientist–practitioner model in the light of a Kuhnian story about science, we would be concerned with questions such as:

- In which paradigm(s) was I trained?
- Which paradigms are most influential in my practice now? How have I got here?
- To what 'community of scientists' (in a broad sense) do I currently belong?

- What types of reasoning, formulation, creativity and intervention does this paradigm encourage and discourage?
- Given that different paradigms emphasize different questions, how would the nature of my enquiries change if I switched paradigm?

For psychology as a profession, similar questions arise, including:

- What are the paradigms in which our profession is embedded?
- With which scientific communities have we allied ourselves at different points in history? What have been the benefits and costs of this?
- What (small-scale) 'revolutions' has psychology successfully negotiated to date and what have the effects of these been?
- How best can we bring together rival paradigms to advance our knowledge in systematic ways?

So far we have considered the implications of three stories, drawn from the physical sciences, which scientist–practitioners can use to critique their work. However, the crisis of rationality has also caused social scientists to reconsider questions about how we perceive human experience, what constitutes legitimate forms of explanation and the types of enquiry to which we should direct our 'scientific' attention. Two responses deserve particular consideration here: social constructionism and critical realism, each of which is predicated upon new purposes, perspectives and processes.

THE CRISIS OF RATIONALITY AND SOCIAL CONSTRUCTIONISM: ELEVATING DISCOURSE TO THE HEART OF PSYCHOLOGICAL SCIENCE

If we accept that there is no such thing as an objective reality then we must remain sceptical about any form of knowledge that purports to uncover it. This has been the position advocated by social constructionism which, as a radical philosophical challenge to the empiricist worldview, posits that any distinction between our internal worlds and the external world is quintessentially problematic (see Burr, 1995; Gergen, 1985, 1992 for an overview).

Influenced by philosophy, sociology and linguistics, social constructionism encompasses a range of worldviews which nonetheless share a common set of perspectives. These are (1) that all knowledge is historically, culturally and socially embedded; (2) that what we regard as truth or reality is in fact the product of on-going social exchanges through which meanings are communicated, negotiated and co-constructed and (3) that different types of social exchange predispose us towards certain types of action over others (Burr, 1995). Implicit in this worldview is the belief that there are no 'facts' which exist apart from our constructions of them; truth becomes relative, and no single perspective (including a scientific one) can have greater validity than any other.

The way in which reality is socially constructed applies equally to our understanding of human experience. Taken to its extreme, for example, the social constructionist position would advocate that there is nothing essentially 'given' about human experience; our nature is not discovered but actively created through interactions within the societies into which we are born and whose prevailing ideas and beliefs shape the way we come to understand the world. In any given interaction, we operate with the generalized knowledge (culture) into which we have been socialized and the specific knowledge (co-constructed) that emerges during the course of the interaction (Lane, 1973). A clear illustration of this would be Gergen's argument for locating self and self-understanding exclusively in the domain of social interaction, rather than assuming that the mind has any enduring properties of its own. As he states, 'The mind becomes a form of social myth; the self is removed from the head and placed within the sphere of social dimensions' (1985: 271).

Social constructionism advocates that the vehicle which enables meanings to be constructed in the context of our social interactions is discourse; that is, the realm of language, metaphor and text. Used by authors in different ways, discourse has been defined by some as encompassing 'all forms of spoken interaction, formal and informal, and written texts of all kinds' (Potter and Wetherell, 1987: 7) whilst others have advocated a more inclusive interpretation that includes 'non-verbal behaviour, Braille . . . advertisements, fashion systems, stained glass, architecture, tarot cards and bus tickets' (Parker, 1992: 7).

Although there are different definitions of discourse, as an over-arching framework on the pursuit of knowledge, social constructionism has radical implications for how we conduct our science. According to most interpretations of the social constructionist movement, human reality is a discursive construction that does not entail material-causal processes. As a result, it is argued that we should abandon our search for causal influences in favour of uncovering the motivations behind specific activities as revealed through common-sense explanations of behaviour. From a social constructionist perspective then, our accounts of our own states, motives, choices and behaviours can be used as devices to suggest possible reasons for the existence of psychological phenomena (Greenwood, 1991).

One implication of this story is that it moves us away from the search for universal laws and from the processes of observation and experimentation, towards non-numerical, contextually-situated data which attempt to make sense of phenomena in terms of the meanings which people bring to them (Henwood, 1996; McLeod, 1994). For the applied psychologist, there may be distinct advantages in doing so. As Henwood and Pidgeon suggest, 'the gathering of non-numerical data . . . frees researchers to explore, and be sensitive to, the multiple interpretations and meanings which may be placed upon thoughts and behaviour when viewed in context and in their full capacity' (1995: 115–16).

Thus, a central purpose of social constructionism is to derive understanding of the social rules, beliefs and norms that shape the reasons for individuals' actions. It is based on a perspective that we operate as social beings in contexts in which there exist multiple truths. Our accounts of our own states, motives, choices and behaviours can be used to suggest possible reasons for the existence of psychological phenomena and thus represent the processes through which we can better grasp human realities.

Social constructionism has found favour within many branches of applied psychology. With its emphasis on embracing multiple perspectives as equally valid, it offers an important response to the cause of both feminist and minority communities to develop a greater awareness of and respect for diversity in practice. Pope and Mays (1995) have also advocated its benefits for examining the perspectives of different stakeholders during times of large-scale organizational or political change. Similarly, Corrie and Callanan (2001) highlight the advantages of a social constructionist framework for 'tapping into' complex and culturally-dependent beliefs about operating as scientist–practitioners.

Social constructionism also opens up avenues for exploring the more intangible aspects of our experience such as our emotions, our relationships and how we come to arrive at certain meanings rather than others. Emphasizing that knowledge is something that people create together adds a vital dimension to our work as scientist–practitioners, not only in our ability to appreciate the multiple realities constructed by our clients and how these constructions shape their lives, but also in enabling us to re-examine our relationship with science as one of many vehicles we use to inform, make sense of and justify our professional activities. This in turn allows us to consider which discourses about science have taken precedence over others, at which points in time and in which scientist–practitioner communities. Specifically, it helps us develop:

- a fuller appreciation of how social and political discourses lead us to regard certain types of knowledge as more rigorous than others;
- greater understanding of how we have been enabled and constrained in our work by the dominant (empiricist) discourse about science;
- a more detailed understanding of how we innovate and intervene through gathering practitioners' 'common sense' accounts;
- knowledge of 'common assumptions' about professional practice that guide our actions and how these relate to a scientist–practitioner discourse.

However, to operate as social constructionist scientist–practitioners raises a fundamental question. Its central purpose is to seek out motivations behind specific activities as revealed through common-sense explanations of behaviour. Yet can we assume that defining our reality exclusively as a function of social processes is sufficient to inform the demands we face in our practice? What are the implications of adopting a perspective that discursive constructions are the only realities with which we should be concerned? Could the adoption of this as the basis for our science, at least in an extreme form, lead us towards what Davison and Gann describe as 'an undesirable solipsism' (1998: 65)?

One of the challenges that social constructionism faces is how to provide frameworks for making sense of the ways in which we negotiate the practical constraints that impinge upon us; that is, how we intervene in the world to bring about the out-comes we desire. In describing some of the challenges facing therapeutic practitio-ners, for example, Efran and Clarfield point out that therapists 'need to know how constructivism might help them deal more effectively with a quarrelling couple, a cocaine-addicted teenager, a suicidal husband, a house-bound agoraphobic, an obsessive hand-washer, or a high-school drop-out' (1992: 215).

Arguably, this quotation highlights the central task facing all psychologists: namely the ability to intervene to facilitate change. This hints at the need to concern ourselves with a world that exists independently of our socially derived concepts and has led some to argue that psychologists need not only a science of discourse, but also a science of intervention.

REDEFINING CAUSALITY IN PSYCHOLOGICAL SCIENCE: THE CONTRIBUTION OF CRITICAL REALISM

Despite the ambiguity and diversity in scientific theorizing that the philosophy of science highlights, science has generally developed our understanding of our physical and social worlds in important ways. It must, therefore, be doing some-thing right. This was the argument posed by Bhaskar (1975, 1979) and Manicas and Secord (1983) whose response to the crisis of rationality has led to a story about science termed 'critical realism'.

Like social constructionism, critical realism recognizes that knowledge is a product of historical and social processes and that discourse plays a central role in shaping human reality. However, critical realism (as opposed to the naive realism of the empiricist worldview) proposes that our experience of the world is based on the interaction of many systems including those that exist independently of our discursive constructions of them. In other words, there is a social reality which exists independently of discourse. This world comprises substantive underlying structures against which any socially constructed reality must be negotiated.

If there are realities which exist apart from socially-embedded discourse, and which shape our experiences and actions, then we need a way to investigate them. This transforms the task of science into one of inventing theories that aim to represent the world. As Manicas and Secord suggest, 'Sciences generate their own rational criteria in terms of which theory is accepted or rejected and can be deemed to be rational because there is a world that exists independently of our ability to know it' (1983: 401).

According to this perspective, material-causal processes create enabling or constraining conditions for how we act (Secord, 1984) and experiments remain critical in advancing knowledge because they are the sole means through which we can come to understand the underlying structures that shape our thought and action. The purpose of a critical realist science is to reveal the underlying structures that are critical in shaping our socially constructed realities.

We must be clear about the definition of 'causal' in this context. Causality as originally defined by David Hume (1739/1985) within the empiricist story refers to the description of observed regularity based on use of the senses to observe how one physical object affects another. Hume was sceptical about society's faith in causality as a gateway to knowledge but nonetheless believed that we could regard objects as having causal effects when they possess three features: contiguity (that is, adjacent in time and space, as in the proximity of one variable and another), priority in time (causes must precede effects) and, most importantly, constant conjunction in sense experience (today understood as association or correlation).

Regular correlation has always been considered insufficient to deduce causality but it has, nonetheless, been considered to be a necessary feature (Greenwood, 1991). However, the critical realist perspective argues that Hume's view of causality cannot be a correct basis for science because causal powers are subject to interference. Bhaskar (1975), for example, argued that some entities never exhibit their causal powers because of regular interference. A frequently cited example here would be the way in which the natural course of viral infection is altered through vaccination, or the process of conception halted through contraception. Causal laws cannot state what will happen if certain preconditions are met, but indicate the potential of an entity to produce a particular effect when certain enabling conditions are present and no other factors interfere. Consequently, causal properties may not manifest themselves on every occasion.

Secord (1984) and Greenwood (1989) differentiate two types of causality in the world: that manifested by physical powers and that manifested by human powers, otherwise termed 'agency'. Physical causes must manifest their power in order to produce a given effect if the facilitating conditions are present and there is no interference. However, this is not the case with social phenomena as there is an important competence-performance distinction in human beings. Individuals may have the capacity to perform a given action but can choose otherwise. Greenwood (1989) proposes that this reformulation of causality can be used to resolve the conflict in psychology between the study of causality and the study of reason and the freedom of human beings as independent from stimulus control. As Manicas and Secord observe:

> psychology as an experimental science is best understood . . . as concerned with the structure of our competencies and not our realization of them in our everyday behaviour . . . . Explaining their actualization requires more than experimental science provides, and thus there is a place for the other psychological sciences that pertain to human action in life settings.
>
> (1983: 406)

For critical realists, then, our story about science must encompass the notion of free will and self-interventions. Qualitative studies remain important for discovering diverse and contextualized viewpoints but they cannot be the sole basis for science because human reality involves intervening in a causal order, independent of language. This causal order either constrains or facilitates our choices and actions. The implications of this for a science of psychology is that it must take account of our capacity to choose.

As Trierweiler and Stricker (1998) point out, what makes this story valuable is that it allows us to pursue realities that exist beyond our socially constructed ones and yet prevents us from becoming over-confident that the knowledge we possess can be translated into generalizable laws. Although critical realism is yet to make its way into the scientist–practitioner debate in any substantive sense, it contributes to a clearer understanding of how we approach the task of intervening in our day-to-day lives. One example of this is given by Baillie and Corrie (1996) who use a critical realist approach to make sense of clients' accounts of their experiences of psychotherapy, describing the 'stream of activity in which we are continually immersed, and which forms an ever present backdrop for our current actions in the form of tasks, challenges, and formative influences' (1996: 302) as a 'practical order', one that is individualized (rather than universal), localized in context and changes over time but which is nonetheless omnipresent.

If we subscribe to a story about science that says we need to know how to intervene as well as represent (to coin the title of Ian Hacking's (1983) book) and whose purpose is governed by a search for material-causal processes in addition to other processes of discovery (such as common-sense accounts), then we can appreciate how action is a separate sphere from language and one with which scientist–practitioners need to be concerned. In addition to the issues raised by social constructionism, questions through which we critique our practice would include:

- As agents of change, how do we go about engineering desirable outcomes in our work?
- What tools, strategies and interventions do we need to achieve them?
- What are the external factors that we need to take into account to maximize the chances of engineering a preferred outcome (including any practical constraints of time, money or context)?
- What are the ways in which different types of professional intervention enable or constrain the self-interventions of our clients?

CREATING CHAOS OUT OF ORDER: THE CONTRIBUTION OF NEW SCIENCE

Stories about representing and intervening are all very well but as Wheatley (1999) argues, if we are to continue claiming that science is the backbone of our practice, then we should identify ourselves with the science of today.

Developments in the field of quantum physics, chaos theory and self-organizing systems are radically altering the way we understand the scientific endeavour. In their expositions of how this so-called 'new science' can inform working with organizations, both Wheatley (1999) and Stacey (1992) highlight the central importance of uncertainty and ambiguity in scientific theorizing. Catastrophe theory, for example, examines how complex results stem from simple interactions and helps us appreciate how sudden and unpredictable changes occur after a period of stability. In the quantum world, it is recognized that energy can appear and disappear unexpectedly (Davies, 1983). As Wheatley explains, 'The quantum world teaches that there are no pre-fixed, definitely describable destinations. There are, instead, potentials that will form into real ideas depending on who the discoverer is and what she is interested in discovering' (1999: xiv).

Stacey (1992) points out how this scientific worldview differs from our Western mindset which favours the notion that progress occurs through a state of equilibrium (that is, stability, predictability, control and consensus). However, he highlights that stability is only possible if there are clear-cut causal relationships. As the systems in which we work and attempt to intervene as psychologists are fuelled by complex dynamics, we can never truly know which interventions cause what outcomes.

Instead of aiming for equilibrium, Stacey proposes that we should maximize our chances of survival by embracing 'bounded instability'. Drawing on chaos theory he highlights how instability is far from chaotic (in the colloquial sense) but constrained by the structures of the law which generate it. There is a coherent pattern or structure in which random outcomes occur. He illustrates this with the example of the snowflake: although each snowflake conforms to the general requirements of the 'snowflake category', each one is unique and its form impossible to predict.

Modern science, then, challenges the notion of an ordered and objective reality which we can uncover with increasingly sophisticated techniques. Its purpose is to understand the non-linear relationships that characterize complex systems, including human ones. Its perspective is that aiming for prediction and control is a misleading basis upon which to build a science. The task is a holistic endeavour in which we seek to facilitate connections that might enhance self-organization. The critical determiner is relationship because the universe evolves in the process of our interacting with it.

One example of modern science in action is the work of David Bohm who developed a model of the universe inspired by holography. According to Bohm (1980), the world we perceive through our senses is merely a fragment of a much larger matrix and can be conceptualized as a projected holographic image. This larger matrix, which can be compared to the hologram, is not available to our senses or direct scientific scrutiny. What we understand to be stable structures are simply abstractions because our best efforts to understand the world are spawned from a wholeness which is immeasurable and ultimately unknowable.

Working in the field of human consciousness, Grof (1993) elaborates Bohm's analogy of the hologram by proposing that the part is not just a fragment of the whole but in some cases reflects and contains the whole. Applied to human consciousness, therefore, we are not separate entities comprised of component parts but each contains the universe within us.

What differentiates new science from other stories about science is its holistic worldview. The importance of viewing ourselves and our world holistically will come as no surprise to those familiar with Gestalt psychology (Perls, 1969; Polster and Polster, 1974). However, basing our story of science upon it may seem more radical. Specifically, it demands that we replace the caution of the empiricist with a worldview that is expansive, innovative and related. It also challenges the perspective that numbers equate to reality through providing us with objective information. Numbers can give us very useful information but they can, according to a new science worldview, provide an illusory sense of control, resulting in a failure to examine our perspectives on numerical data with sufficient clarity. For example, as scientist–practitioners, to what extent do we equate numbers with a measure of truth? To what extent do we see them as a way of opening up new discourses about possibilities for change? How do they facilitate (and inhibit) divergent thinking and creativity? If numerical data do not generate the answers we seek, how should we respond?

Of course, this is not to suggest that psychology should abandon methods which aim at measuring specific variables nor is it an invitation to relinquish our commitment to quality control, target setting and ongoing evaluation (Stacey, 1992). Moreover, we should not confuse measurement with the empiricist worldview. We only stray into empiricist territory when we believe our findings somehow replicate the 'truth' of a particular phenomenon (Miller, 1999). Nonetheless, if the physical world does change in response to our interacting with it, then we must find ways to reflect this in our conceptualization of science. Such a position raises new types of questions including:

- As the profession of psychology expands and our methods become increasingly sophisticated, how will we capitalize on this rich potential and avoid intellectual, methodological or scientific dead-ends?
- Who are the people and professions with which we now need to ally ourselves? What kinds of connections do we need to make? How can we break down any barriers and overcome differences (including those that exist between applied psychological areas) to enhance cooperation?
- How do we establish a direction for the future of the profession, and develop strategies for promoting our services, when the future is unpredictable and unknowable?
- How can we best interact with different organizations to create models of practice for the future (including ones that can address the questions of the future and of which we are not yet aware)?

WHERE TO FROM HERE?

Ending this Chapter with a brief description of some of the insights from chaos theory is perhaps fitting; what this chapter reveals is that science itself is more chaotic than we often like to believe. However, as Wheatley (1999) observes, what appears to be chaotic often develops into distinct patterns, partnering with order in unexpected ways.

Having described some of the most influential stories about the nature of science, we find ourselves confronted with a range of ideas, each of which is built on a different purpose and set of perspectives and processes. For now, perhaps a useful starting point is to consider each story as residing somewhere along a continuum of 'closed' to 'open' perspectives, according to its position on truth. Thus, empiricist science, with its search for universal laws and belief in an objective reality would occupy the most closed position, whilst new science, with its belief that there are not even any pre-fixed destinations would occupy the most radically open. Our use of science will clearly look very different according to which point along the continuum we locate ourselves. Each story offers unique opportunities for reflecting on our practice and each is bound by particular constraints. If we are to break down the science–practice schism that has dominated the scientist–practitioner debate, we need to embrace a multidimensional outlook.

Re-examining our commitment to one particular model of science may be an uncomfortable prospect in a climate that favours speedy solutions over journeys of discovery (Zander and Zander, 2000). In such a climate, it can feel safer to operate as though reality is 'out there somewhere'. However, to relinquish the notion of science as a pathway to truth is not to suggest that psychology cannot be a science (Manicas and Secord, 1983). The issue is rather one of definition which, as this chapter has revealed, is far from straightforward.

Part of the challenge is that science is, amongst other things, a social enterprise. Each story about science has a distinct history that is grounded in context, debate and rebuttal and is an endeavour fraught with tacit ideas, values and assumptions that bear more than a passing resemblance to the world of practice. Indeed, Kuhn suggested that the evolution of science is sufficiently complex to require the input of psychologists to explain how paradigmatic shifts occur (Chalmers, 1982). It is perhaps ironic that while we have looked to science to secure our credibility, science may turn to psychology to better understand itself.

If we accept that science is a complex, contextualized and at times even chaotic endeavour, then it behoves us to hold our personal definitions up to scrutiny. At this point, therefore, we invite you to re-examine your own scientific purpose, perspectives and processes through considering the questions presented in the conclusion of this book (see the Reflective Tool). We hope that these questions might inspire you to consider the ways in which different 'sciences' might inform your work.

Finally, it will be obvious to the reader that we have steered clear of any single conclusion about what science should be. Such conclusions, we believe, would be premature and misguided, showing a disrespect for the complexity of the phenomena we seek to understand. We have aimed instead to engage you in a broader conversation about the landscape of sciences, so that we can begin to identify questions that help us clarify what it means to be scientists in the twenty-first century. As John observes, 'Science is not to be comprehended in terms of a method, but in terms of its cultivation of, and respect for, the principle of unfettered free enquiry' (1998: 28). It is the spirit of free enquiry that we encourage you to pursue because it is this which makes the science of psychology – however defined – such a valuable framework for generating creative, meaningful and ultimately transformational solutions with our clients.

Chapter 6

Defining our identity as scientist–practitioners

First say to yourself what you would be: and then do what you have to do.

(Epictetus)

Whatever you are, be a good one.

(Abraham Lincoln)

The concept of the scientist–practitioner started as a way to delineate the profession of psychology as a clinical practice. Based in rationality it marked the desire of the fledging group of those who used psychology in clinical settings to be seen as a distinct profession rather than as a technical adjunct to psychiatry. It also provided a rationale for the methods we used. As noted in Chapter 1, the emergence of this fledgling group differed in the USA, where treatment represented an area of practice, from the UK where it was experimentally led in pursuit of rational diagnosis. The concept provided a justification for our place in clinical work and our differentiation from others who were not psychologists.

The development of professional training in psychology as distinct and subsequent to our academic training emerged to underpin and legitimize our claim to professional status. Thus, we developed theoretical knowledge of practice related to our underpinning academic theory. We assumed codes of practice and in clinical and educational and later other applications, defined specific areas of competence which we claimed as our own. We had an identity as professionals but it was an identity based on the methods we used. So this leaves us with the question, 'Who are we?'

In this chapter, we consider what it means to claim an identity as a scientist–practitioner, over and above adherence to any activity or method. In inviting you to consider what this might mean for your own practice, we consider both the work of the psychologist and the conceptual perspectives that inform it, within the broader context of social identity. We also explore how social representations within our peer group and of the broader profession might inform and direct our practice.

SOCIAL IDENTITY AND THE PRACTICE OF PSYCHOLOGY

Work is typically a major source of social identification in people's lives. In professional and occupational groups, this identification includes colleagues, professional bodies, and unifying beliefs. It involves long-term social contacts and forms a context in which occupational or professional category can be a major determinant of interpersonal interaction. Similarly, it has been suggested that the scientist–practitioner model represents an identity through which we organize and make sense of our professional beliefs, actions and communications with others (see Aspenson et al., 1993). Thus we have claimed the identity but in claiming it, we need to consider the implications of that identity in practice.

Identity is itself an area of psychological study. In looking at what it means to be a scientist–practitioner we must, therefore, also look at social identity processes and the emergence of a concept of the professional.

Studies investigating social identity and the link with the organizational processes underpinning professional activity have emerged over the last two decades (Ashforth and Mael, 1989; Fox et al., 1984; Lane et al., 2000; Oaker and Brown, 1986; Schiffmann and Wagner, 1985; Siporin, 1984; Zani, 1987). In addition to exploring social identity, work on the social representation of professional practice has been used to explore the development of shared beliefs and the ways in which these shared beliefs direct social action (see, for example, Amerio and Ghiglione, 1986; Hayes, 1991; Herzlich, 1973; Hewstone, 1983; Lalljee et al., 1984; Michael, 1989; Moscovici and Hewstone, 1983).

Work on the social discourse which underpins professional identity also indicates that professional identities are never unified but consist of multiple processes of identification (Lo, 2004). These are constructed by different, intersecting and sometimes antagonistic, discursive practices that make particular identifications possible. Thus, identity formation is both a strategic and a context bound process (Chappell, et al., 2003). The theoretical work in this field (Billig, 1987) has given rise to an analysis of a wide range of professionals from medics to clergy (the latter including comparison of professional identity and relationships to God, see Vignoles et al., 2004). Recent work has taken this analysis into the field of determinants of organizational behaviour through the use of the concept of organizational citizenship behaviours (Feather and Rauter, 2004). These fields of study make it imperative that we understand the implications of the claims to be a profession on our practice when we are with our clients.

IDENTITY AND THE SOCIAL EMBEDDEDNESS OF PROFESSIONS

Early studies of the professions emphasized their position as functional specialities, specifically as designated carriers of rationality. As a consequence, professions were seen as impartial and indeed this is the role they are still assumed to play (consider, for example, the case of the psychologist as an expert witness called upon to give evidence in court cases). Yet later commentators (see Lo, 2004, we draw heavily on this work here) point out an alternative view in which professions are institutionalized forms of power. The knowledge to which professionals lay claim is arrived at and sustained through relationships with the state and capitalist market. We cannot, therefore, lay claim to an independent status.

As Larson (1977) argues, professions can be seen as interest groups engaged in a collective mobility project to improve their economic and social standing. Freidson (2001) also makes the point that power is gained through the attainment of professional autonomy by state licensing, which enables monopoly supply. Hence professionals can be seen to represent agents of the state empowered to define our needs as clients and to exercise a disciplined control of our behaviour as citizens. We need, therefore, to understand the processes of identity formation within professions which enables us to recognize the consequences of (1) being seen as practitioners that provide rational and scientific solutions to social problems while (2) being employed as agents of the state or capital and (3) engaged on a constant drive for economic and social prestige. Within each of these positions we can potentially act tyrannically by defining what is in another's best interest. We can create a series of silent conspiracies with those in power against the interests of the powerless but feel good about ourselves since we believe that we know what is best for them (Miller and Lane, 1993). Our ability to work from a place of ignorance about other people's lives yet adopt the expert stance has been clearly illustrated in work with marginalized groups such as refugees, asylum seekers and clients living with HIV (Epstein, 1996; Stern *et al.*, 1994).

This integration of the interests of the professional and the state sees its most recent embodiment in the prioritizing of certain forms of knowledge over others, forms that are unlikely to be available to anyone working outside of state authorization. In the British health-care system, for example, knowledge is weighted according to perceived legitimacy with the controlled trial being seen as the gold standard and user and expert censuses being seen as a limited form of evidence (Department of Health, 2001). This could be seen as the continuation of the historical trend noted by Johnson (1972) who sees the rise of professionalism as directly linked to the new techniques of ruling by the modern state. Seen in this light, the jurisdiction of professions such as law and psychiatry are granted only is so far as they work as convenient and useful techniques of state rule. Based on studies in Europe and the USA, Krause (1996) goes as far as arguing that professions are engaged in a final surrender to capitalism and increasingly pass control to the state.

Arguably, the history of psychology has tended to follow each of these steps. It has insisted on a form of identity predicated on rationality and science and has developed a form of credentialing which codifies which types of knowledge are legitimate and which ones are not. It has also, at least traditionally and in the context of official discourse, downgraded the importance of user experience. Additionally, psychology has demonstrated dependence on the state and engaged in the 'final surrender' noted by Krause by handing autonomy over to state licensing rather than professional control. This perhaps can be seen in moves by many health professions, including psychology, to give up autonomous control of credentialing to licensing by an agency of the state, such as the Health Professions Council.

While we can observe these processes from the outside, their influence may seem less clear in our daily practice, where our sense of professional identity and encounters with individual clients seem driven by priorities other than those of the state. It is this ambiguity that has been the subject of most recent study. In particular, Lo (2004) highlights the social embeddedness of professions and the need to recognize that embeddedness as a site of identity formation. This distances us from a more traditional view of the professional as an identity based on the rational, scientific, impartial use of knowledge in the service of the public, to one in which the relationship between client and professional is central. It recognizes that our professional practice happens in specific social contexts and that our sense of our self 'identity' is generated in those contexts based on relational discourses. In line with social constructionist models of science, we create our identities out of the conversations we have within our practice. This has three major implications:

1 We must confront the roots of our theories as predominantly originated by white males

This issue was particularly potent in the report by the British Psychological Society *The Future of Psychological Science* (1991) which resulted in a number of changes in practice. These included attempts to recognize the impact on minority professionals of the dominant rhetoric and the impact on marginalized groups of the imposition of white, male and colonial theories on deviant behaviour and access to services. The rise of a Black and Feminist Psychology in opposition to the dominant position, recognition of the over-representation of black youth in services designed to exclude them from access to mainstream education (that is, special education as a means of social control) and the role of psychiatry in discriminatory diagnosis and treatment of marginal groups combined to create a major challenge to psychology as practised during the closing decades of the last century (Miller and Lane, 1993).

2 We must confront the priority given to certain forms of knowledge over others

Foucault (1983) framed the ways in which priority is given to certain forms of knowledge over others as regimes of truth. These regimes lead to practices within disciplines that become internalized and serve to align behaviour with socio-economic objectives. We work, think and act within the targets set by others because we have internalized those regimes of truth. The narratives we use when we define our selves as scientist–practitioners impact on how we assign meaning to events and how we then act. The permitted narratives embedded in the identity determine what can be considered legitimate or true, which views can be expressed and who has the authority to express them (Chappell *et al.*, 2003). The types of narrative that are dominant depend in part on the distribution of power (Sommers and Gibson, 1994) or which profession or part of it aligns itself to that power.

Significantly, a number of authors are now calling on us to draw upon a much wider range of evidence to inform our practice than has traditionally been the case (Milton and Corrie, 2002; Newnes, 2001; Stern *et al.*, 1994). In doing so they are contesting that power. Thus, we may move from evidence-based practice to practice-based evidence (Barkham and Mellor-Clark, 2000) and even to non-academic sources to guide our work (Coleman, 2001; Spinelli, 2001). These sources and our own experience may draw us towards more implicit or 'intuitive' knowledge, as well as to greater creativity in our practice (see Chapter 4). As we look to these alternative forms we increasingly, as Miller Mair (1988) suggests, define ourselves in terms of the stories we tell.

3 We must confront the way we construct stories about our identity as psychologists

If the stories we create about our identity as psychologists are socially embedded, it follows that it is through the multiple discourses carved out of the settings in which we work that we come to construct a narrative of our identity. To the extent that we choose to frame that identity as scientist–practitioners, we must be mindful of the influences that shape our choice of the name and our modes of practice. Whilst we claim that our solutions to human problems are grounded in science, we have to understand how they are also shaped through social networks. This forces us to address the social construction of expertise (Larson, 1977). An expert cannot exist without a lay public which recognizes the badge of expertise and is prepared to engage with it. However, the lay public is expert in other ways and for which we have often failed to give sufficient credence. Some would argue that this has limited professional understanding. Lane (1990), for example, has claimed that by failing to legitimize clients' stories (or rather, by requiring clients to conform to our way of telling them), we have come to favour technical solutions which do not challenge those in authority. In doing so, we are not recognizing how we might become part of the problem, rather than part of the solution.

MOVING BEYOND THE NOTION OF PSYCHOLOGIST AS EXPERT

How does our expertise manifest itself in the encounter with clients? Just one example illustrates this. Clinical psychology, amongst other disciplines, has traditionally espoused an approach to practice which moves through a cycle of assessment, formulation, treatment and evaluation. This framework can be seen to be grounded in traditional Western medicine generally and the notion of diagnosis specifically, as a basis for determining appropriate treatment. The theories on which this approach are based are those in which the expert administers knowledge to the client who does not have this knowledge. We need to consider the implications of this framework carefully as we may have adopted this stance without fully grasping the ways in which it could deny agency to the client. For example, it presupposes that we can know another through assessment based on categories not of their making. It places a premium on sifting information to fit those categories. We assume a story about our role and identity predicted on the expert–lay relationship. The client is asked to provide data in the form we require and as long as they conform to that role, will be assumed to be eligible for the services for which we act as gatekeepers (Davies, 1995; Green, 1980).

So how might it be different? We would suggest that one way in which we might better understand the implications of our socially constructed expertise and accommodate our clients' expertise accordingly is by recognizing the nature of the encounter between us. If we follow the same example it could be argued that we cannot, in spite of all our training, start with assessment. It predetermines too much. The alternative is to start with the encounter. If we accept the social embeddedness of our profession then we must embrace the connection between the scientific and the social.

A first step would be, therefore, to define the nature of the encounter. Our initial engagement with the client (whether an individual or organization) has to create the possibility of a dialogue by which we agree the shared concern on which we will work. This will include a debate about the forms of knowing we bring and the respective roles we will play. In that conversation we can place the concern in the context of the system in which the client and the psychologist operate and jointly define their piece of work together. What occurs next is flexible and uncertain and acknowledges that the work encompasses both cognition and emotion, the rational and the intuitive. It recognizes that we are engaged in a social process to provide a service that is fit for purpose and encompasses a duty of care.

In accepting that our work comprises a social encounter in which we co-construct the process, we cannot then move to assessment. Rather we are engaged on an exploration together. We might bring to that exploration tools of assessment predicated on the rational, but they are there as an offer from us which requires acceptance. Similarly, we cannot 'present' a formulation to our clients but rather co-construct it as a way of creating a framework that makes sense to all parties involved.

We would argue that this empowers the client so that the intervention is jointly agreed. However, other implications follow. Because we have placed the encounter in the social context, the intervention could include any part of the system. The client might not be the source of change; other features of the system might be preferred. Similarly, the impact of the intervention may be evaluated at the personal, interpersonal and systemic levels. However, since this is a co-constructed process each party will be able to reflect on what was learned as well the implications of this for our future practice. This includes our sense of what is and is not included in our definition of our identity as a scientist–practitioner.

Many practitioners working in diverse and complex settings have adopted a more broadly-based definition of the scientist–practitioner model underpinned by individualized case formulation (see Chapter 3). While not the most common form of practice, it could be argued that this represents a viable narrative for a more diverse identity as a scientist–practitioner (see Bruch and Bond, 1998; Gray *et al.*, 1994; Lane, 1978, 1990; Lane and Miller, 1992; Scherer, *et al.*, 1990; Turkat, 1985). There is, however, an increasing recognition that multiple forms of knowing (or modes of knowledge) are critical to our continued role as scientists and practitioners. We will consider this in relation to practice and research which will lead us into a reconceptualization of what it means to embrace a scientist–practitioner identity at the current time.

HOW DO MODES OF ACADEMIC AND PROFESSIONAL KNOWLEDGE INFORM OUR PRACTICE?

The distinction between science and practice has been highlighted in the idea of a typology of knowledge modes (Gibbons *et al.*, 1994). This rests on the separation of disciplinary knowledge (mode 1) constructed in the university (science) and transdisciplinary knowledge constructed in the world of practice (mode 2). According to Gibbons, disciplinary knowledge is typically linear, causal and cumulative. Applied to solve problems through technology outside of the university, the source of knowledge nonetheless always originates within the discipline; the discipline itself determines what is appropriate for society. Practice is an application of knowledge derived elsewhere; it is not itself a source of knowledge generation. Mode 2 knowledge is transdisciplinary and sees the source for identifying problems and solutions in the practice setting. Technology, therefore, is seen as autonomous rather than being preceded by science.

The distinctions between mode 1 and mode 2 knowledge have profound effects since the world of the researcher is based on judgements that are different from those of the practitioner and these judgements have important consequences for the collaboration between them. Underpinning mode 1 is the assumption that disciplinary knowledge is superior to knowledge produced in the workplace and that professional contexts are merely research sites. The common pattern of published papers between practitioners and scientists in which the practitioner simply collects or provides the information upon which the real work in undertaken illustrates this.

This distinction is somewhat ideal (hybrid activity clearly does exist) but perhaps can be best illustrated by assuming that the traditional PhD programme used to train scientists operates to a mode 1 knowledge framework. In contrast, the emerging professional doctorates which now form the basis of our training as practitioners are underpinned by different epistemologies which draw upon different strengths of disciplinary boundaries, utilize different understandings of the relationship between theoretical and practical knowledge and have varied ways of operationalizing these constructs in the development of their programmes (Scott *et al.*, 2004).

Looking at the emergence of professional doctorates, Scott *et al.* (2004) argue in favour of four rather than two modes of knowledge. Outlined below, this perhaps better represents the value of the contribution that practitioner-generated knowledge brings:

- *Mode 1: Disciplinary Knowledge.* Scientific description is seen as the superior form of knowledge and the only possible way of seeing the world. It implies that there are correct ways to gather data and if properly applied will lead to value-free authoritative knowledge. The practice setting may be a source of data but knowledge is valued for its own sake, not for its application.
- *Mode 2: Technical Rationality.* This is based in the rational and scientific beyond the specific practice setting. The practitioner is required to divest themselves of personally derived practice knowledge in favour of knowledge that transcends their local and particular knowledge. This framework supports the idea of evidence-based practice in that the concern is not to understand the political, ethical or consequential contexts for work but rather 'what works'. The emphasis is on efficiency, not knowledge for its own sake.
- *Mode 3: Dispositional and Transdisciplinary Knowledge.* This is based on the assumption (post-crisis of rationality, see Chapter 5) that knowledge is non-predictable, non-determinist and contextualized. Practice is a deliberative action concerned with making appropriate decisions about practical problems in specific situations. The emphasis is on knowledge developed by the individual through reflection on practice.
- *Mode 4: Critical Knowledge.* This is based on the critique of existing forms of knowledge. Its purpose is explicitly political and the emphasis is on change. Individuals are seen to be positioned within discursive and institutional structures which influence how they understand themselves and others. Critiques of that understanding are encouraged and there is an attempt to undermine the conventional knowledge discourses with which both scientists and practitioners work.

The need for new forms of collaboration that respect different modes of knowledge is urgent. As scientist–practitioners, we must be able to recognize different modes of knowledge and forms of scientific practice that create alternative worldviews. As Zander and Zander (2000) suggest, problems appear unsolvable because we perceive them through a particular frame of reference: what we have termed here modes of knowledge. They suggest that if we create a new framework, new possibilities emerge. So what implications might follow from a scientist–practitioner model that takes account of a much broader range of approaches to knowledge and its development? We would argue that through such a framework we could:

- Appreciate more fully how decisions about scientific activity and the most appropriate questions to ask are shaped by the predominant zeitgeist and seek a greater appreciation of the discourses that have shaped our professional identity.
- Reflect on the pressures to make ourselves appear in a particular way and consider how we negotiate those demands.
- Understand the way in which our ideas are shaped (for example, about what to investigate and what resources we have).
- Ponder how our interactions with our clients might become enabling or constraining conversations, because we adopt a particular mode of knowledge.
- Enquire about the historically and socially contingent factors within which our discourse has become lodged.

RECONCEPTUALIZING THE SCIENTIST–PRACTITIONER MODEL AS A DIVERSE AND MULTIPLE IDENTITY

The need to attempt a reconceptualization of the scientist–practitioner model as a form of identity is now appearing from a number or sources. Abrahamson and Pearlman (1993), for example, have observed an emerging consensus that the scientist–practitioner model is less connected to a distinct activity or role than to an inner professional 'compass' which carries with it a moral injunction to distinguish between sources of knowledge on the basis of their origins. This echoed the earlier statement made by Singer who elevated the relationship between research and practice to a matter of ethics:

> The ethical practice of psychotherapy must reflect the current status of knowledge . . . The practitioner who has not examined recent developments in the research literature or who has not kept abreast of evaluation studies of various forms of treatment may well be violating a central ethic of the profession.
>
> (1980: 372)

Aspenson et al. (1993) also found this to be an important feature of psychology trainees' attitudes towards the scientist–practitioner model. In particular, they found that a distinctive feature of post-graduate clinical and counselling psychology students with positive attitudes towards the model was the belief that ethical and effective practice was dependent upon therapists keeping themselves informed about theoretical and empirical developments. Over time, these values appeared to become internalized, suggesting that for some, commitment to the scientist–practitioner identity equates with commitment to a set of beliefs and values.

Of further interest is Crane and McArthur Hafen's (2002) developmental perspective in which they propose that each of us travels through a distinct series of scientist–practitioner stages. During training, the aim is to produce effective practitioners who are able to implement what has been established by others (that is, work as evidence-based practitioners or mode 2 knowledge). In the second stage, practitioners can be taught how to use research through evaluating the contribution of different studies (i.e. developing discriminatory consumer skills to arrive at a sense of what is helpful in the applied domain). Practitioners then learn to collect data from clients which introduce them to using specific scientific methods they will need when they qualify. Finally, they become 'translators' of research for other practitioners in the field.

Whilst this approach raises further questions (for example, whether it is possible for practitioners to consume research effectively if they have not conducted it themselves), a developmental trajectory highlights how interpretations of the scientist–practitioner identity may vary according to the career stage. Novice practitioners may prefer a more concrete definition of what it means to be a scientist–practitioner as this offers a specific (and perhaps containing) 'lens' through which to view the development of effective professional practice in specific areas. In contrast, highly experienced practitioners may want the flexibility to determine how they define the model and how to implement it. This would appear to be consistent with the literature on the stages of professional development more broadly, whereby it is recognized that our relationship with diverse sources of knowledge, both formal and informal, acquires different meanings and emphasis at different points in our careers (see Eraut, 2000; Skovholt and Rønnestad, 1992).

Indirect support for a more identity-based outlook on what it means to be a scientist–practitioner comes from work by Rajan *et al.* (2000) who, looking at organizations more generally, make the point that how individuals act is partly a feature of the organizational culture in which they work. Specifically, they identified preferences for different patterns of management of choice:

- Actors – who prefer to follow a script, thus they welcome cultures that provide quality systems or specific models to guide practice.
- Adaptors – who, while working within agreed frames, prefer to adapt their approach to meet specific needs or aim for higher levels of service beyond the usual. Adaptors prefer cultures that provide options from within a range of models or performance-led systems, which grant choice in how the work will be carried out.
- Innovators – who will experiment with a range of ideas to develop new possibilities for generating high levels of service. Innovators use multiple models and will work outside of existing frames if necessary to achieve high levels of practice. They prefer cultures which allow for wide discretionary action and encourage innovation.

The way in which professional identity is socially embedded and may vary as a function of developmental stages points to a vision of the scientist–practitioner that is very different from that proposed by our predecessors in 1949. In offering our reconceptualization at this time in our history, we propose that the scientist–

practitioner in psychology is not and cannot be defined as a model in any static sense, but is better understood as a narrative framework in which the discipline of psychology is paramount but individualized and self-reflective. This identity will be expressed in diverse forms based on the specific choices made within the context in which the encounter with the client takes place, as well as personal values, objectives and career opportunities. This clearly requires close attention to the contextual factors that impact on the construction of our activity and a willingness to engage with a range of modes of knowledge. It also requires a relational narrative in which practice is socially constructed in conversation with our clients, not predetermined by us.

In choosing such an identity, we believe it is the responsibility of each psychologist to hold in mind explicit frameworks for differentiating ways of knowing and a general set of psychological principles for informing the selection of modes of knowledge to assist with the creation of a systematic approach to professional decision-making. One of the principal tasks facing the scientist–practitioner, as we see it, is to articulate and justify the reasons for using one version of science (and practice) over another in any particular context. In this way, being a scientist–practitioner becomes a system through which we can better evaluate the limitations of our chosen model and also be clear about the purposes it can fulfil.

WHAT DOES THE SCIENTIST–PRACTITIONER IDENTITY MEAN FOR PRACTICE?

Psychologists are employed in academia, research institutes, the public, voluntary and the commercial sectors as well as private practice, acting as clinicians, advisors, and consultants to a diverse range of individuals and organizations. Even within defined fields such as occupational psychology, two occupational psychologists with similar qualifications and levels of experience might share little in the way of activity and function beyond a generic consultancy or problem-solving approach (Crawshaw, 2000). This diversity of practice and identity can be considered a strength, enhancing the range of skills which we bring to our enquiries. However, it raises a number of issues for the profession as a whole. One issue is the lack of any clear public profile with typically poor public understanding of the role of the profession. A second concern is the significant overlap with other professions where selected psychological skills may be used without recourse to the standards and ethical frameworks of the psychologist from which they have been drawn.

Arguably, the public definition of the identity of the psychologist will come from within the profession, from peers, from the consideration with stakeholders of the external 'face' of the profession within the present context and also through a clear understanding of how it aspires to develop in the future. Thus, we need to be concerned not only with what we are but what we aspire to become. Curiously, psychology is ideally placed to consider the development of our identity within a rapidly changing work environment: that is, after all, our expertise. Yet we also need to be proactive in identifying and developing the competencies we need in the future so that the profession might fully embrace the opportunities for providing added value and impact. Without this, we may fail to ignite a vision for the profession or engender a passion for our work among our stakeholders.

So what questions might a reformulated scientist—practitioner model offer now? We believe that an identity as a scientist—practitioner continues to add unique value to our work as psychologists. However, as originally conceived it was but one narrative. Multiple narratives are possible that provide for rigour and value in practice. We would see key questions from this multiple perspective as including:

- Why is this enquiry worth pursuing? Who else might believe this enquiry is worth pursuing and why?
- What kinds of solutions will my intervention yield and not yield? Who will benefit from it and who will lose out?
- How does pursuing this enquiry in this way enhance or damage my credibility as a psychologist?
- How does pursuing this enquiry in this way enhance or damage my sense of professional integrity?
- How does the pursuit of this enquiry bring me closer to or further away from the kind of practitioner I wish to be?
- How does the pursuit of this enquiry bring me closer to or further away from the kind of scientist I wish to be?
- What questions has this enquiry now left me with and how might I go about investigating them?
- What have I learned about my assumptions and beliefs as a result of participating in this enquiry? Which assumptions have been upheld and which have been challenged?
- What have I learned from this situation that will change my future practice? Who else should be included in my reflection on my practice?
- Have my assumptions and beliefs enabled me to become more or less connected to the clients I was aiming to help? Who has been excluded by my choices?

Finally, it should be noted that much of our work is engaged in socially critical areas and with marginalized groups, including those members of the profession who themselves are marginalized from the debate. In the pursuit of answers to the above questions, and in line with a contemporary reformulation of the scientist—practitioner model we see a need to engage in an active debate that includes the involvement of (1) practitioners at all levels of development, from pre-qualification level through to those holding senior positions; (2) researchers and educators seeking to inform and train the practitioners; (3) the appropriate learned societies and professional organizations concerned with the development and impact of the profession and (4) those who use our services, those who are excluded from our services and commentators on our services.

Psychology must ensure not merely a gesture at inclusion but a radical reform of how the profession is shaped in the future, in order to legitimize all voices. We hope increasingly to be able to address these issues as a profession. However, we believe that if each practitioner were to engage with these issues in relation to their own practice and to share them with their practice community, this would represent an important starting point in enhancing the contribution of the profession to the societies we seek to serve. A reformulated scientist–practitioner model is viable, retains rigour and acknowledges the social and scientific in our work. However, it will necessitate promoting multiple narratives and emergent identities rather than being bound by a set of activities based on a 50-year-old definition of what it is to be a professional.

Chapter 7

Generalizable findings and idiographic problems: struggles and successes for educational psychologists as scientist–practitioners

Andy Miller and *Norah Frederickson*

INTRODUCTION

There are around three thousand educational psychologists (EPs) working in the United Kingdom, the vast majority of whom are employed by Local Education Authorities with a small proportion working in private practice or specialist settings. By virtue of studying psychology as undergraduates, these EPs have been inducted into the experimental method. And yet it is noticeable that practitioner EPs in their publications hardly ever use an experimental approach. Accounts involving single case quasi-experimental designs also very rarely appear in the profession's major journals.

A number of possible explanations for this suggest themselves. Apart from those in Scotland, EPs have traditionally been socialized into the teaching profession as a requirement of their training, in which, until very recently, little premium was placed upon having a scientific mindset. Also, an early location within child guidance clinics tended to encourage an individualized approach towards clients, which was often 'pathologizing' in its nature. Statutory duties, especially those concerning the identification and assessment of special educational needs (DfES, 2001) have reinforced an individual approach, despite long-standing ambitions within the profession for a wider role.

However, an alternative explanation for the dearth of experimental studies carried out by individual EPs concerns the clash between the canons of what might be seen as good science and those of effective practice – the tension implicit in a modern conception of the scientist–practitioner that forms the subject matter of this book. As in other branches of applied psychology, the relationship between research and practice in educational psychology has been recognized as problematic (Phillips, 1999; Sigston, 1993).

Tensions for the scientist–practitioner EP

A useful model for conceptualizing the tensions for EPs in the scientist–practitioner role has been provided by Clarke (2004) in the context of a discussion about research methodology in psychology. With a few minor alterations to terminology,

	Single Case	Multiple Cases
	Description (a)	Description (A)
	Explanation (b)	Explanation (B)
	Intervention (c)	Intervention (C)

Figure 2 Clarke's model demonstrating pathways from problem descriptions to generalized explanations and interventions (from Clarke, 2004)

Clarke's framework highlights two frequently occurring areas of dilemma for EPs, namely:

- The incomplete or inappropriate nature of many research findings and theoretical formulations within psychology as a basis for understanding the complex problems with which EPs are frequently presented.
- The imprecise and tentative relationship often to be found between 'assessment' and 'intervention' within professional practice.

Understanding general processes and understanding individual problems

Clarke points out that the general task of *research psychologists* in understanding and explaining unseen processes is:

> to get from descriptions of individual instances of the product (be they individual cases, problems, people, events, or whatever) to a generalized account of the underlying processes. There are two steps involved, from the particular to the general, and from description to explanation. In most research they

are taken in that order. First the data are aggregated. Then in the aggregate, explanations are sought and checked. But the data-coding and aggregation stage tends to obscure the structure of each case, making it harder for the researcher to use real-world knowledge and domain expertise. Very often the comprehensibility of the research material which is apparent at the outset is lost early on, and then laboriously recovered or replaced by the use of large data sets and elaborate statistics.

(2004: 86–7)

Clarke's areas of dilemma are illustrated in Figure 2. In this description of much conventional research in psychology, the route to understanding is from cells a to A and then on to B. The intention is that such an understanding of general psychological processes (cell B) – and without this, psychology would cease to possess a discipline-defining body of knowledge and explanation – will permit a fuller understanding of the individual problem (cell b), whether this problem is judged to be located with an individual pupil, organization, family or whatever. So cell B (the psychological theory and research base) feeds into cell b – the case formulation (see Chapter 3 in this book) or problem analysis (Woolfson *et al.*, 2003) phase.

An alternative route (from cells a to b and then to B) is sometimes seen as a preferable route for research in complex real-world settings, in the form of detailed case studies (cell b), the results of which are somehow amalgamated with those from other case studies once completed (cell B). However, while there is increasing interest and work in this area (Doyle, 2003), as yet there are no obvious or straightforward *methods* for combining the findings from a series of individual case studies. The 'richer' the data and the more complex the understanding of the individual case, the harder it is to compare and combine such findings into a full and generalized understanding or explanation of events.

Basing interventions on theoretical understandings and research evidence

In general, practitioners in the 'helping professions' have been concerned with interventions, either at the particular level with individual clients (cell c) or at a general level if contributing to group interventions or policy developments that aim to benefit a larger number of clients (cell C). For those aspiring to be *scientist–practitioners*, there is judged to be an imperative to link such interventions with evidence-based understandings, and even theoretical formulations, concerning the problems being addressed. But factors such as the availability of resources, conflicting professional cultures, and the degree to which various participants adopt or understand research perspectives, all mitigate against a straightforward relationship between research findings (cell B) and palliative action on the part of EPs (cells c and C). Tizard (1990), in the era before the drive for 'evidence-based practice', pointed out that there were many reasons why research findings did not

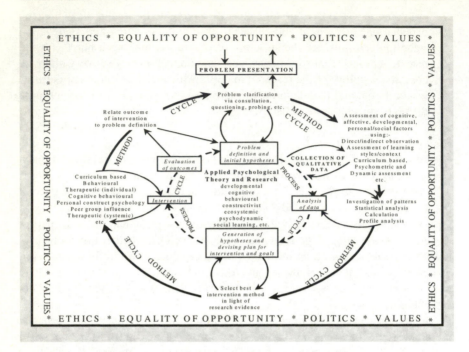

Figure 3 A framework for the psychological assessement of children (Division of Educational and Child Psychology, 1999)

simplistically exert an influence on the development of social and educational policy.

However, by drawing on *craft knowledge* developed through *reflection in action* (Schön, 1987) the practitioner can construct from complex, messy, ill-structured real-world problems, problems to which the existing psychological evidence-base can be applied. Additionally, EPs frequently work in domains where there is no one set of universally accepted and uncontested research findings. In such cases, and because Education and other Services are still mandated to intervene, 'best guess' interventions are often suggested and enacted, as incorporated into the BPS Division of Educational and Child Psychology's (1999) framework for psychological assessment (Figure 3). The outcomes from these tentative and hypothesis-testing interventions (cells c and C) then have the potential to feed back into and inform individual and general problem explanations (cells b and B). To date, the small amount of experimental research conducted by practitioner educational psychologists has typically followed this route. Paired Reading (Miller *et al.*, 1986) and Circles of Friends (Frederickson and Turner, 2003) provide two such examples where the efficacy of innovative interventions, developed through work with individual cases, was subsequently investigated through quasi-experimental designs in applied settings. In the future a greater demand for the systematic evaluation of local innovatory programmes and local implementations of national initiatives is likely, given the increasing focus on accountability requirements and evidence-based practice in education (Sebba, 2004).

The 'What Works' school of thought assumes very reasonably that getting to cell C is the goal (Carr, 2000). A generalized knowledge of interventions that work reliably with specific individual problems is seen to be the 'gold standard' (for example in the case of a particular student with dyslexia or with a particular school deemed on inspection to be 'failing'). Whilst this linking of 'cell C interventions' to 'cell a' individual, or 'cell A' group problem descriptions is a highly desirable goal, it must be acknowledged however that even those interventions judged the most effective do not work with around 33 per cent of young people (Carr, 2000).

The structure of this chapter

This chapter uses Clarke's model as a unifying structure within which to discuss the challenges, dilemmas and achievements of, or for, British EPs attempting to work as scientist–practitioners. These will be exemplified by four distinct and very different phases and styles of practice:

- the use of psychometric testing;
- behavioural approaches;
- systems work;
- consultation.

The chapter will conclude by defining the extent to which this model suggests EPs might develop further as scientist–practitioners.

PSYCHOMETRIC TESTING

The early history of the EP profession displays a strong association with psychometric testing, particularly intelligence testing, a feature also true of school psychology in the USA as reported for example by Davis *et al.*, (2004). Gillham (1978) in fact remarks that, in Britain on a one-year training to be an EP in the mid-1960s, he performed the Stanford–Binet test around 100 times! Although dissenting voices within the profession grew throughout the 1970s (e.g. Burden, 1973; Gillham, 1978; Leyden, 1978; Maliphant, 1974), and practice slowly changed away from such a reliance on intelligence testing, there remained, and still remains today, a common perception among the general public, other 'helping professionals' and some academic psychologists, that this represents the dominant activity of EPs.

A major purpose to which the use of intelligence tests was put was to 'ascertain' the suitability of some pupils for segregated special schooling. A widely used criterion for placing a young person in an ESN(M) ('educationally subnormal – moderate') school was an IQ measured at 70 (two standard deviations from the mean) or below. One of the authors began his career in a Service in the mid-

1970s in which there was a requirement that all students referred to the Service, for whatever presenting problem, should undergo an IQ assessment. Further, any such student found to have an IQ of 70 or less should be recommended for an ESN(M) school placement, whatever the other circumstances. Conversely, any student scoring a point or two above this cut-off figure could or should not be admitted, however strong the requests or demands from other quarters.

In terms of Clarke's model, an explanation deriving from the study of large groups (cell B) was used to determine a general policy or intervention for groups of young people (cell C) and hence as a clear yardstick in individual recommendations (cell c). On this approach, the particular constituents of the IQ test were assembled so as to produce scores normally distributed across age stratifications on the standardization sample, and correlated with academic attainment, However, as Clarke points out, the early aggregation process whereby a very limited amount of information is collected from a large number of individuals (i.e. from performance on a set of 'sub-tests' by the standardization sample) immediately strips away the possibility of building an explanation on a far wider set of aspects of each particular individual and the complexity of each of their personal environments.

Given all the attention given to IQ tests by many professionals, and certain academic psychologists, it is striking how little research was also carried out into the efficacy of the interventions that they were argued to imply. Scientist–practitioners of that time might have been expected to be researching whether segregated special schooling could be demonstrated to have *any* beneficial effects, whether such provision had any *differential* benefits between categories of pupil (defined by means of such tests), and whether *cost-effectiveness* of any benefits could be demonstrated once compared to the outcomes from a similar resource investment in other, less segregated provision (cell C). Despite considerable methodological shortcomings, a fairly consistent overall conclusion from different reviews in the USA in the 1970s and early 1980s (Baker *et al.*, 1994–1995; Madden and Slavin, 1983) was that there was no evidence that pupils in special school placements made any greater academic or social progress than did comparable pupils in mainstream placements. Indeed there appeared to be some advantage to mainstream placements, though only if a suitably individualized or differentiated educational programme was provided.

Advances in conceptualizations of intelligence within psychology (see Ceci, 1996; Gardner, 1993) and within the professional practice of EPs contributed to a waning of the use of IQ tests by this specific group. Within the professional context, not only was the efficacy of segregated placements increasingly questioned but sociologists (e.g. Tomlinson, 1978) were accusing EPs in their practice of being complicit in 'social control'. In addition, black parents saw EPs as displaying 'institutional racism' – a challenge that came as a shock and a salutary lesson to a group of mainly liberal-minded and socially progressive EPs (Booker *et al.*, 1989). More latterly, the growing prominence of the movement for a fully inclusive school system has further challenged such previously established practice as undesirable (Thomas and Vaughan, 2004).

Amongst EPs themselves, there was an accelerating interest in methods of assessment intimately linked to the nature of the curriculum itself (Ainscow and Tweddle, 1979). In particular, task analysis came to prominence (Gardner and Tweddle, 1979), as did an interest in Precision Teaching (Raybould and Solity, 1982; Williams and Muncey, 1982) and Direct Instruction methods (Branwhite, 1986; Miller *et al.*, 1985). The value of such approaches had been demonstrated in cell C-type research into *interventions* with multiple cases (Haring *et al.*, 1978) but, in the context of this discussion, the prominence of a scientist–practitioner stance was to be seen in EPs employing methods with teachers in which a daily evaluation of the efficacy of individualized teaching programmes was a central feature (cell c-type research).

Whereas EPs were to be found rapidly abandoning their professed allegiance to the use of IQ tests by the mid-1980s (Lokke *et al.*, 1997), other professionals in medicine, education and psychology were turning towards them in their work in the area of dyslexia and specific learning difficulties. In essence, notions of statistical atypicality, based on large samples, were again being used to justify individually targeted interventions. In these instances, the atypicality was between an IQ measure and another standardized measure, usually a 'reading quotient (RQ)'. This highly sensitive and contentious area of practice generated many arguments between Local Education Authorities, various professionals and parents and made it difficult for EPs to leave behind a high degree of involvement in IQ testing. However, Stage *et al.*, (2003) draw attention to the fact that little, or no cell c-, or cell C-type research evidence exists to demonstrate that students with and without IQ/RQ discrepancies, but with similar levels of reading performance, actually respond any differently to various interventions.

It is now widely recommended that such discrepancy definitions should be eliminated and replaced by definitions based on a response-to-intervention approach where teachers implement evidence-based interventions and carefully monitor pupil progress (British Psychological Society, 1999; Office of Special Education Programs, USA Department of Education, 2002).

Atypicality of measured discrepancies between sub-tests *within* an IQ test have fared no better. Frederickson (1999) reviewed the evidence on a number of sub-test profiles on the Weschler Intelligence Scale for Children that have been claimed to be diagnostic of dyslexia. While these profiles, for example lower scores on the ACID (Arithmetic, Coding, Information and Digit Span) profile, were found to differ statistically between typically developing children and those with literacy difficulties, the differences were not diagnostically or educationally significant. For example, 5 per cent of children with literacy difficulties were found to have an ACID profile, as compared with 1.1 per cent of typically developing children. If used diagnostically this would mean both that 95 per cent of children with reading difficulties would not be identified and that 1.1 per cent of the much larger group of children who did not have literacy difficulties would be incorrectly identified. In one study (Prifitera and Dersch, 1993) only 25 out of the 612 children with reading difficulties were correctly identified. At the same time 24 of the 2,158 typically developing children were identified in error.

In summary, as far as the use of psychometric, and especially IQ, tests by EPs has been concerned there appears to have been a recurring element of unjustified reasoning. In essence, this is the assumption that the study of the distribution of IQ scores, or of the distribution of discrepancies between IQ and other measures, or of the distribution of discrepancies between various sub-test scores within an IQ test, yields crucial information for deciding upon the desirability of certain interventions with individuals. In Clarke's model, cell B-type explanations based on the study of multiple cases were far too readily assumed to support certain cell c-type individual interventions. An EP does not become a scientist–practitioner merely by virtue of carrying out a high degree or large amount of measurement.

Conversely, the trends that seemed to most successfully challenge this practice drew on findings from large-scale intervention studies, but then recommended individual approaches, such as Precision Teaching, that incorporated very rigorous attempts to evaluate efficacy within each individual intervention – multiple case research (cell C) informing individual interventions (cell c) carried out with a scientist–practitioner's strong concern and enthusiasm for evaluation.

BEHAVIOURAL APPROACHES

Applied psychologists looked to behavioural approaches as one possible route out of the dilemmas posed by, and shortcomings of approaches allied strongly to, psychometric testing. Early British proponents (Presland, 1973; Ward, 1976) were strongly influenced by the landmark American study carried out by Madsen *et al.*, (1968). The basic tenets of Learning Theory – concepts such as reinforcement strengthening the occurrence of behaviour and the notion of extinction – were developed from experiments from the 1930s onwards. These multi-subject experiments (cell B) often involved animals learning in simplified environments such as mazes (Hill, 1971).

Applied behavioural analysis represented an attempt to translate such conceptualizations into the more complex environments inhabited by humans, particularly in the case of this discussion into classrooms and other educational settings (e.g. Wheldall, 1987). The usual method for formally reporting problem formulations and intervention strategies within this paradigm was by means of the single case experimental design. Early proponents, Madsen *et al.* (1968) investigated the effects of teachers' praise, ignoring and clear statements of rules on the behaviour of students deemed difficult to manage.

However, by attempting to understand the behaviour of these individual students in terms of these cell B-type formulations, crucial features of the educational context were overlooked or not recognized as crucially salient. Within applied behavioural analysis, the statement of classroom rules was construed as a 'setting condition', paralleling aspects of the environments in which experiments on pigeons and rats were carried out. In fact, even the 'simplest' of rules in educational contexts require considerable negotiations concerning meanings, exceptions and relative importance. Once this is accepted, the paradigm shifts dramatically towards the social and the constructionist.

One of the major findings after a decade or so of British activity in the use of behavioural approaches (Merrett, 1981) was that teachers seemed very reluctant to abstract the principles behind specific interventions devised with EPs and to devise similar but new approaches when attempting to manage the behaviour of other students – the problem of generalization (Presland, 1981). When interventions devised within a behavioural paradigm were studied in depth (Miller, 2003), the systemic nature of schools, and home–school interactions, and the cognitive and emotional responses of the various participants were brought to the fore.

Within a psychosocial perspective such as this, cell-B type formulations from classic Learning Theory could no longer hold. Other cell-B theoretical frameworks, such as those concerned with attribution theory, were found to have considerable explanatory value, but it was also recognized that fuller and further attention to individual interventions (cell c) would be necessary before it might be possible to make more general pronouncements about 'What Works' (cell C) in managing difficult behaviour in classrooms.

SYSTEMS APPROACHES

While behavioural approaches enjoyed considerable success with discrete classroom-focused problems, more difficulties were experienced where home–school interactions were involved. The involvement of different school staff, holding different roles within the organization and bringing different perceptions, attributions and values to the description and interpretation of problematic situations served similarly to increase the complexity of the situation in ways that highlighted the insufficiency of classic behavioural approaches (Douglas, 1982). Yet a major aspiration of educational psychologists, in pursuing both more effective intervention and prevention, was to increase work 'through the organisation, policy and structure of schools and through the attitudes and behaviour of adults towards children' (Gillham, 1978: 16). Systems approaches were identified as a means of dealing with the organizational and interactional complexity involved (Burden, 1978; Miller, 1980). As Checkland observes,

> Systems thinking is an attempt, within the broad sweep of science, to retain much of that tradition but to supplement it by tackling the problems of irreducible complexity via a form of thinking based on wholes and their properties which complements scientific reductionism.
>
> (1999: 74)

The essential distinguishing features of a systems approach are: a holistic rather than a reductionist emphasis and explanations in terms of circular rather than linear causality. Just as there are different types of behavioural theories, different strands of systems thinking can be identified. One major strand is General Systems Theory (Bertalanffy, 1968) which is biologically based. Within this strand a number of approaches developed that feature in the practice of educational psychology, such as systemic family therapy (Palazzoli *et al.*, 1978) and the Tavistock Institute model of joint family–school intervention (Dowling and Osborne, 1994).

A second major strand, Systems Analysis, developed from a mechanistic basis in engineering and operational research (Jenkins, 1969). This approach formed the starting point for an influential series of studies in schools conducted by Burden and his colleagues (Burden, 1978; Burden, 1981; Burden, *et al.*, 1982). From this work it emerged that the systems approach developed by Jenkins was not sufficiently flexible to deal with the reactivity of systems involving human participants and the spiral model of an action research approach was recommended as an alternative (Elliott, 1981; Lewin, 1951).

The same conclusion was reached by Checkland, Jenkins' successor as professor of systems at Lancaster University, from attempts to apply the systems analysis approach beyond 'hard' engineering contexts to 'soft' commercial, health and social care settings. As a result Checkland (1981) developed Soft Systems Methodology (SSM) which utilizes a framework of systems ideas within an action research approach. Designed especially for use with social systems, SSM adopts an interpretative stance. It deals with situations that those involved perceive to be problematic or to present an opportunity for improvement. The task is not to narrowly define a problem to solve. Rather, the aim is to build up the richest possible picture of the situation presented, drawing on the disparate perspectives of all involved, and then, by means of a systemic analysis, to help those involved identify feasible improvements which they could make to the situation in which they are all enmeshed.

SSM has been applied in a range of contexts in educational psychology practice (Frederickson and Cline, 2002; Miller, 2003). Specific foci have included: supporting schools in special measures (Bettle *et al.*, 2001), inclusion of pupils who have special educational needs (Frederickson, 1993), establishment of a case management database (Forrester, 1993) and screening programmes in schools (Gersch *et al.*, 2001). The studies describe a flexible, yet systematic approach which starts from a rich picture description of a particular organizational situation perceived to be problematic, cell a in Clarke's model. At cell b, systems that may be relevant to understanding and improving the situation are identified and modelled. Finally desirable and feasible changes generated from the systems models are identified, implemented and evaluated (cell c) through the collation of perceived changes (intended and unintended) from those involved in the problem situation. The general conclusion is that the approach is useful in dealing with complexity inherent in working with and in schools and other organizations.

Reflecting on systems and other work undertaken in schools, educational psychologists (Frederickson, 1990) and clinical psychologists (Douglas, 1982) have concluded that the scientific approach remains the approach of choice in tackling well-defined problems, but that such problems tend to be rare in applied psychology practice that is carried out in real-life environments. Where does this leave the applied psychologist as scientist–practitioner? Naughton (1979) claims that SSM fits within a technology, rather than a science paradigm because its primary goal is effective action rather than understanding *per se*. This is highly congruent with Schön's (1987) view that practitioners are primarily interested in changing situations. However Naughton's definition of technology involves the systematic application of scientific, as well as other organized knowledge to practical tasks.

While Checkland presents systems work as complementary to a scientific approach, he does place it 'within the broad sweep of science' (1999: 74). Checkland and Holwell (1998) argue that replicability, essential to science, is not achievable in research in complex social contexts. However neither do they accept a weak constructionist criterion where 'there seems to be virtually no difference between writing novels and doing social research' (Checkland, 1999: 39–40). Similar conclusions are drawn by Stoker and Figg (1998) who identify action as an important *modus operandi* for EPs who aspire to operate as scientist–practitioners. They highlight difficulties with both traditional positivist and constructionist approaches. The distance required in the former approach between the researcher and the researched is seen as untenable in the world of the practitioner while 'constructivism suggests no strong methodological position and a relativism that seems equally indefensible' (Stoker and Figg, 1998: 55).

Checkland and Holwell (1998) suggest 'recoverability' rather than replicability as a suitable criterion for practitioners. This involves the use of an explicit intellectual framework and process which makes it possible for others to follow the research and evaluate or re-evaluate the findings and interpretations presented. It is suggested that this allows learning from successive implementations of the approach, learning about the focus area of the research, the framework of ideas applied or the methodology used. It fits well with the arguments made in Chapter 2 of this book for the importance of systematic frameworks for professional reasoning. In terms of Clarke's model the claim is that this kind of systematic and rigorous approach to the study of a particular aspect of a particular organization (e.g. academic motivation in Year 9 in St. Monica's secondary school) can lead to learning about the use of the approach (from cells a to b and on to c).

A series of studies of a particular issue using SSM may offer the possibility of learning whether patterns can be identified across studies in the area of interest. It is unlikely that clear generalizations about interventions (cell C) would emerge from such a systematic comparison of organizational case study data. However description (cell A) and hypothesis generation (cell B) across cases should both be possible. This is a very different matter from collecting shelves full of diverse, impressionist cases, or action research studies which lack an intellectual framework to which their findings can be related and whose implications, therefore, tend to be limited to their individual contexts.

CONSULTATION

Consultation has been widely embraced by EPs in recent years as a means of dealing with the complexity inherent in work focused on individual children, where self-referral is extremely rare. In general terms consultation can be defined as a process of 'collaborative problem solving between a mental health specialist (the consultant) and one or more persons (the consultees) who are responsible for providing some form of psychological assistance to another (the client) (Medway, 1979: 276). It received a cautious endorsement in the DfEE (2000) report on the role and practice of educational psychologists in the UK. Central to all consultation approaches in EP practice is an appreciation of the importance of engaging the participation of the concerned adults in developing an understanding of the situation and in bringing about change. There are many parallels when applying systems approaches to issues identified at an organizational level and when applying systems approaches to issues in consultation work with teachers and parents who have concerns about children.

As in the case of systems approaches, there are variants of consultation and a key distinguishing feature is the extent to which the concerned adults are the direct focus. Organizational level consultation approaches, such as process consultation (Schein, 1969), which are focused on relationships between adults will not be considered here. Mental health consultation (Caplan, 1970; Figg and Stoker, 1990) is an example of a predominately adult-focused approach in which psychodynamic concepts are used in case discussion to assist teachers to identify and overcome personal blocks to more effective working. By contrast, in behavioural consultation (Bergan and Kratochwill, 1990) the case discussion draws on social learning theory and follows a problem-solving approach focused primarily on effecting change in the behaviour of the child about whom the consultee is concerned. However, as Gutkin and Curtis (1999) point out, while the emphasis differs, all models of consultation aim to some extent to affect positive change for clients and to enskill or empower consultees to effectively manage or even prevent similar situations in future.

A number of authors (Gutkin and Curtis, 1999; Wagner, 2000) have argued that neither of these approaches is adequate and that an interactionist, systemic model of consultation is required that acknowledges the effects of, and aims to impact on, adult attributions and problem-solving skills as well as pupil outcomes. Consequently both sets of authors advocate a comprehensive approach. Wagner's interrelating systems approach to consultation (1995, 2000), developed in the UK, draws directly on systemic and social constructionist perspectives in framing enquiries about situations perceived to be problematic. However the frameworks that are offered to facilitate 'conversations that make a difference' include elements from problem-solving and social learning approaches and incorporate follow-up in evaluating progress, all these aspects involving the family and psychologist as well as teaching staff.

Gutkin and Curtis (1999) term their approach, developed in the USA, 'ecobehavioural', signifying the incorporation of ecological, systemic and interactional thinking into the long established behavioural consultation framework. There are many parallels between the developments over time described by Gutkin and Curtis (1999) in a North American context and those described by Woolfson *et al.*, (2003) in the UK. Woolfson *et al.* (2003) extend the problem analysis framework (Monsen *et al.*, 1998) which emphasized hypothesis-testing, intervention and evaluation, into an integrated framework that 'provides a practical tool for informing systemic EP practice within an interdisciplinary, collaborative context by employing ecological analysis of problems . . .' (Woolfson *et al.*, 2003: 301). The five-phase approach described by Woolfson *et al.* (2003) has much in common with the four-step approach described by Gutkin and Curtis (1999), comprising problem identification, problem analysis, plan implementation and treatment evaluation.

These steps, particularly if conceived as stages in a cycle, provide a generic description of the consultation process. However the starting point in the cycle and the focus of the work with clients may differ considerably in different approaches. For example, approaches to consultation in educational psychology based on the principles and practices of solution-focused brief therapy (Rhodes and Ajmal, 1995) will focus in with the clients on identifying goals rather than problems, will analyse exceptions in sharing guiding assumptions and formulating prescriptions for action, will place great emphasis on working out the detail of implementation and on measuring change in evaluation, often through the use of scaling techniques. In addition to its strong cognitive-behavioural orientation, this approach is also based on systemic principles such as the assumption that behaviours interrelate across contexts. This drives a willingness to begin work where there is easiest and legitimate access, irrespective of the setting in which concerns have been identified, and to work with the person who most wants change.

Gutkin argues that while:

> an ecological perspective can improve on a narrow view of behavioural psychology for school-based consultants, there can be little doubt that the reverse is also true . . . The hard-nosed empiricism and extensive knowledge base that have developed under the behavioural 'umbrella' must not be lost.
>
> (1993: 97)

Gutkin's argument receives support from a review of outcome research in consultation between 1985 and 1995 (see Sheridan *et al.*, 1996). Convincingly positive outcomes were reported from studies where behavioural approaches (including the ecobehavioural variant) to consultation had been used. Although the number of studies using mental health consultation was very much smaller, outcomes were also predominately positive. However outcomes from studies where no clear model of consultation was used were much more equivocal and, in some cases, negative. This suggests the likely importance of adopting coherent models of consultation and using clear practice frameworks to support them, such as those proposed by

Gutkin and Curtis (1999), Rhodes and Ajmal (1995), Wagner (1995) and Woolf-son *et al.* (2003). It also raises concern about reports that much EP consultation practice in the UK is not based on a coherent approach (Farouk, 1999).

Thus, the available evidence suggests that unsystematic approaches to consultation, where a Service embraces a vague conceptualization and leaves individual interpretation to practitioners, is less likely to lead to effective outcomes than a clear ecobehavioural or interrelating systemic model, supported by practice frameworks to guide implementation. The adoption of a coherent approach to consultation is also a prerequisite for the collation of evaluative data to allow validation and further development of the approach. Clearly the collection of evaluative data is also important in ensuring that the needs of particular individuals are effectively met. Yet evaluation is often omitted as EPs cite time constraints (Kratochwill and Stoiber, 2000; Leadbetter, 2000), despite the requirements of the duty of care EPs owe to their clients (Garland, 1997) and the availability of appropriate approaches for collating information from individual cases for audit and evaluation purposes.

One such approach is Goal Attainment Scaling (GAS) (Kiresuk and Sherman, 1968) which has been applied by psychologists in the UK to date in only a small number of educational contexts, for example in evaluating a behaviour support teaching service (Imich and Roberts, 1990) and the provision of conductive education (MacKay *et al.*, 1993). Of particular relevance is an account from the USA by Sladeczek *et al.*, (2001), in which the technique was incorporated into a behavioural consultation framework in evaluating the outcomes of consultation.

GAS is individualized to each client or problem situation and encourages collaboration with all involved in identifying a manageable number of priority areas to target for intervention and in setting goals to which there is broad commitment. The goals identified are then scaled to produce measures of rate and adequacy of progress. Key measurement properties are established sufficiently to allow for defensible use in decision-making about individual progress and in collating outcomes from many individuals in evaluating aspects of service effectiveness (see Frederickson, 2002, for further information). With a small number of additional refinements, the techniques for collating information on outcomes from individuals may provide a means of moving from cell c to cell C in Clarke's model. For example, if collations were focused on particular types of interventions and examined in relation to various individual characteristics and/or circumstances, it may be possible to begin to address important applied research questions about which interventions work best in practice with which client groups.

CONCLUSION

The notion of the scientist–practitioner holds great appeal for many EPs but, as this chapter and indeed the whole book have shown, beyond the superficial appeal of this concept lies a complex web of issues involving epistemology and the nature of science as well as the complex social and political environments in which EPs have to practise ethically and reflectively. For the academic psychologist, science has generated theoretical explanations and understandings by studying multiple cases, each stripped of their messy individual complexities. Whilst this approach has furnished academic psychology with many achievements, these have some-times served practitioner psychologists less well.

In their use of psychometric tests, for example, drawing on cell B-type explana-tions, EPs encouraged a set of practices that many have come to rue for reasons given above. In essence, these explanations have provided impoverished or incom-plete understandings of individuals (cell b) and yielded little by way of helpful individual strategies (cell c) or wider policy implications (cell C). Understanding within behavioural psychology appeared to fare somewhat better, in that theo-retical developments again based on the study of multiple (often animal) studies yielded the conceptual tools that were incorporated into explanations of the behav-iour of individuals (cell b) and intervention strategies (cell c). However, the limited nature of such theorizing was exposed once more systemic considerations were applied to the practice of EPs.

However, if the theoretical understandings from cell B have proved disappoint-ing, or even misleading for EPs, the study of such matters in their initial under-graduate training in psychology has equipped EPs with many valuable tools and perspectives. For example, the study and practice of the scientific method has gen-erated a respect for hypothesis testing, the conditions necessary for demonstrating causation, and an appreciation of the reliability and validity that may be accorded to measures. In addition, undergraduate training also teaches an awareness that 'findings' in social science research are usually probabilistic rather than certain in nature, and that generalizability, and near and far transfer are important con-siderations. These and related insights are not necessarily widely shared in educa-tion and other areas of social policy. However, as an evidence-based approach is increasingly advocated and debated (Hargreaves, 1996; Thomas and Pring, 2004), EPs have the opportunity to make a significant and necessary contribution where otherwise 'data', rather than evidence, knowledge and understanding, may come to drive local policy and practice. Hence, the interest within the profession in system-ic approaches such as soft systems methodology which, whilst acknowledging and addressing the complexity and, often hidden, cultural aspects of organizations, nonetheless proceed in a logical, ordered and 'transparent' manner. Similarly, systematic approaches to consultation have provided frameworks within which a broad range of psychological theory and research can be drawn on to inform practice. The incorporation of systematic evaluation methodologies such as Goal Attainment Scaling enables the collation of data in cell (c) which can be meaning-fully collated in drawing tentative generalizations (cell C).

This chapter has argued that EPs can and do operate as scientist–practition-ers. They do this in an idiographic fashion moving down the left-hand column of Clarke's model, from the presentation of an individual problem, through to a formulated understanding and on to an individually-targeted intervention. EPs are wise to be cautious about expecting research findings in academic psychology to be readily applicable to their work. While their practice will be informed by both psychological theory (cell B to cell b) and research on the efficacy of interventions (cell C to cell c), it has long been recognized that this is not a matter of direct translation. As James observed:

> You make a great, a very great mistake if you think that psychology, being the science of minds' laws, is something from which you can deduce definite programmes and schemes and methods of instruction for immediate classroom use. Psychology is a science and teaching is an art: and sciences never generate arts directly out of themselves. An intermediary, inventive mind must make the application, by using its originality.
>
> (1899: 23–4)

While many elements of the research psychologist's mindset and approach are to be found within the practice frameworks that distinguish the successful EP, it should be recognized that additional systematic methodologies are also involved. Schön uses terms such as 'professional artistry' and 'reflection in action' to refer to systematic and rigorous processes developed through practicums or training workshops in professional education. As he explains:

> In the terrain of professional practice, applied science and research-based technique occupy a critically important though limited territory, bounded on several sides by artistry. There are an art of problem framing, an art of implementation and an art of improvisation – all necessary to mediate the use in practice of applied science and technique
>
> (1987: 13)

It is only by applying 'comparable-to-science' standards of rigour to issues of practice that the scientist–practitioner concept can carry conviction as a marriage of equals.

By looking to structured and sensitive approaches such as the use of GAS within a systematic consultative framework in individual casework, and SSM in organizational and inter-agency work, EPs will be able to collate, compare and contrast examples of single interventions in complex settings, leading to greater and more widely generalizable knowledge of successful interventions. In doing so, EPs will then truly be in a position to consolidate and celebrate their identities as modern scientist–practitioners.

Chapter 8

The scientist–practitioner in a counselling psychology setting

Dennis Bury and *Susan Maise Strauss*

INTRODUCTION

The human psyche is influenced by an extraordinary complexity of experiences. Many would therefore maintain that we can never completely understand another human being. As scientist–practitioners, is our purported allegiance to, and reliance upon, 'official' sources of knowledge (including theory and scientific evidence) sufficient for us to be confident that we can construct consistently helpful solutions from the myriad clinical data at our fingertips? Should we as psychologists accept that full understanding of causality is simply not an achievable objective? If we adopt the position that we can never fully explain causes, however, what role do we actually play? Can our interventions even be considered valid, let alone scientific?

The question of how practitioners reflect upon their activity, and of the scientific assumptions behind their work, has occupied much debate in the field of psychology, and the many different strands of this debate are woven throughout the fabric of this book. In this chapter, we consider some of the many implications of this debate for counselling psychologists.

Specifically, we begin by exploring the position of counselling psychology within the profession more broadly, and consider its place in the current controversy about the scientist–practitioner role. Next, we articulate some of our own practice in this regard, attempting not only to take note of the systematic approaches that we employ in counselling psychology but also to incorporate the wide range of expectations and experience that comes to the therapeutic endeavour. Finally, we try to define the type of scientist–practitioner that we envision in a counselling psychology setting.

THE COUNSELLING PSYCHOLOGIST

Counselling psychology has been recognized by the American Psychological Association for some time but it was only in 1982 that the British Psychological Society established a section of counselling psychology, leading to full divisional status in the UK in 1994. The identity of the counselling psychologist as scientist–practitioner, already established in the United States, has come to be endorsed in the UK as well (see British Psychological Society, 2004). The recent emphasis upon evidence-based practice has, however, led practitioners in both countries to re-examine the meaning of the scientist–practitioner model within counselling psychology and the extent to which this remains a viable framework for guiding professional practice. In fact, some would argue that it is precisely because of the broadening of the field of applied psychology, to include areas such as counselling psychology, that this re-examination of the relationship between science and practice has come about (Strawbridge and Woolfe, 2004).

As Strawbridge and Woolfe (1996) observe, the activities, role and identity of counselling psychologists cannot be explored separately from the economic, political and social contexts in which they operate. As counselling psychologists occupy progressively varied roles in an expanding range of work settings, we must address questions such as: 'What is it that makes counselling psychology unique amongst the psychological disciplines?' 'What is it that brings 'added value' as each discipline within psychology seeks to define (and redefine) itself in an increasingly competitive marketplace?' (See Chapter 13.)

At its core, counselling psychology privileges respect for the personal, subjective experience of the client over and above notions of diagnosis, assessment and treatment, as well as the pursuit of innovative, phenomenological methods for understanding human experience. At the same time, however, we find ourselves working within mental health teams and other health-care settings, where notions of 'sickness' and the associated labels that go with the concept of mental illness prevail. How (if at all) can these types of activity be reconciled with the humanistic values underpinning the counselling psychologist's philosophy of practice? How should we position ourselves, as a profession, in relation to matters as contentious as psychological testing (Sequeira and van Scoyoc, 2004), diagnosis and standardized approaches to 'treatment' delivery? As Golsworthy (2004) observes, this is part of an ongoing debate within counselling psychology as our methods and roles come to attract greater political recognition.

We are, of course, not alone in having to address these dilemmas. Our sister profession of clinical psychology is grappling with similar issues about the relative merits of standardized vs. individualized treatments and the role of diagnosis. It is important to recognize that there are substantial areas of compatibility and many ways in which our work draws from a similar array of theoretical frameworks and interventions. However, unlike clinical psychology which evolved alongside a medical model, counselling psychology in both countries has traditionally been associated with phenomenological and humanistic concerns (Rogers, 1961), and in America this has included a focus on prevention as well as community-based interventions (Sue, 2001; Vera and Speight, 2003). We do not work from an assumption of pathology. Our clients typically come because of their own desire to better understand and explore some aspect of their lives. Strawbridge and Woolfe (2004) suggest that, in addition to a more subjective focus, it is the emphasis on the quality of the therapeutic relationship that distinguishes counselling psychology from a more clinical model. The therapist's role as collaborative helper is considered crucial, as is the reflexivity afforded through ongoing supervision. While individual counselling and clinical psychologists may in fact fall along a continuum in this respect, the significance of the therapeutic relationship is central to the identity of counselling psychology as a profession.

In the ongoing debate about definition, some would argue that the traditional scientist–practitioner model simply cannot capture the essence of the therapeutic relationship that is so integral to counselling psychologists' work and that, as a framework of practice it is, therefore, unsustainable (Carter, 2002; Wakefield and Kirk, 1996). Others maintain that our therapeutic work can indeed be seen as taking place within the realm of the scientist–practitioner model, and that we must recognize this by enlarging our definition of what constitutes the scientific aspects of our identity (Corrie and Callanan, 2000, 2001; Strawbridge and Woolfe, 1996). Hage (2003) reminds us that much is at stake for counselling psychologists as the scientist–practitioner identity undergoes a re-examination. A move toward a more medical model could threaten precisely those attributes that make counselling psychology distinctive.

Wilkinson (see Chapter 3) addresses the importance of 'psychological mindedness' in guiding our interventions, whereby our goal is to arrive at a meaningful personal narrative, rather than trying to fit our clients' experiences neatly into particular theoretical models. She addresses the risks we otherwise run in reaching 'premature foreclosure'. These views have much in common with Schön's (1987) image of the 'reflective practitioner', advocating the importance of a holistic, one could even say artistic, approach.

Several alternatives to the traditional empirical, positivist model have been put forth in order to better understand the science of our practice. Many have favoured the argument that we arrive at our understanding of our clients through a social construction of reality, whereby social and cultural influences define multiple human realities (Gergen, 1985). The critical realist approach, on the other hand, while acknowledging these multiple social, cultural and language-based constructions, maintains that there is a human reality that exists independent of social context. It retains the idea of a causal order that can be subjected to experimental analysis (Bhaskar, 1975; Manicas and Secord, 1983; see Chapter 5). Could it be that counselling psychology can draw upon a different definition of science than that initially suggested by the term 'scientist–practitioner'?

Corrie and Callanan (2000) maintain that, not only does the concept of the scientist–practitioner remain very relevant to our practice of therapy, but it may also be a vital part of counselling psychologists' professional identity in a larger sense. In order to acknowledge this aspect of our role, they suggest a broadening of the definition of scientist–practitioner, thereby more accurately reflecting the role that scientific research plays in our work. They note our ethical responsibility, for example, to keep informed of current research, as it relates to theory, practice implementation and outcome. Moreover, they point out that many of our activities of evaluation and analysis are very much in keeping with the scientific aspects of the scientist–practitioner model. While the dominant paradigms of psychotherapy outcome research (typically embodied in the randomized controlled trial) seem at odds with our humanistic roots, there are alternative questions worth asking. As Goldfried and Eubanks-Carter (2004) point out, a focus on principle and strategies helps to bridge the practitioner–researcher divide. Basic psychopathology research focuses on what needs to be changed. For us this is a question about problem setting, not pathology. Outcome research in randomized trials focuses on whether change has occurred, whereas for counselling psychologists the more interesting question relates to how change occurs. The interaction and exchange across the research–practice divide that Goldfried and Eubanks-Carter seek is certainly one to which we can respond as counselling psychologists.

WHERE DO WE START?

In writing this chapter we engaged in a dialogue, comparing, contrasting and critiquing our own views towards science and practice. This enabled us to address some of the salient issues and draw out our particular practice and understanding. We came to realize that we each came from different stances, not only in terms of theoretical perspective, but also in our focus on science and practice. Rather than attempting to iron out these differences, we saw this chapter as an opportunity to test out whether there were commonalities between us – almost an experiment in equivalence – that might highlight aspects of the debate in the field. Indeed, we began to suspect that some of our differences were in fact mirroring – or even recreating – aspects of the debate itself: science and practice as opposed to science vs. practice.

We were struck by the fact that, as much as we readily delve into discussions about such things as theoretical perspective, assessment technique, conceptualization, and intervention strategies, seldom do we stop to ask as simple a question as, *what is it that we actually do?* The changing role of psychology as a profession and the reality of marketability makes this question pertinent. In co-constructing this chapter we have, therefore, elevated this question to the heart of our discussions as we saw it as central to the examination of our role as scientist–practitioners. Through our discussions, we hoped to arrive at some broader conclusions by means of addressing (1) the key elements we consider as we begin our therapeutic work with a client, (2) whether our practice is guided by one main theoretical perspective or by multiple models, and (3) whether other theories or principles might be particularly relevant to our practice.

WHAT IS IT THAT WE ACTUALLY DO?

What key elements do you consider as you begin your therapeutic work with a client?

We began by addressing the role that we play in the objectification of meaning, given that a core element in our work is our clients' desire to make sense of their distress. We agreed that, while offering interpretations, we must be mindful of not imposing our own reality upon our clients, but rather empowering and respecting autonomy.

The therapeutic framework is often surprisingly all about not knowing, about bringing into awareness previously undiscovered knowledge of oneself. This awareness is often in the realm of affect and human relationship, areas not traditionally considered in the scientific sphere.

Nonetheless, our exploration is very much guided by definite scientific methodology and principles that influence the way in which meaning evolves in the therapist–client relationship. As scientist–practitioners, we question the reliability and validity of clinical measures and the treatment methods we employ. But even sound measures and methods, while they may suggest patterns, only present us with hypotheses to 'try on'. No matter how much we attempt to bring objectivity to our interventions, the relationship aspects push the boundaries of that objectivity. We strive to manage a balancing act.

This gives rise to two possible domains of exploration and enquiry. The first, akin to our science, relates to notions of what we can do. The second, true to our humanistic roots and the notion of encounter and relationship, is more akin to what we can be. These are discussed in turn.

What can I do?

Our diagnostic and research systems originate with preconceptions and attempt to seek a universal replicability. Frameworks such as the Diagnostic and Statistical Manual of Mental Disorders (American Psychiatric Association, 1994) may be valid but only in certain contexts (Neimeyer and Raskin, 2000). Similarly, we found that we utilized one type of scientific enquiry for understanding people's responses to physiological arousal, and a more idiographic approach for personal representations of meaning. We acknowledged, moreover, that people come to therapy with their own constructs of what might loosely be termed causality (Watson and Winter, 2000; Winter and Watson, 1999).

We noted how the development of an objective perspective is enhanced by means of off-site resources – supervision, books, journals, traditions of therapy and case examples, in addition to a self-reflexive dimension. The benefit of a good on-line database affords us the chance to import perspectives, thereby linking *local science* with a bigger picture of supporting or contrary evidence. We have a knowledge base built from research from which we 'can do' practice.

However, looking into a system alters it. There are social science parallels to

Heisenberg's propositions about observer effects on physical systems. The system within which we operate, the relationship, allows that emotion and reasoning are aligned, suggesting a *reasonable* basis (Robinson, 2004), but imported rationality may become oppressive. The structuring effects it imposes grants power to psychologists that they may not seek but do need to recognize. Recent developments in science in the form of chaos theory are beginning to incorporate this concept (see Chapter 5), and may provide the parallel to the consistent voice in counselling psychology that has advocated a practice-led, phenomenologically focused approach to enquiry. This potentially radically reshapes the concept of science in counselling psychology practice.

Thus, the task becomes not to find the exact measurement to fit, but rather to locate tracks that will allow us to play and work (Newman and Holzman, 1999). Reality, therefore, becomes loosely defined and confoundable. Falsification is now 'serial reconceptualization' – 'critical thinking' (Gambrill, 1993; Phillips, 1992) and scepticism (Kurtz, 1992). Decisions and intuitions are not to be trusted alone for too long, for neither are representations of the truth. Both practitioner and scientist are incomplete, always in a dance between a localized science and wider traditions.

What can I be?

Recent models of science help us mould a scientist–practitioner identity more akin to our underlying values, and help us appreciate how our work is indeed in the realm of science. Where, however, do other variables sit, those that we more traditionally consider when we define what we do as therapists, such as affect and therapeutic relationship? We would argue that these aspects are just as central to the science of the scientist–practitioner model, as they too help give definition to the larger framework in which we operate. In particular they address some of the key elements that impact on how change occurs. We focus here on some significant aspects of the therapist's use of self.

We would see a focus on client affect as pivotal in effective practice. We see our role as that of a facilitator for the emergence of that affect, in order that our clients might allow themselves to be vulnerable, to access powerful emotions within the safe limits of the therapeutic hour, and thus to work through relevant emotional material.

In this we draw on many of the principles that emerged from the humanistic research tradition, whereby the taping and analysis of sessions created research paradigms that looked at the process of change. This research established the competencies that are essential for any good therapeutic work, including unconditional positive regard and the skills of listening, reflecting and conveying accurate empathy (Rogers, 1961). The trust built up through empathy and guidance was identified in this research as the key to treatment success. It is the relationship that allows it to happen.

However, we must remain sensitive to the inevitable power differential, and the inherent vulnerability of the client. In addition to obvious ethical violations, there are countless ways that we as therapists, albeit at times unconsciously, can seriously violate treatment boundaries. Given the frame of therapy and the natural focus on the client's issues, it can be easy to be blind to how our own countertransference may dramatically interfere with our client's work, whether it be unwittingly using the therapy at some level for our own gratification, satisfying our own needs for connection, or perhaps portraying a hostile attitude toward a particular client, no matter how subtle. Many believe the answer lies in part in personal therapy before undertaking a profession like ours, as well as the continued monitoring of our own mental health throughout our career. Such monitoring, in addition to self-examination, includes continued case consultation with colleagues.

The importance attributed to relationship arises from research on therapeutic process as well as our experience of it as counselling psychologists. It would be a danger to underplay that importance to fit more into an empirical model of outcome research. A standardized manual that lays out the questions to ask to create the *relationship*, ready for the application of predetermined interventions, may only be of use in certain circumstances. Carol Gilligan (2003) reminds us that the human world is essentially relationally responsive. And, as Miller and Stiver note, 'Most theorists have long agreed that people develop only in interaction with others . . . To talk of participating in others' psychological development, then, is to talk about a form of activity that is essential to human life' (1997: 17).

Is practice guided by one main theoretical perspective?

We know from our own experience that we may be influenced by various models while having one model as a core framework. One of us (DB) has been influenced by three profoundly different approaches – the cognitive-behavioural, the personal construct and the person-centred. This raises key questions for practice, since they are in many respects irreconcilable. It might be possible to follow an integrative route or, at any one point in time, to be informed by the theoretical perspective that makes sense for the client journey (see Chapter 2). However, this requires us to be competent in the 'doing' of the procedures, the tools that help define the approach or model. These may be very diverse. Types of language often accompany specific practices. Some instruments are statistically validated, and some are profoundly idiographic. Each embeds ideas about human behaviour and in using them we have to be aware of the assumptions that inform their use. Theoretical perspectives tend to adopt particular instruments. For some, the assumptions that accompany a focus on instrumental reality may be unacceptable (we will never know about people or things except by mediation of instruments) (Ihde, 1991, 2003). Yet instrumental reality, or knowing performatively, or 'thing knowledge' as one view has it (Baird, 2004), does form part of the knowledge base of counselling psychology.

For one of us (SMS), work as a therapist is most informed by a psychodynamic view, while still drawing from eclectic training in both cognitive-behavioural and person-centred approaches. Within this frame, much importance is placed on a thorough diagnostic interview, taking into account the client's family history and other relevant personal background, in addition to a comprehensive exploration of the presenting problem and the client's current functioning. There are times when, even within a single frame, therapists may take a multifaceted approach. Ideas from a cognitive-behavioural intervention to teach children self-management skills, for example, or behaviour modification to help a student conquer test anxiety, may find their way into more dynamically influenced frameworks. Such approaches might be an adjunct to more psychodynamic exploration, or at times they might be the sole intervention. However, always within a psychodynamic view there will be a continued eye toward relevant underlying factors that may emerge through the client's personal narrative.

Are there other theories or principles that are particularly relevant to your practice?

If, as counselling psychologists, we are to represent the very broad range of our clients' experience, then we have to place limits on our use of any one framework. Systematic evidential investigation is relevant only to the range of usability of the tools employed. Science is always on the move. Theory is pro tem and causation gives way to new levels of inference.

Arnold Lazarus, (see Dryden, 1991) concludes that it all depends, and this perhaps expresses our use of science as being dependent upon its value for a particular client. Reality with the human range of usability is negotiated between things and people and is reality only in so much as it can validate similar things: 'It is the interaction of persons with objects via beliefs that gives meaning to events and objects, not the autonomous creation of reality by persons' (Mackay, 2003: 380). This of course places the relationship and our use of self at the centre of our work; it is what we do.

Highlighting the therapist's use of self, Jordan (1999) addresses the notion of vulnerability as a positive construct, not only in the client but also in the therapist. She speaks of the profound caring that is a part of our work as therapists, and also our need to allow ourselves to be vulnerable in examining our own work and in seeking consultation. In their relational approach to psychotherapy, Miller and Stiver (1997) use a sense of connection as their gauge in timing interpretations. They say it is that moment when the patient recognizes that the therapist feels moved by him or her that something important occurs.

These issues have been explored in much of the recent psychological literature on women's development. We learn that, through deepening our understanding of women, we can better understand the human psyche, thus broadening our ways of viewing psychotherapy, and, moreover, the world in general. Studies of women suggest that traditional models of psychotherapy are gendered and patriarchal, making false assumptions about the value of separation and autonomy. Gilligan (2003) advocates that we instead employ an active and responsive manner of listening and questioning, taking voice as the 'barometer of relationship', the 'footprint of the psyche', bringing out our clients' voices without either distancing or imposing our own agenda upon them. Her concern is with the 'landscape' between the person and the researcher, and she sees the new person as a 'new terrain', a 'new voice'.

Is it possible that these views offer some objective ways of handling such meaningful experience within a new scientist–practitioner narrative? Perhaps we can avoid the traps in traditional empirical research methods which, in setting up certain parameters, can end up distorting objectivity. Gilligan (2003) has argued that data gathering can be subjected to quantitative or narrative analysis, yielding a 'logic of the psyche', with reliability being found in the diversity of the interpretive group, and validity in the relational context, and in not assuming a cultural framework. Similarly, in their book, *Women's Ways of Knowing*, Belenky and her colleagues discuss 'constructed reality', referring to a 'narrative sense of the self – past and future', whereby 'different perspectives and different points in time produce different answers' (Belenky *et al.*, 1986: 136). They note that women who reach this stage of knowing are 'a far cry from the perception of science as absolute truth' (1986: 138), and yet it seems this narrative sense of the self could still be subjected to objective analysis.

SOME PRELIMINARY CONCLUSIONS

We would both agree that the essence of our work as therapists is in striving to help our clients lend meaning to their own personal stories. And yet how do we, indeed how can we, reconcile the seemingly disparate views expressed here? While as individuals we might either lean toward an explanation based in the science of our practice, or focus more on our role as practitioner, taken together, we may highlight the fuller picture of what it is that counselling psychologists actually do. We have, through writing this chapter, come to appreciate how much we blend practice and science.

We have attempted to test our own diversity against extant literature, both to seek some sort of unity and to attempt to offer some sort of guide for the future. The conclusions that follow represent suggested dimensions for retaining the scientist–practitioner identity while noting its potential transformation.

In defining the scientist–practitioner from a counselling psychology perspective, Strawbridge and Woolfe speak of the 'critical task of problem setting' as opposed to 'problem solving' (2004: 6). They address the knowledge that we gain not only through research but also through experience. They note that it is reflection and 'monitoring of practice in process' (2004: 6), both individually and together with colleagues, that guide our interventions, and they acknowledge the 'significance of stories in human experience' (2004: 10). They maintain that not only are skills of empathic listening and reflecting essential to good practice, but in fact these skills define the practice of science within a psychotherapeutic context. It is by listening to and reflecting upon women's and men's voices that we can gain a clearer vision and a deeper understanding of our clients.

Not only do we learn within a context of a single case conceptualization, but also we continually build a body of knowledge that informs all of our work as scientist–practitioners. In a similar vein, Hage reminds us of the 'fundamental tenets' of the field of counselling psychology, 'which has emphasized respect for the personal, subjective experience of the client and multifaceted approaches to knowing' (Hage, 2003: 557). In acknowledgement of such reflection and experience, and the sort of knowing that encompasses our work, Corrie and Callanan suggest that 'it no longer makes sense to construe the scientist–practitioner model as representing a single method or doctrine' (2000: 424). In posing critical questions for further investigation, they ask whether different therapists do indeed 'interpret the scientist–practitioner model to mean different things', and they query as to the possible 'nature and range of these more idiosyncratic definitions' (2000: 424).

As we reflect upon our own practice in the context of the above definitions, we note many commonalities. We both see ourselves as 'problem setters'. We suggest our own example illustrates the concept of 'multifaceted approaches to knowing'. We strongly acknowledge the importance of allowing our clients' subjective reality to guide our interventions.

Our assumption, based in current ideology, had been that we practise and theorize in one way. In fact, we found that the literature supports increased use of diversified scientific resources and identities in counselling psychology. Moreover, a key component of counselling psychology is the capacity to observe meanings objectively (Mackay, 2003; Pelling, 2000), making adaptations as time proceeds. As with reading a text, meaning is not clear at first, rather it evolves. A diverse, comprehensive and fully epistemological view of science offers value to practice and research. Counselling psychology in practice requests it, and it will aid adapting the practitioner identity for workplaces that we have not yet explored.

We acknowledge that we cannot get away from importing our own meanings, as our system of interaction is one in which we intervene whether we like it or not. People do react to norms. As practitioners we must know when to import what sort of scientific perspective or tool, and how to limit its range of usability. Even quantitatively we have available to us multiple models of probabilistic prediction, because adequate modelling for diverse and non-linear systems does now exist (Song and Lee, 2004).

Just as science has benefited from the examination of what it is that scientists do (Fuller, 1993), so too may counselling psychology benefit from a focus on what practitioners actually do when claiming to be scientists. There is no reason why empirical research cannot address psychological practice in this way.

Counselling psychology makes a considerable contribution to the broader field of psychology in its focus upon the moral and idiographic dimension. We would note, for example, the theme of oppression; while science can lead practice in oppressive directions, oppressive practice can sometimes resort to science to justify itself. Peer review and other off-site tools give a two-way balance. Indeed, counselling psychologists need to be active in disseminating research to develop this aspect of their identity (Bor and du Plessis, 1997; Cowie and Glachan, 2000).

We both agree that gender plays a substantial role in our work. We see it in practice, and also in the literature on the gender component in science (Keller, 1995; Rose, 1994). We could envision counselling psychology taking the lead in directing scientific attention to gender issues and formulating suitable methods by which to undertake such research.

Although it is difficult to quantify and replicate generalized results in counselling psychology practice, we have seen the value of reporting from the early process studies. These provide a public account of what we do when we practise, thereby opening our work to scrutiny and research. Falsifiability in its strictest sense gives way to accountability. Failure is as important as success. Contextual failures may then help us develop more sensitive forms of research and practice.

Counselling psychology may in fact come to be distinguished through building broad traditions of research surrounding its core tenets. As the field develops further complexity, *What Works for Whom* (Roth and Fonagy, 1996) becomes *what works for whom, when, where and how*. Counselling psychologists will wish to account for their revised use of scientific methods to the public, and may demonstrate accountability by reporting trends rather than using over-defined probabilities. This may be a contribution that counselling psychology brings to other areas of psychology.

It is in the focus on the full extent of the experience of the client (rather than splitting the client into diagnostic categories) that counselling psychology has much to contribute (Elliott and Williams, 2003). This will, however, certainly bring more ethical quandaries, as some methods use processes that impinge upon the interpersonal environment (Bowen and John, 2001). As Hopf indicates, qualitative approaches, 'in comparison to quantitative research – are more radical and also more difficult to solve' (2004: 335). We endorse methods that articulate the science of what we do when in practice. We do not want research to diminish the significance of experiential material by forcing it into an empirical mode. We support the core argument of this book for a broadening of the definition of scientist–practitioner. In doing so, it is likely that counselling psychologists will have to find ways in which adherents of incompatible paradigms can learn to validate each other. Without this, fragmentation within the discipline will occur.

In summary, the sort of 'science with practice' we envisage is one in which there is a comprehensive range of tools. We are not limited to standardized modelling only. Human complexity means that the standard model of experiment and evidence will inevitably be confounded. This requires us to access forms of scientific modelling that are sensitive to context as well as an existing empirical literature. If we can do so, we will create a more dynamic interaction between science and practice.

Chapter 9

Feeling one's way in the dark: applying the scientist–practitioner model with young people who sexually offend

Val Haarbosch and *Ian Newey*

INTRODUCTION

Sexual abuse is not a new topic and much has been written about children as victims of adult perpetrators. The awareness of children as *perpetrators* is less developed. Kelly *et al.*'s (1991) study of 16–21 year olds found that one in three women and one in five men have some kind of unwanted sexual experience before the age of 18. It has been, and remains, more difficult for people to recognize and accept that the perpetrators of sexual abuse can also be children and young people. Professionals and families alike have reframed abusive behaviours to 'fit' into the more acceptable realm of 'adolescent experimentation' and minimized the significance of what has taken place (see the report of the National Children's Home, 1992). Cunningham and McFarlane's epilogue to their practice manual for pre-teens aptly describes why so many people find the concept difficult:

> We live in a society that would like to believe that the children who are the subject of this manual do not exist. Perhaps we would all rather pretend that sex offenders are alien beings who arrive, full grown, from another planet. Often the implausible is easier to accept than the unthinkable. Certainly none of us wants to look into the eyes of young children and see the seeds of potential destructiveness. Even when we do see it we are naturally reluctant to affix labels of deviance and criminality to ones so young.
>
> (1991: 232)

Within this chapter we will explore how the tensions and challenges inherent in the emerging field of service delivery to these children requires a multidisciplinary, robust but responsive model of practice as epitomized by that of the scientist–practitioner.

Table 2 Incidence of sexual offending behaviour

| Total number of sexual offences reported: | 29,500 |
| % of those cautioned or found guilty of offence: | 9,900 |

Age	Percentage of offenders
Under 21 years	30
17–20	14
14–16	12
10–13	4

Source: Home Office (1993) *Criminal statistics for England and Wales 1992*

Notes:
Of all rape offence – 20% under 21 years of age
Overall 1% of sexual offences attributed to females

CONTEXT

This resistance by society to recognize that children can be perpetrators of abuse has, in our opinion, had an effect on the level of provision for young people who exhibit inappropriate or abusive sexual behaviours. These are the children society does not want to acknowledge. No wonder they and their families are often reluctant to seek help, as they are largely unaware of the consequences of ignoring such behaviour. Therefore, the practitioner in this field must also be a diplomat, helping these young people, their families and sometimes even other professionals to recognize the need for assessment and intervention, without causing alienation, despair or over-reaction.

The prevalence of abusive behaviours perpetrated by young people clearly indicates that they should not be ignored. By amalgamating a range of studies and Home Office statistics on the incidence of recorded sexual offences, it can be shown that between one-third and one-fifth of sexual crimes are committed by people under the age of 21 (Table 2). This, of course, does not take into account unreported incidents, which may be even higher than those for adult sexual abuse.

Although there is a continuum of sexually aggressive behaviours, from genital exposure to penetrative acts, the statistics above do not include exploratory behaviours that are appropriate within normal sexual development (see Table 3). Those who attend projects like ours are not young people who are engaging in healthy sexual experimentation.

Table 3 Type of offence and sexual behaviour in young people

Type of Offence	Percentage of reported incidents
Indecent assault	59
Rape	23
Exhibitionism	II
Other non-contact offences	7

Source: Fehrenbach, et al., 1986 (American Journal of Orthopsychiatry, 56: 225–33. Copyright 1986. American Medical Association. All rights reserved.)
N=305 <18 years

Type of sexual behaviour	Percentage of young people
Penetration	59
Intercourse	31
Oral-genital contact	12
Genital touching	16
Non-contact	12

Souce: Wasserman and Kappel, 1985
N=161 <19 years

The range of factors associated with the onset of sexually abusive behaviour is as yet unknown. However, the developing research on adolescents in the UK is starting to provide valuable indicators. For example, it is known that witnessing physical violence, experiencing physical violence/abuse, family rejection and experiencing discontinuity of care are all significant factors (Skuse et al., 1998; Watkins and Bentovim, 1992). Nonetheless, it is important to note that the experience of childhood sexual abuse is not sufficient to account for the development of sexually abusive behaviour, even though exposure to violence between parents increases the likelihood of a non-sexually victimized adolescent male developing sexually abusive behaviour (Skuse et al., 1998). Unsurprisingly, where a young person lives in an environment of neglect or parental disinterest they are likely to struggle to recognize self-empathy, let alone empathy from others. Ryan and Lane (1997) suggest the development of victim empathy in a young person is only possible where a young person has experienced 'empathetic care' from a trusted caregiver.

In the late 1980s, a group of interested workers from Social Services and the Health Service in Norfolk recognized the need for a professional response to these behaviours and set up a project to develop a service for these young people. At this time it is important to note that there was no framework in place to address these types of behaviours. Even today, this remains an emerging field of work which presents a range of challenges for the practitioner.

Currently the project, now called the Sexually Appropriate Youngsters project (SAY), is part of Norfolk's Youth Offending Team (YOT). SAY's move from the field of social care to the criminal justice system echoes a tension that has, and still, exists in this field. Specifically, the difficulties and dilemmas focus around where to appropriately place these young people within existing systems. The client group's 'dual status' as children and young people who have exhibited sexually abusive behaviour but who also have needs from having experienced abuse (all categories) themselves means they straddle two domains. This tension has been evident in differing agency responses and guidance and within the legal provisions, which create another hurdle for the practitioner to negotiate.

Norfolk YOT has taken a pragmatic view: namely that if a child or young person exhibits sexually abusive behaviour they need a service regardless of whether the criminal justice system is involved. We work with young people who engage in the same sexually abusive behaviours, some will have their names placed on the Sex Offender Register and others will not. Being on the Register has significant life consequences for young people who are Schedule 1 Offenders as defined by the Sex Offenders Act 1997.

The stigma of having any form of identification as a 'sex offender' is difficult for young people and their families. Society's vilification of all sexual offending irrespective of age of the person, context or the actual behaviour involved fosters shame, denial and minimization rather than help-seeking behaviour. Similarly it is hard for families to seek support from friends or relatives for fear of repercussions.

The project offers a variety of services:

* a consultation service to all Area Child Protection Committee (ACPC) agencies, by telephone, face-to-face meetings, and by providing material for other agency workers;
* a fast track response/assessment for criminal cases to assist in decision-making following Police interviews (Police/YOT Protocol);
* full assessments, preventative and criminal cases;
* intervention programmes, preventative and criminal cases;
* educative sessions to young people who deny allegations of abusive behaviour but agree that guidance on appropriate sexual behaviour would be helpful;
* reports for court;
* presentations to school staff, Social Services teams and other agencies.
* in-house training for YOT workers and health workers;
* inter-agency joint work.

Throughout all services offered, one of the central messages we aim to convey is that our clients are young people, not adult sex offenders. They differ significantly from adults and early intervention is positive. The key in this work is to be able to strike a balance between engaging with clients and agencies without minimizing the risk a young person may present to others. A robust risk analysis is clearly an essential component of the work as it ensures (a) that the right level of intervention is recommended to address the sexually abusive behaviour and (b) that this intervention is conducted in the most appropriate setting (community or residential). The safety of known or potential victims is critical in the risk analysis and should not be diminished by the needs of the young person being assessed. For young people assessment should not solely be a hunt for risk factors; careful compilation of information from families or the wider external systems can provide valuable ameliorating protective factors.

Assessments involve four to six individual hour-long sessions with two project workers, ideally mixed gender. Participation of parents/carers is currently limited to the initial and final sessions. The involvement of other agencies in this process is best practised as detailed in *Working Together to Safeguard Children* (Department of Health, 1999) but constraints on local Social Services often mitigate against this. When joint working takes place care is required to ensure everyone speaks the same language. In our opinion, this combination of agencies working together enriches practice and is perhaps at the core of the modern scientist–practitioner approach.

During assessment, the scientist–practitioner in this setting engages in hypothesizing and formulating within an iterative cycle of reflection – a process that highlights the cognitive distortions, internal and external factors that maintain the young person's inappropriate and abusive behaviour. We will address assessment in more detail later but it is these areas which form the basis of the intervention phase. Not all young people need this; for some, the work done during assessment with the support of parents/carers proves a sufficient and proportionate response given the offence and the length of the order imposed by the court. The majority of programmes last from 12 to 18 months, which research supports as the optimum length.

Having established the need for a professional response to these behaviours care needs to be taken in how we define such behaviour in children and young people. Affixing arbitrary labels to the 'whole person' is unhelpful and potentially damaging to any change process being envisaged. Recognition needs to be given to the transience of childhood and adolescence. Each of us has moved on from the child we once were. Simply stated, it is a particular behaviour that is the issue and one type of behaviour does not (or should not) define the young person. The language we use at our initial meetings where we define the reason for our involvement and broker the agreement to engage in the assessment process is pivotal. Calder (2002) and Hackett (2003) have addressed this area highlighting the importance of using the following terminology 'young people who sexually abuse' as opposed to 'adolescent offender' or 'young abuser'. 'You are a young person who has sexually abused' acknowledges from the onset that those we see are first and foremost young people. It establishes that they have done something wrong in the past but this does not mean that they will always be an abuser and gives a strong message that they could change if they want to. Critically it states I, the practitioner, am taking your behaviour seriously; it is abuse but I am interested in you as a young person as well.

Writing this section of our chapter has led us to revisit, reflect and re-discuss the impact of the project name (which was at that time the 'Sexually *Aggressive* Youngsters Project') on young people and their families. This is an issue that has been ongoing within the Project for some time and was identified through the angry reactions to it from the young people's families which contrasted with our internal team debates which centred on our dogged belief that we should not collude with any minimization of the behaviours we dealt with. Our title was our statement. It is with slight blushes that we admit that even aspiring reflective practitioners such as ourselves can get stuck! However, reflection is also creative and it seems simple now that we have emerged as the 'Sexually *Appropriate* Youngsters project'. This new title better reflects the behaviour we hope our clients will gain from working with us rather than the behaviour that precipitates their referral.

The success of our programme is heavily influenced by how we address our clients in the initial stages of the intervention. Here our reflections as scientist–practitioners identify that we must never underestimate what we bring to any interaction. McKeown (2000) examined factors which influence successful therapeutic outcomes. He established that the therapist–client relationship has 30 per cent influence and the area of client hopefulness 15 per cent influence.

Hopefulness about the outcome is one of several areas that differentiate this group from adults. Young people who sexually abuse differ from adults in a number of areas including the following:

- They are not as fixed in patterns of sexual arousal and interest. Their cognitive distortions are less well-developed and the role of fantasy as a precursor to abuse, although not as clearly understood in young people, nonetheless appears to be less significant.
- Motivating and engaging with young people needs a different approach and is generally more difficult with adults (Richardson and Graham, 1997).
- Behaviour change is more likely in young people.
- Emotional maturity is less developed and their sophistication is generally lower.
- They have committed fewer offences.
- Their ability to learn is better.
- Young people experience and expect significant degrees of external control over their behaviour by parents or carers.
- Unlike adult offenders, adolescents are not independent beings; they are dependent on others and more open to influence by those around them.

Working with young people at an early stage to break the pattern of learned and habitual behaviour reduces the likelihood of it becoming part of future adult behaviour. However, whilst not treating our clients like adult offenders, it is also vital that the victim of the sexual abuse remains at the core of our work. We should never forget that the impact of sexual abuse on the victim is no less because the perpetrator is not an adult (Ryan, 2000).

THE JOURNEY TO DEVELOP A FRAMEWORK OF PRACTICE

It was in 1989, whilst working in a child sexual abuse team, that Val Haarbosch was invited to join a pilot project working with adolescent sexual offenders. The knowledge base around this client group was sparse. At this time, North America was the leader in the field with only a handful of similar projects in this country. The major part of the literature and all of the research considered adult offenders based in North America. The practice models that existed also only related to adult offenders. Practitioners dealing with young people usually adapted them to 'fit' adolescents. In contrast, our approach was informed by what we saw as a truly scientist–practitioner approach: the critical appraisal of existing research and drawing upon our own professional expertise to develop a robust, evidenced-based framework, which could be tested and modified in light of experience.

The journey began to gather momentum: voracious reading of texts on cognitive-behavioural therapy and sex offending was the order of the day to enable us to understand current theories underpinning work with this client group. The broad theoretical models that informed work with sex offenders at that time included the addiction model which traces its roots to learning theories. According to Breer (1987), for example, reinforcement can occur as a result of actual behaviour or in response to a fantasy model about molesting behaviour. Carnes (1983) applied the addiction model directly to disorders of sexuality expounding a seven-point guide to addictive behaviour. Finkelhor (1984) also drew up 'Four Preconditions to Abuse' which illustrates the difference in the build-up to sexual offending and other types of offending. The 'cycle of sexually abusive behaviour' expounded by Ryan and Lane (1997) was the lynchpin of most of our work with young people. Whilst cognitive-behavioural models of therapy, which modified distorted thinking (including expectations and attributions) and improved problem-solving skills, were deemed to be the most effective way of addressing sexually abusive behaviour, all programmes had to work in this way to be credible.

With this background reading and our professional knowledge we embarked on developing a working model. Originally there were four professionals involved, two social workers, a consultant clinical psychologist and a consultant child and adolescent psychiatrist. In our existing work with young people we all used a variety of approaches to help clients effect change recognizing that differing approaches were needed for different individuals. Therefore from the onset we all held the view that a one-theory or method approach to these young people would not be the most effective way of addressing their sexually abusive behaviour. The mix of health and social care professionals gave us a breadth of knowledge to pool together to produce an eclectic model offering a holistic approach to each young person. This combination of styles included incorporating aspects of systemic family therapy, the statements victims of sexual abuse made about their experiences of abuse, youth justice approaches to addressing criminal behaviour, the effects of trauma on children and young people and an over-arching social care perspective. The philosophy of 'one size does not fit all' still remains a major driver for the current way we work with young people.

The other main driver for us was acknowledging our lack of expertise in this field, which led us to reflect constantly on what we were doing, why we were doing it, how effective it was and what it told us about these young people. From the outset we adopted a pattern of working that included a meeting between co-workers, 30 minutes before each session, to draw up a plan of action recording the aim of the session, how to deliver it, and its intended outcome. Approximately one hour was spent delivering the session with a further 30 minutes to reflect on the process including recording outcomes, what had worked and not worked and key learning points for workers. This reflection was shared between practitioners enabling us to increase our own learning as well as ensuring our model was adapted according to evidence-based practice rather than adhering to the existing adult models of intervention. This method of working for practitioners continues to underpin the project.

Since then, further research has taken place which has informed and enhanced practice. The way young people who abuse are viewed and the approaches used to work with them have been influenced by the recognition that they have more similarities than differences with other young people who have significant emotional and behavioural disorders (S.A. Rich, 1998; Ryan, 1998). This has enabled practitioners to increase the literature base they draw upon and has led to an expansion in the methodologies used with young people.

When we began as a 'pilot project' in Norwich under the name The Adolescent Sex Offender Group (ASOG) we estimated we would receive approximately seven referrals per year for young people who came to the Police or court's attention. Imagine our surprise and panic when several months into the work we had seventeen young people in our service and professionals around the county were anxious to refer more. We offered assessments at any stage in the process but held the view that a criminal sentence was needed to give us a legal mandate to carry out the work.

The learning curve we underwent was steep: the more we came to understand the young people, the more we began to realize how unhelpful or untypical some of the assumptions about adult offenders were for these adolescent males. It is noteworthy that the vast majority of young people referred to us are male. Additionally, young people were referred to the programme who had committed acts of serious sexual abuse but avoided the criminal system, as the victims (often in their own family) did not want to make a criminal complaint. It was a shock to realize some of these young people presented with more worrying behaviour than those on orders and quickly led us to change our referral criteria. This flexibility of referral with an emphasis on preventative work is still retained today and made Norfolk a somewhat unusual Youth Offending Team in 2000. Priority does have to be given to criminal cases, which creates tension, as preventative cases have to wait for a service to be available.

We also recognized our clients' sense of hopelessness. Irrespective of their commitment to change their behaviour and regardless of how well they worked with us to address their abusive behaviour, these teenagers were labelled as sex offenders 'for life' by the court process and the Schedule 1 status it incurred. Today it is unusual for those attending the SAY project to have a court order, even though the project is now part of the Youth Offending Team. We divert most young people from court to receive a Reprimand or Final Warning, or if appropriate, away from the criminal system altogether, offering educative sessions if required. The work with this group and its duration (12–18 months) remains the same but we do it by voluntary agreement or begin it as part of a Reprimand or Final Warning programme.

In North America, group work was common in this field. However, based on one team member's observations and our viewing of tapes that illustrated some confrontational sessions, we initially decided to offer individual programmes. Our rationale was based on our discomfort with the combative approach of some American programmes and worries that young people may learn new methods of abuse from group discussions and potentially form new abusive networks. When we did expand from individual work to include a group work component we were guided by the principles of 11 curative factors in psychotherapeutic groups as expounded by Yalom (1975). We were astonished that this proposal was met with huge parental resistance. All parents expressed the same fears; they did not want their child mixing with sex offenders, and worse, they were terrified they would meet someone they knew and other people would know what their son 'had done'. It was a timely reminder of the difficult situation these parents faced and the reality of the constraints and fears with which they now lived. With such a small team we had concentrated our limited resources on seeing the young people as often as we could, involving parents at the initial session and at reviews, with the attendant cost of unresolved parental needs. We know that taking parents with you is essential, recognizing the stages they go through and adapting input without disempowering them. Parents need to understand their child's sexually abusive behaviour, to feel confident in helping them in their resolve not to repeat the behaviour and to act as a support team member once the programme is over.

Increasing parental involvement in our work continues to challenge us organizationally. Although there are more staff (12 YOT workers from three units around the county give hours with two psychologists) we, like many services, have a constant waiting list. Since 2000, SAY has covered the whole of Norfolk, which is a large rural county that does not facilitate group sessions for parents or young people. We have not run group sessions since our initial venture into this type of intervention as our referrals have not given us a compatible mix of young people within a commutable distance. This is a current deficit in our programme. We are, however, about to offer parental educative sessions in our three YOT offices.

The 'pure purpose' of intervention in this area would be to prevent future sexual offences. However, a more realistic goal is to assess areas of risk, to reduce opportunities to re-offend and to reduce recidivism as much as possible whilst enabling the young people to live free and positive lives. A targeted assessment of all allegations is required as:

An apparently isolated incident may well be part of a much more entrenched pattern known only to the young person who abuses. Some will spontaneously self correct, but we do not know which ones will and which ones will not. Prolonged work may be needed in some cases but assessment is needed in them all.

(Calder, 2002: 8)

To try to achieve this aim of assessing all cases the SAY project is underpinned by two protocols. The first is with the Police and states that, apart from grave offences, all young people alleged to have committed sexual offences should be interviewed by the Police then bailed for a SAY assessment. Whilst in principle this appears ideal, the swift administration of justice as laid down by the Crime and Disorder Act 1998 means that we have 28 days to achieve this. This is insufficient time to complete a full assessment, given variable referral rates and other demands on staff. The second protocol is an Area Child Protection Committee policy, which clearly defines the stages from consultation with the YOT, if there is concerning behaviour, to involvement in the Child Protection system. It might be assumed that this system is more conducive to the process as it potentially offers a multi-agency approach to assessment. However, new timeframes for Social Services and constraints on service delivery, combined with our waiting list for preventative cases, often mean delays in achieving this. Thus, our practice must be constrained within the legal requirements whilst providing a defendable assessment of risk.

MODEL OF PRACTICE

For us, the key to the scientist–practitioner model is solving the puzzle. Why has this young person behaved in this way? The process begins with formulating a hypothesis from the initial data and the first client contacts.

Aims of Initial Assessment

- to ascertain if professional intervention is required;
- to ascertain if the young person is safe enough to remain in the community;
- to consider placement options during treatment;
- to ascertain whether the child/young person is motivated to engage in treatment;
- to gauge whether he or she is likely to respond to treatment;
- to decide on the most suitable type of treatment;
- to establish a young person's available treatment resources;
- to recommend necessary protective restrictions (e.g. concerning baby sitting contact) to protect further potential victims and the young person from future abusive behaviour.

Assessing the behaviour alone is insufficient; the context of the behaviour must be considered with regard to the relationship between those involved. As Calder observes:

> The risk of sexual abusing is likely to be present unless the opportunity to further abuse is ended, the young person has acknowledged the abusive behaviour and accepted responsibility for it, and there is an agreement by the young abuser, his/her family, to work with the relevant agencies to address the problem.
>
> (2002: 9)

Tailoring the programme

Whilst reflecting on this contribution to the scientist–practitioner debate we identified the core process informing our work with young people. It can be considered as an iterative cycle of reflection around the emerging needs of the young person (Figure 4). This cycle will become evident as we detail the stages within our work from assessment, clinical formulation and closure in the following pages.

Assessment

Traditionally, assessment has often been seen as a stage in a linear 'flowchart' of working with a client: referral, assessment, formulation, action plan, intervention, evaluation and discharge. Whilst it is fair to say that this linear model is over-simplistic for the vast majority of client groups, it is particularly inadequate when attempting to work with young sexual aggressors.

Assessment has to be an ongoing process and formulations constantly revised accordingly (see the section below for more on this). Continued assessment of young people should, of course, include assessment of risk to inform other agencies for planning of safety of siblings, other family members, friends and community. Other essential components of assessment are a developmental history and a 'life map' whereby a young person writes down a timeline of his (or her) life with relevant life events, both those perceived as negative and positive. Along with these life events, a young person needs to describe the interpretations of those events.

Once the basic assessment data, as defined above, are collected the assessment continues.

As described in Chapters 2 and 3, a scientist–practitioner as we interpret this term, has a strategy guiding the questions asked about a person's history and their offending behaviour. The questions asked are linked to the iterative cycle as shown in Figure 4: there is a constant cycle of formulating hypotheses and testing hypotheses by asking questions. The aim is to be mindful of models and theories that are relevant to the area of difficulty, from wherever they have been drawn. Thus,

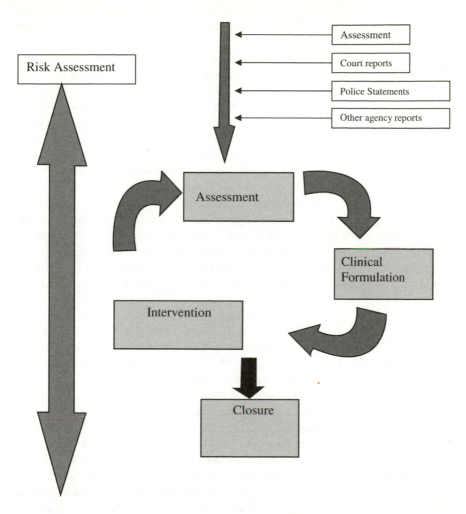

Figure 4 An iterative cycle of reflection around the emerging needs of the young person

although one might expect 'relevant' models and theories to relate to the broader literature on sexually aggressive behaviour, it is important to look farther afield to any approach that might usefully inform the work. This is why a broad reading of clinical literature is desirable before a specialist area is chosen.

Although models and theories guide the assessment process, the scientist–practitioner cannot be restricted to asking only those questions directly implied by them. It would seem that there are factors which mediate between the literature and the lines of questioning we choose to pursue. In our work with young people who sexually abuse (and where definitive evidence remains sparse) we would argue that something less tangible often guides the style of questioning and reasoning we use. This 'something' seems to be akin to intuition; a practitioner senses that a line of questioning is appropriate but may have difficulty explaining why in rational terms.

Intuition is, of course, a terribly unfashionable concept. However, it may not be as unscientific as first appears. What is termed 'intuitive' may in fact arise out of personal constructs assembled from accrued professional and life experience as well as knowledge from the scientific and clinical literatures. Although many practitioners are unable to source the reason for following a particular line of questioning, there is clearly some resonance here with Schön's (1987) and Polyani's (1967) belief that experienced practitioners and scientists typically know more than they can articulate. However, therein lies the tension. Intuition may be underpinned by solid scientific and clinical knowledge that enables us to move closer towards the elusive concept of expertise. Alternatively, it may be inaccurate and misleading, based on heuristics (see Chapter 2) and other reasoning biases that are detrimental to our clients' well-being and our capacity to respond to their needs.

In this regard, we would argue that supervision is essential to keep clinical intuition honed (in addition to many other benefits). In the current context of 'clinical intuition', supervision can help practitioners make links between the decisions they make and the sources that inspired those decisions. This process of supervision should take place regularly with a colleague, but we should also be mindful of 'internal supervision' (Casement and Wallerstein, 2004) whereby a clinician asks questions of their own clinical practice as it is occurring. Relevant questions then become: 'What am I trying to do here?'; 'Why did I ask that?'; 'What information do I need to check out this hypothesis based on this particular model?'

Once sources that inspired clinical decisions are made explicit, it is possible to check on the validity and currency of those sources. Without staying abreast of recent literature, it is possible that a clinician's intuition may become outdated or blunt. The process of intuition and one's reading of the current literature is circular: not only is intuition guided by reading and experience, one's reading is also guided by previously acquired 'intuition'. Sometimes a clinician reads an article that does not 'fit' with their clinical view, and may initially disregard certain pieces of literature for that reason. However, after several articles making similar points that are incongruous with the practitioner's existing view, such personalized 'knowledge' might need to change to accommodate the new literature. This is a process similar to the way in which Piaget (1966) described sensory information being incorporated into a baby's understanding of the world which we saw as occurring in a 'scientific manner'.

For example, Piaget argued that babies go through the stages of assimilation, where they acquire new information, accommodation, where that information is put with existing knowledge and disequilibrium, when it becomes apparent that the new information does not 'fit' with existing models about the world. Finally, equilibrium is restored when rules are modified so that the new information does fit.

It would seem to us that one of the main differences between babies and scientist–practitioners (amongst others of course!) is that the latter are more likely to reject seemingly reliable new information. Scientist–practitioners have to be in possession of a cynicism about new information, with an ability to accept new contradictory models only when there is almost irrefutable evidence. As scientist–practitioners we hopefully maintain a critical mind whereby we know about the context of research, including errors and methodological constraints. Babies are not capable of this before they have acquired theory of mind and thus, the idea of perception, interpretation, and deception.

Formulation

Formulation is a key task in working with this group of people. The specific needs of an individual are defined by the clinical formulation; one size does not fit all. Interventions need to be tailored to the specific (probably changing) needs of each client. A formulation is made by bringing together the following components:

- the best current information available from assessment data;
- the best models, theories and research data from the scientific and therapeutic literatures.

The clinical formulation is a series of working hypotheses based on assessment information and relevant psychological (and other) models. It is a means of trying to understand the person's difficulties, in terms of the biological, psychological and social factors and events, which may have contributed to the current behaviours (see Chapter 3 for a broader discussion of formulation and also Persons, 1989, for a review of the case formulation approach).

To be more specific about this client group, it is necessary to draw upon developmental theories (what is developmentally normal in terms of cognitive, moral and psychosexual development?), personal history and comparison with theoretical models.

Interventions

The (evolving) conclusions derived from the (ongoing) assessment phase suggest the level of intervention programme that is either suitable or required. The main goals of intervention are:

- the protection of victims;
- the prevention of further offences;
- the development of self-control; the concept of 'cure' is not appropriate. Note that intervention should be at the least invasive level, commensurate with the protection of actual or potential victims.

A holistic approach is taken when designing the individual programmes. The areas covered are interlinked and provide each young person with:

- an understanding of their sexually abusive behaviour;
- an understanding of the effects of their behaviour including victim empathy;
- an ability to recognize warning signs (antecedents) to the target behaviours;
- developing a range of alternative behaviours;
- creating a list of identified high-risk situations that should be avoided with strategies to deal with life;
- helping build on positive areas and strengthening resilience;
- reframing clients' fantasy scripts where appropriate;
- helping clients acquire a range of skills they can use to assist them in their resolution not to repeat such behaviour in the future. This could include sessions on problem-solving, anger management and work on self-esteem, amongst others.

For us as scientist–practitioners working in this under-researched and relatively poorly understood domain of clinical practice, intervention programmes provide an ongoing challenge. The continual assessment of risk allied to the ongoing process of rigorous questioning and challenging requires the constant use of the iterative cycle of reflection. This process is also linked to the continual evaluation and measurement of change that runs throughout the intervention stage.

At the conclusion of the programme, a comprehensive individual relapse prevention plan will be drawn up for each young person. A copy of the plan will inform and assist clients' parents or carers in their role as monitors and supporters in preventing further sexually abusive behaviour. Responsibility always rests with the young person to continue to implement what they have learned; the programme is about equipping young people so they are able to control their behaviour. It does not aim to 'cure' sexually abusive behaviour.

IN CONCLUSION

To summarize, we have drawn out what we perceive to be the main issues associated with working with young people who sexually abuse. We must reiterate that work with this client group is an emerging field. When one of the authors (VH) started working in this area in 1989, there were no frameworks in place and clinical literature in the field was severely limited. This is still the case, although the body of evidence is growing, albeit slowly. Perhaps the societal resistance to the idea of children who sexually aggress may be one of the factors limiting the development of knowledge in the area.

Despite the past reliance on adult offender based literature to inform work with young people who sexually aggress, it is essential that we see and acknowledge the differences between adult offenders and our client group. The evidence suggests that we can be much more optimistic about the prognosis for young people who sexually offend. This is partially accounted for by the less fixed pattern of sexual arousal and interest (due to fewer offences), the less developed and rigid patterns of cognitive distortion, the increased level of motivation and engagement and overall improved ability to learn. There are also systemic factors that reduce opportunities for recidivism: young people expect significant degrees of external control of their behaviour by parents or carers.

There are, of course, some similarities between adult offenders and young people who sexually abuse. There is a significant stigma associated with being identified as a sex offender. This stigma can extend to the young person, their family, and other members of the wider system. It can have a massive impact on a young person's peer relationships, and on their family's peer relationships. This is, again, likely to be related to the societal difficulty with acknowledging the problem, and associated fear and ignorance. There are, however, genuine risks that need to be managed around a young person who has perpetrated a sexual offence. There is a difference between the essential robust risk analysis and management that is needed to keep potential victims safe, and blanket scaremongering. Society can certainly adopt a positive role in the future management of young people who have offended, but the predominant view that the only solution is to lock up offenders is not helpful.

Finally, to crystallize our message from the chapter, we would argue that one central characteristic of the scientist–practitioner role with this client group is to engage in an on-going process of formulating. The act of pulling together knowledge from the assessment and from years of experience and study to make a series of fluid working hypotheses is, as we see it, the defining act of the scientist–practitioner over adherence to any particular method, activity or role. The mistake, of course, would be to see formulation as an end goal, whereas it should remain a process, from the very first contact with a young person to the time of discharge, and beyond. Formulating is an act of curiosity: an iterative cycle of reflection on the emerging needs of the young person. The flexibility of thinking in children that improves their prognosis compared to their adult counterparts is a trait that we should adopt to improve our practice. We think that we all should take Patrick Casement's advice, and learn from our patients.

ACKNOWLEDGEMENT

We would like to acknowledge the invaluable contribution to this chapter from Dr Annette Fillery-Travis who not only made our involvement possible but who also encouraged two practitioners who had no problem talking the chapter but needed a rigorous researcher to ensure that we completed our task and wrote something.

Chapter 10

Coaching psychology and the scientist–practitioner model

Michael J. Cavanagh and *Anthony M. Grant*

INTRODUCTION

This chapter considers the application of the scientist–practitioner model in the area of coaching psychology. There is growing interest in coaching as a form of psychological intervention aimed primarily at non-clinical populations. The scientist–practitioner model is presented as an important differentiator between the coaches who practise from a background in professional psychology, and coaches whose experience is not informed by formal training in the behavioural sciences. After describing coaching psychology and then briefly considering the main theoretical models we employ, we critically assess the strengths and limits of the scientist–practitioner model in the light of complexity theory. Complexity theory provides a useful description of the iterative and organic nature of psychological interventions, and provides a corrective to a linear reductionist understanding of the scientist–practitioner model. Rather than seeing the role of science and practice as developing prescriptive models of psychological practice, we argue for an evidence-based approach to coaching psychology. This approach values the contribution of both science and practice in the process of informing coaching interventions.

Executive, workplace and life coaching have received much coverage in the popular media (see Garman *et al.*, 2000; Wyld, 2001). Coaching as an intervention for personal and organization change is growing in popularity in government, business, healthcare and the community. While the roots of coaching go back decades, it is only in recent years that coaching has drawn the attention of researchers and practitioners in psychology. Unlike other areas of applied psychology, there is not a large coaching-specific scientific literature. While the process of developing a coaching-specific literature evolves, the lack of detailed, empirically validated and easily accessible coaching-specific studies has forced coaching psychologists to adapt theories and techniques drawn from across the wider behavioural science literature. This process has shaped our view of the scientist–practitioner model.

WHAT IS COACHING?

There are a plethora of definitions of coaching and the words 'coach' and 'coaching' have been used in relation to a staggering variety of issues and populations. Topics include reference to coaching individuals to overcome Attention Deficit Hyperactivity Disorder (ADHD) (Ratey, 2002), improving sales performance (G. A. Rich, 1998), job interview (Maurer *et al.*, 1998), cognitive training in schizophrenia (Twamley *et al.*, 2003), improving orgasms (Goodstone, 2003), career coaching (Scandura, 1992), stress management (Busch and Steinmetz, 2002), life coaching (Grant and Greene, 2001) and executive coaching (Kilburg, 2000), to name but a few.

Definitions of coaching are similarly varied. Parsloe (1995: 18) proposes that coaching is 'directly concerned with the immediate improvement of performance and development of skills by a form of tutoring or instruction'. In contrast, Whitmore (1992: 8) proposes that 'coaching is unlocking a person's potential to maximise their own performance. It is helping them to learn rather than teaching them.'

While Parsloe and Whitmore might fall at opposite ends of the 'facilitation vs. telling dimension' most definitions of coaching are process-oriented and include: a helping, collaborative and egalitarian rather than authoritarian relationship between coach and coachee; a focus on constructing solutions in preference to analysing problems; the assumption that clients are from a population without significant levels of psychopathology or emotional distress; an emphasis on collaborative goal setting; and the recognition that the coach needs clear expertise in facilitating the client's learning.

A good general definition of coaching sees coaching as a goal-directed, results-orientated, systematic process in which one person facilitates sustained change in another individual or group through fostering the self-directed learning and personal growth of the coachee (Grant, 2003).

A TRIPARTITE MODEL OF COACHING IN THE WORKPLACE

As practitioners, the type of coaching we are most engaged in is executive or workplace coaching. Drawing on the work of Witherspoon and White (1996) we can delineate three key categories of workplace coaching: skills coaching, performance coaching and developmental coaching.

Skills coaching focuses on developing a specific skill set. This kind of coaching might be a fairly short intervention, perhaps one or two sessions. Coaching for skills often requires the coach to focus on specific behaviours and the coaching sessions are often highly detailed. The coach may model the required skills, and coaching sessions usually encompass a rehearsal and feedback process. It could involve improving communications skills, sales skills or rehearsing for presentations or negotiations.

Performance coaching is about improving performance over a specific timeframe. In the workplace this could be between one month to two years. Here, the coaching is more focused on the process by which the coachee can set goals, overcome obstacles and evaluate and monitor their performance over time as they work towards their goals. A typical approach is to outline the *c*urrent situation, detail the *i*deal outcome, then analyse what lies in the *g*ap between them, and formulate an *a*ction plan and a *r*eview process – the CIGAR model. This kind of coaching tends to be more strategic than skills coaching, and in the workplace may take place following a performance review.

Developmental coaching also takes a broader, more holistic approach, often dealing with more intimate questions of personal and professional development. This kind of coaching may focus on enhancing emotional competencies, or working more effectively with team members or developing the executive's human potential. Developmental coaching is rather like therapy for the people who don't need therapy and often involves the creation of a personal reflective space where the coachee can explore issues and options and formulate action plans in a confidential, supporting environment.

It should be noted that these typologies are not discrete and separate from each other. There is often a degree of overlap between them. For example, a coaching intervention which focuses on enhancing presentation skills for a shy or introverted coachee would have a substantial developmental element, and a developmental coaching programme which is targeted at enhancing emotional intelligence or leadership competencies may well include some skills coaching.

COACHING AND THE SCIENTIST–PRACTITIONER MODEL

Despite a clear focus on human behaviour, psychology has been slow to embrace coaching as an area of professional practice. Only in the last two years have formal groups for coaches been established in the Australian and British Psychological Societies. (It should be noted that these appear to be among the fastest growing areas of interest for members.) Nevertheless, the coaching industry at large is populated by coaches from a range of backgrounds, including business, education, health and the helping professions. Indeed, there are currently no barriers to entry into coaching practice, and no commonly accepted body of knowledge from which coaches draw their practice (Garman *et al.*, 2000). In short, coaching lacks the two key hallmarks of a profession (Bullock *et al.*, 1988; Williams, 1995).

The scientist–practitioner model (Raimy, 1950) enables us to draw an important (and controversial) distinction between the claims made by non-psychologically trained coaches and those made by coaching psychologists. Both non-psychologically trained coaches and coaching psychologists aim to assist individuals and organizations in achieving goals via behavioural, cognitive and emotional self-regulation. However, in this undertaking the scientist–practitioner model of training exhorts the coaching psychologist to develop interventions based on a well-researched and continually developing body of knowledge and techniques. The psychologist is said to be able to understand and evaluate their interventions against a background that incorporates significant training in the production and interpretation of scientific knowledge. This lends epistemic authority to the claims of the coaching psychologist.

The same cannot be said of those in the wider coaching industry, where many of the interventions involve untested proprietary models built on ideas and beliefs drawn from a wide range of sources, both credible and spurious. There is often little or no understanding of the scientific merit of these interventions or the claims made about them. Hence, the scientist–practitioner model legitimizes and differentiates coaching psychologists from the wider body of coaches operating in the field.

The fundamental tenet of the scientist–practitioner model as defined at the 1949 Boulder Conference is that primary training of clinical (or applied) psychologists should be as scientists and researchers, and then secondly as clinicians or purveyors of psychological services (Raimy, 1950). The Vail conference of 1973 revised this when it endorsed the formation of professional degrees which embodied a practitioner–scientist approach, that is, an approach in which the formation of practitioners was given primacy over education in the scientific method. Subsequent conferences have sought to reverse, replace or modify this model (Belar and Perry, 1992; O'Gorman, 2001; Wollersheim, 1985).

Volumes have been written supporting and challenging the respective adequacies of these models. It is not our intention here to weigh in on either side of the scientist vs. practitioner debate. Whether one gives greater educational emphasis to the practical or scientific components of applied psychology does not appear to us to be the central or most interesting question. As most often presented, both perspectives are based on a Newtonian model of science, which assumes that causation is essentially linear and can be adequately revealed by scientific methods. Furthermore, it also assumes that armed with this knowledge we are able to predict and control reality. The uncritical acceptance of these assumptions (and, as we shall see, their postmodernist opposites) may not well serve either the science or the practice of psychology. Rather, a much more critical issue is how practising psychologists understand the strengths and limitations of the scientific and practical knowledge they carry, and how they bring both to bear in the service of their clients and profession.

To this end, we would like to discuss some of the issues we see as scientist–practitioners in our area of applied psychology – the field of coaching psychology, and more specifically, executive coaching. We shall discuss these on two levels: the philosophical or epistemological, and the practical. We will begin this by describing coaching psychology and the type of coaching we practise.

COACHING PSYCHOLOGY

The term coaching psychology is relatively new and, as yet, not well understood. One reason for this may be that each of the established areas of applied psychology (clinical, counselling, organizational, health and sports) rightly identifies significant similarities between what they do and coaching. At the same time, there are significant differences which mean that coaching psychology does not seem to fit neatly into these areas of psychological practice. The Australian Psychological Society Interest Group in Coaching Psychology defines coaching psychology as an applied positive psychology, which draws on and develops established psychological approaches. It can be understood in terms of the systematic application of behavioural science to the enhancement of life experience, work performance and well-being for individuals, groups and organizations who do not have clinically significant mental heath issues or levels of distress that could be regarded as abnormal (Australian Psychological Society, 2004).

The first thing one might notice about this definition is that coaching psychology uses theories and techniques developed across the breadth of the psychological enterprise. In addition, the coaching psychologist may need to develop skills and knowledge in areas typically unfamiliar to many psychologists. These include business, management, teaching and workplace training. For example, executive coaching encompasses a vast range of services and specialties including coaching for enhanced strategic planning; presentation skills; anger and stress management; team building and leadership development. Each coaching application requires the coach to have a specialist skill and knowledge set. Indeed, most good coaches tend to develop specialities over time.

Hence, the breadth of knowledge-base, rather than its uniqueness, is one of the features that distinguishes coaching psychology from other forms of psychological practice. The second important distinguishing feature of coaching psychology is its client population. Coaching psychology typically deals with non-clinical or non-distressed populations. This makes the context of coaching quite different to other clinical and counselling interventions. While coaching psychologists may use theories and techniques developed in clinical settings (e.g. cognitive restructuring, brief solution-focused interventions), the content, style and tempo with which these techniques are used is often dramatically different in coaching.

Clinical and counselling interventions tend to have a pathological orientation – they are largely concerned with categorical diagnosis, containment and the amelioration of dysfunctional behaviour patterns. Coaching clients typically do not display the level of distress and impairment seen in clinical patients. For coaching clients the use of pathology-laden terminology and a clinical style of approach can be alienating (Drewery and Winslade, 1997; Shazer and Lipchik, 1984), and may even contribute to the creation and maintenance of problem behaviours (Walter and Peller, 1996).

Of course, the distinction between clinical and non-clinical issues is often a difficult one to make in practice. As Figure 5 represents, clients fall along a continuum

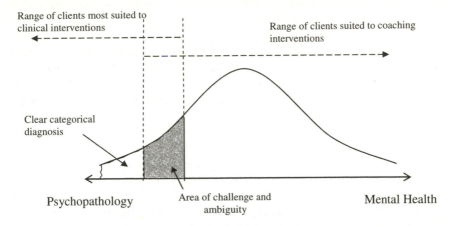

Range of clients most suited to clinical interventions

Range of clients suited to coaching interventions

Clear categorical diagnosis

Psychopathology

Area of challenge and ambiguity

Mental Health

Figure 5 The coaching client-base and psychopathology

of clinical need. Precisely where a client is situated on this continuum will vary with time and according to the particular issues under consideration. The width of the grey area in the diagram is similarly variable. However, it varies as a function of both client characteristics and the ability of the coach to develop an accurate and useful case conceptualization. Here the coach's knowledge base and ability to formulate and test hypotheses are at a premium.

For example, a key coaching skill is the ability to distinguish between depression and a lowering of mood in response to the presence or absence of a significant challenge. Similarly, the ability to tell the difference between clinically significant social anxiety and normal anxiety around public speaking is important for the coaching psychologist. In executive coaching, or coaching in organizational settings, the grey area frequently revolves around personality issues. Many executives and teams do not realize their potential or are derailed by behaviours and communication patterns associated with sub-clinical yet problematic personality patterns.

One way to circumvent the potential problems associated with the use of problem-focused clinical techniques with non-clinical populations is to integrate a solution-focused approach (Shazer, 1988, 1994) into a cognitive-behavioural framework, and use this to form a basis for a psychology of coaching. This is the approach taken at the Coaching Psychology Unit at the University of Sydney.

Brief solution-focused therapy (BSFT) has its roots in Milton H. Erickson's approach to strategic therapy. Erickson's work was highlighted by the foundation of the Mental Research Institute (MRI) in Palo Alto, California in 1958, and the publication of *Strategies of Psychotherapy* (Haley, 1963; see Cade and O'Hanlon, 1993 for further details of the development of BSFT and Erickson's contribution). O'Connell (1998) cites the following as being central characteristics of Erickson's approach and these form the basis of BSFT (Shazer, 1988). These may well prove to be the essential constructs underpinning a psychology of coaching.

- *Use of a non-pathological model*. Problems are not indications of pathology or dysfunctionality, rather they stem from a limited repertoire of behaviour.
- *A focus on constructing solutions*. The therapist/coach facilitates the construction of solutions rather than trying to understand the aetiology of the problem.
- *Use of existing client resources*. The therapist/coach helps the client recognize and utilize resources of which they were unaware.
- *Utilization*. The mobilization and utilization of any part of the client's life experience which could help resolve the presenting problem.
- *Action-orientation*. There is a fundamental expectation on the therapist/coach's part that positive change will occur, and the therapist/coach expects the client to act to create this change outside of the coaching session.
- *Clear, specific goal setting*. Setting of attainable goals within a specific timeframe.
- *Assumption that change can happen in a short period of time*. This stands in contrast to therapeutic schools that assume that the problem must be worked on over a long period of time.
- *Strategic*. Therapeutic/coaching interventions are designed specifically for each client.
- *Future-orientation*. The emphasis is more on the future (what the client wants to have happen) than the present or the past.
- *Enchantment*. The therapy/coaching process is designed and conducted in a way that is attractive and engaging for the client.
- *Active and influential therapist*. The therapist/coach is openly influential.

Underpinning these facets are a number of philosophical assumptions.

- Self and others are essentially able.
- People make the best choice for themselves at any given time.
- Discourses and conversations shape our experience of reality.
- Therapy/coaching is a dialogue between therapist/coach and client in which both co-jointly construct the problem and the solution.

POSTMODERNISM AND SCIENTIFIC TRUTH

The above philosophical assumptions indicate that BSFT embodies a constructivist philosophy. Constructivist approaches are based on the assumption that individuals construct their experience of reality – experience is not a direct response to sensory stimulation, rather one's experience is mediated by the beliefs one holds about oneself, others and the world. Cognitive approaches to therapy similarly embody a constructivist philosophy (e.g. Beck, 1995; Beck *et al.*, 1979; Ellis and Harper, 1961).

However, a number of brief-solution focused therapists have sought to link a radical anti-realist, postmodernist philosophy to BSFT (e.g. O'Connell, 1998; Shazer, 1988; Walter and Peller, 1996; White, 1993). A postmodernist position argues that because reality is constructed through conversation and language, there can be no objective reality and therefore all views are equally valid. This argument leads to a position which is antithetical to science. If all views are equally valid then there can be no basis for legitimizing claims about the world. In the post-modernist view science, which claims to have valid methods for discovering the truth, is a fraud, and the scientist–practitioner model is little else than a political manoeuvre for legitimizing claims to epistemic authority (John, 1998).

It is important to consider whether these arguments are conceptually sound. If so, there is little ground for upholding either the scientist–practitioner model or a psychology of coaching based on an evidenced-based, cognitive-behavioural and solution-focused approach.

There are a number of serious conceptual problems associated with such an anti-realist, philosophy, and these conceptual issues have ramifications for a psychology of coaching (for a more detailed exposition of such problems see Held, 1995; 1996). Firstly, the postmodernist position is self-refuting – if there is no objective truth then the claim that there is no objective truth is itself not true. In response to the self-refuting dismissal argument Walter and Peller (1996) argue that the claim that there is no truth is a belief rather than a statement of fact, and we cannot objectively know what is apart from us, we can only know our beliefs. This response is not a satisfactory rebuttal because it leads to a position of 'unspeak-ability' and solipsism – that is I cannot know anything about anything, and cannot meaningfully communicate any concepts to anyone apart from myself.

Secondly, if all perspectives are equally valid, there is no ground for claim-ing expertise or skill in any area of life. Yet the postmodernist therapist typically undertakes training to enhance their expertise and therapeutic skills (Presbury, *et al.*, 1999; Wetchler, 1990).

Thirdly, if science is a fraud and there really is no means of conducting evalu-ations, postmodernist therapists cannot make claims as to the effectiveness of their therapeutic practice. According to this position the client would be just as well served therapeutically by receiving therapy from the garbage collector or the butcher. It is difficult to see on what ethical basis a postmodernist therapist or coach would charge payment for their services. Indeed, ethics cease to have mean-ing in a postmodernist world.

Clearly, the postmodernist construal of the world needs be rejected on the basis of its internal incoherence. This does not, however, provide evidence for the veracity of the philosophical assumptions inherent in the Boulder formula-tion of the scientist–practitioner model. Here too, there are a number of important assumptions and questions that bear examination.

THE SCIENTIST–PRACTITIONER AND COMPLEXITY THEORY

Much has been written on the validity of the assumptions of the scientist–practitioner model and it is not our intention to replicate that discussion in detail here (for example, see Barlow 1981; Frank, 1984; John, 1998; Rennie, 1994) and this debate is covered in Chapter 1 of this book. Similarly, much has been written on the practical difficulties associated with conducting research in private practice and other non-university clinical settings – not least of which are basic differences in temperament and inclination between clinicians and researchers (see Haynes *et al.*, 1987; Zachar and Leong, 2000). Rather, we will focus here on three assumptions underlying the scientific worldview seen in the scientist–practitioner model: the assumptions of linear causality, predictability and control. To do this we shall look at these assumptions in the light of complexity theory.

Fundamental to the scientist–practitioner model as traditionally conceptualized is the notion that the world is structured by deterministic linear causality and that, at least theoretically, the causal structure of reality is accessible or discoverable via the scientific method. The pre-eminent scientific method used in psychology is the hypothetico-deductive model. This model is presented in psychology courses as the centrepiece and foundation of scientific orthodoxy for the true scientist–practitioner. It holds that scientific knowledge advances via the formation and testing of hypotheses. Hypotheses are said to be scientifically valuable if they are able to be falsified by the tests applied to them. In clinical research, the scientific method is most fully embodied in the randomized controlled trial.

The notion of experimental control is important here. The task of the researcher is to create conditions which can isolate a particular putative causal chain in the experimental system. This is done through controlling for as many potential sources of extraneous causation as possible. Large sample sizes, homogenous groups, random allocation, standardized presentation of stimuli and many other measures are adopted in an effort to reduce potential confounds to interpretability of results. The researcher then acts on the system (the experimental manipulation) and observes whether the causal structure operates as predicted. When done well, exploration of reality via the scientific method is assumed to lead to knowledge which enables the informed psychologist to more accurately predict and control events. This is the fundamental core which provides the scientist–practitioner with epistemic authority.

Experimental method attempts to create, as much as practically possible, a closed mechanistic system. Systems and complexity theory radically challenge the assumptions of linear causation, predictability and control. According to complexity theory, most natural systems, including human systems, are open systems that interact in complex non-linear and adaptive ways with their environment (O'Connor and McDermott, 1997; Stacey, 2000). The non-linearity of causation in complex system results in a number of important features. These include sensitivity to minute differences in initial conditions, radical long-term unpredictability and the emergence of unexpected and unintended patterns of system behaviour (Stacey, 2000). An oft-quoted example of sensitivity to initial conditions is the emergence of weather patterns. Computer modelling has shown that minute differences in a few key factors can lead to major impacts as the system develops. These differences are of such a miniscule magnitude as to be effectively undetectable for the purpose of prediction. This is one of the reasons why, beyond a few days, the prediction of weather patterns becomes highly problematic (Haines, 1998).

The coaching relationship is essentially a complex adaptive system that exists within, and forms part of, a network of other complex systems. This creates a dynamic system of influence which often renders the causal structure of an event unknowable except in hindsight (Stacey, 2000). What takes place at any given point in time in the coaching relationship is determined by an almost infinite causal field that is, in the final analysis, unpredictable at anything but a short-term and relatively gross level. For example, the response a client may have to a simple question may differ dramatically depending on the client's mood, which itself may be shaped by something as simple as having been cut off in traffic on the way to the coaching session. Any number of seemingly innocuous events may impact significantly on the coaching conversation, shaping the content, tone and outcome of the discussion.

This radical unpredictability does not mean that coaching, or any other psychological intervention or research, should be abandoned. The adaptive capacity of systems can also produce relatively stable and predictable patterns of behaviour at a macro-level. For example, our inability to predict the weather with any accuracy beyond more than a few days means that we cannot know whether or not we will need an umbrella in Sydney on January 16, 2009 (or even in three weeks' time). However, at a macro-level, the relative stable pattern of seasonal temperatures means that we can be almost certain that we will not need to wear overcoats on that day. Similarly, in a coaching context, it is impossible to predict the precise impact a particular mode of communication will have on a manager's direct reports, but it is possible, given adequate knowledge of the prior relationship between manager and staff, to have a relatively good idea of the expected tenor and range of responses that may ensue.

Herein lies the central weakness of the scientist–practitioner model. The unique, dynamic adaptive nature of the system formed in coaching relationships means that coaching (along with most practical psychological interventions) is a radically unpredictable, almost iterative process in which the next step is informed, in large part by the conditions immediately preceding it. This process cannot be adequately replicated in laboratory studies, or even in field trials. Each coaching intervention develops in a unique way. Prescribing or predetermining at a micro-level the type of intervention to be used reduces the intervention to a mechanistic and dehumanizing transaction, and substantially reduces its chance of success.

This is true even in the most simple case of skills coaching. For example, coaching a sales person in how to greet a new customer may involve much more than simply telling the person to make eye contact, smile and offer a firm handshake. Unexpected issues may emerge which necessitate departure from a standardized model of training. These may be as simple as differing notions of what is meant by a firm handshake, or as complex as the disclosure of fear of contamination should there be physical contact.

As coaching moves into the performance and development areas, the level of complexity and unpredictability increases dramatically. There is no prescription for the manager who presents at coaching with the goal of becoming a better manager. The precise nature of the intervention will be negotiated and renegotiated as the coaching relationship develops and as the parties come to understand in more detail the nature of the issues to be addressed and skills to be developed.

This ongoing shared development of understanding is a process of case conceptualization (or formulation as in Chapter 3). It is at this point that the scientist–practitioner model comes into its own. A coach's ability to arrive, with a client, at a suitably accurate, clear and useful case conceptualization will depend to a large degree on the coach's ability to access, explore, evaluate and apply a range of mental models to the data at hand. The psychological theory and research provide the models and information needed to undertake this task. Training in production and interpretation of research provides the coach with the mental tools to sift and sort this body of psychological knowledge. Within the coaching engagement, the coach needs also to apply the scientific mindset as part of the reflective process. This involves an ability to observe data, form hypotheses, and critically test them in the coaching session. It also involves an ability to select, evaluate and appropriately interpret psychometric assessment tools. All of these activities involve the coach as both scientist and practitioner.

TOWARDS AN EVIDENCE-BASED COACHING PSYCHOLOGY: SOME CONCLUSIONS

The above discussion suggests that, rather than adopting a linear understanding of the Boulder model, an informational or evidence-based approach to coaching psychology is to be preferred.

Adapted from its use in the medical context, the term 'evidence-based coaching' means far more than simply producing evidence that a specific coaching intervention is effective, or being able to demonstrate return on investment. The evidence-based approach is not merely about the use of randomized clinical trials, or the use of manualized interventions. A more sophisticated understanding of the term 'evidence-based' refers to the intelligent and conscientious use of best current knowledge in making decisions about how to deliver coaching to coaching clients, and in designing and teaching coach training programs (Sackett *et al.*, 1996).

Best current knowledge is up-to-date information from relevant, valid research, theory and practice. Because there is at present a somewhat limited academic coach-specific literature, best current knowledge can often be found in the established literature in related fields of knowledge, theory and practice. The scientist–practitioner coach needs to be able to draw on such existing knowledge, adapt and apply this knowledge, and in the light of their own reflective practice develop grounded frameworks that further inform their methodologies.

The strength of the scientist–practitioner model is not in developing prescriptive models of psychological intervention which can be applied with unquestioning confidence in their scientific veracity. Rather, its strength is that it provides both information and methodological rigour that the practitioner can use to negotiate the ever-changing waters of psychological intervention.

Coaching psychology has the very real potential to become a powerful methodology for individual, organizational, social and systemic change. The use of theoretically based, psychologically grounded coaching is increasing. Ten years ago there was very little coach-specific research or theories for coaches to draw on. This paucity of previously developed interventions has had the benefit of forcing coaching psychologists to go back to basic psychological principles and re-examine the wider body of psychological knowledge in order to create interventions that meet the needs of coaching clients. This process integrates both the scientist and the practitioner in a way that incorporates the needs of the client and intimately involves them in the process. This approach means that coaches are increasingly able to draw on and contribute to an informed and intelligent coach-specific literature. But there is still a considerable way to go. An evidence-based foundation for coaching psychology can move away from the proscriptive linear approach too often associated with the scientist–practitioner model, and towards a methodology that incorporates both rigour and the lived experience of practitioners and clients.

Chapter 11

Roots, relativity and realism: the occupational psychologist as scientist–practitioner

Richard Kwiatkowski and *Barry Winter*

INTRODUCTION

In this chapter we explore how a modern occupational psychologist can be a scientist–practitioner. We shall approach this discussion from a critical realist perspective (see Chapter 5) and argue that, whilst we as psychological scientist–practitioners have to understand that we operate in a complicated socially constructed world, this knowledge has to be implicitly subsumed into practice rather than dominating it. This means that, in order to act in the world, we must accept this world exists, and matters, outside our own social frameworks. This world is one of industry, commerce and organizations. We shall describe our (unavoidably personal) model of science, provide some examples of practice and stress the notion that, whilst acting in the world requires co-existence within multiple realities, it necessarily means that action which occurs within our clients' version of reality is the only action that, initially at least, will be perceived by them as legitimate. This interactive and relativist position and our notion of science, we suggest, has its roots in formulations of applied psychology in the last century, particularly in the seminal work of the National Institute of Industrial Psychology (NIIP). It also resonates with more modern notions that espouse a return to a pragmatic model of science in psychology. Thus, we shall examine some of the underlying humanist roots of our profession, the importance of context and relativity in formulating and executing our interventions, and finally, the importance of realism, pragmatism and utility in acting in the world as psychological scientist–practitioners.

We entirely agree with the critical realist perspective that there is a social reality which exists independently of discourse (see Chapter 5 for an overview). This world comprises substantive underlying structures and any socially constructed reality has to be negotiated in the light of these structures. We hope to show that the position adopted by modern occupational psychologists recognizes the importance of these underlying structures and that, based on the history of our endeavour, thoughtful psychologists today operate not as technicians or naive empiricists but with full awareness of the complexity of applying their version of science in a multivariate, chaotic and ever-changing domain.

A HUNDRED YEARS OF APPLIED PSYCHOLOGY

Who we are is inevitably influenced by our past. In 2001, the British Psychological Society celebrated its centenary and the long and important history of British Occupational Psychology was demonstrated at a symposium at the centenary conference. For example, the Industrial Fatigue Board, applying what we would call ergonomics and physiological principles to workers, made great advances during the First World War. Then, shortly after the war, the National Institute of Industrial Psychology was founded (1921) with its founder, Charles Myers, giving up his position of first Reader of Experimental Psychology at Cambridge University (a position he had largely invented and endowed himself) in order to concentrate on applying psychology to the world of work (Bunn, 2001a).

Early applied psychologists in the UK had no doubt as to the importance of their profession. 'Of the four main determinants of industrial and commercial efficiency – the mechanical, the physiological, the psychological, and the social and economic – the psychological is by far the most important and fundamental,' (Myers, 1920: v). Luckily, they were amassing evidence that could substantiate such assertions, including significant cost savings, rises in output and data on increases in workers' happiness.

Further afield, Munsterberg had published what may well have been the first true Industrial Psychology text in 1912 and his subsequent career in America served to shape the discipline there. Having trained at the laboratory of Wilhelm Wundt, Munsterberg's emphasis was initially on measurement, statistics and physiology, since at that time (and indeed subsequently) psychology strove for parity with the physical sciences. Additionally Munsterberg's interest in groups influenced Moede and thence Allport and made a significant input into social and group psychology (Murphy, 1949). Munsterberg devoted a good deal of energy to trying to persuade the American government of the importance of psychology to the economic welfare of the USA (Landy and Conte, 2004) and, as was common for the time, his emphasis was often on gauging the fit between the person and the job; an influence that is still present in industrial/organizational psychology today.

Experimental psychology

Experimental psychology at this time was relatively new but psychologists were quite clear about its relation to the then, better established, applied psychology:

> Experimental psychology has sometimes been styled the new or scientific psychology. It has been spoken of as if it were quite distinct from, and independent of, the older or general psychology, in which experiment finds no place. Now these are manifest errors. The experiment in psychology is at least as old as Aristotle, and scientific work is possible under conditions which preclude experiment . . . Far from being independent, experimental

psychology has arisen as a refinement of general psychology. Familiarity with the latter is essential to success in the former.

(Myers, 1920: 104)

Thus, more than 80 years ago experimental psychology was seen very much as a servant of applied psychology but sadly, from being the servant, experimental psychology became the master (Bunn, 2001a, 2001b). After the Second World War, for a range of political reasons (Lovie, 2001), a scientific and experimental model held many psychology departments in its thrall. It was a break with the past. It allowed a 'scientific' status to be claimed for psychology and avoided messy multivariate external reality by bringing psychology into the laboratory. This rejection of the applied for the experimental caused a divide between academic and applied psychology which to some extent continues to this day (Anderson *et al.*, 2001).

How the past shapes the present

Before we consider the implicit relativism present in early occupational psychology and its links with modern deconstructionist appraisals both of psychology and organizations, let us dwell for a moment on the past as it informs the present.

Occupational psychology, perhaps the original UK applied psychology, was initially enormously successful and commercially astute. Princes and Prime Ministers attended fund-raising dinners for the NIIP. Psychologists were consulted at the highest levels of government, and crucially, numerous commercial enterprises either sponsored the NIIP, or employed the Institute to help with their work and their workers. It would be somewhat gratuitous to reproduce the whole list here but the range of members was astonishing, ranging from the Bank of England and Rowntrees, to Nobel Industries and numerous unions.

Humanitarian antecedents and progressive methodology

As well as the financial success and commercial improvements it created for its sponsors, the NIIP was perhaps unique in the annals of consultancy in that it relied heavily on qualitative accounts of work produced not by managers or foremen, but by the workers themselves, or by staff from the Institute working alongside them. Perhaps as a result, early NIIP annual reports are littered with verbatim quotes, collected literally on the shop floor from workers whose lives had been improved by the application of psychology and who often expressed a moving level of gratitude. For example, a shop steward, quoted by Balchin (1933) says: 'They tell me you've saved the firm a lot of money,' she said. 'But you've done something better than that. You've made the girls here feel that they were being considered as human beings, not machines. And that's the most valuable thing you could have done, for the firm as well as for them.'

We believe that the underlying ethos of the NIIP had a profound influence on the development of and thinking in occupational psychology. From the outset, the NIIP focused on applying psychology to a variety of work contexts. As many of its investigators had been trained as scientists, usually psychologists, they naturally enough applied what we might think of as the scientific method relying on observation and naturalistic (*in vivo*) experiments. However, they also utilized anthropological and ethnomethodological techniques. NIIP researchers did not rely on second- or third-hand reports. Instead they either observed the workers at first-hand, often for periods of many weeks, or else actually did the job in question. The climate of the workplace was long considered as a variable and investigators were well aware of its importance and pervasiveness (Bevington, 1924). Similarly, the impact of leadership, group cohesion, the environment, external factors and so forth entered into their thinking, their discussions, their reports and recommendations. Thus from the beginning, the NIIP researcher had moved beyond the 'traditional' scientific laboratory-based model. This same tradition informs the best of UK occupational psychology today. It is from this tradition that occupational psychologists view themselves as scientist–practitioners but this is a million miles away from simple positivistic notions of science.

Let us give another example of how the past informs the present practice of occupational psychology. Whilst many psychologists will identify the Hawthorne effect as meaning that, when people are observed their behaviour changes, the Hawthorne studies also led to the growth of humanistic and group relations considerations in the workplace (Roethlisberger and Dickson, 1939). The whole of the Human Relations movement, and arguably much of personnel psychology, was based on the notion of people as human beings rather than as cogs in a machine. Interestingly, this latter position was adopted by Taylor and his followers in the United States and still (dare we say unconsciously) has an impact in much of the Western world, particularly the United States. This topic is beyond the scope of this chapter, but may well have a link to underlying religious (Protestant) notions of work. Indeed, Americanization of the UK via acquisitions has, in some cases, led to change in working practices based on an implicit philosophical difference between American and European models of work.

Elton Mayo, an Australian who obtained a tenured post at Harvard in 1926, is certainly the psychologist who first comes to mind when considering the 'Human Relations' movement. Mayo's humanistic notions regarding the importance of considering the 'whole' person in the work environment have been very influential both in the USA and Great Britain. However, Charles Myers and other members of the NIIP held similar views. They denounced Taylorism and time-and-motion studies as early as the 1920s (Myers, 1923a, 1923b) and as we have already seen, applied humanistic notions of fairness and equality to the workplace at the beginning of the last century. Thus, on both sides of the Atlantic a humanistic ethos, based on respect for the whole person, informed applied psychology for the first part of the twentieth century.

RELATIVISM, MULTIPLE REALITIES AND THE CONSTRUCTION OF SOCIAL REALITY

We shall move on to the topic of what occupational psychologists do with their science later but before we do so, we must point out that occupational psychologists' implicit understanding of the world has, of necessity, always been a complex one. Much of the organizational world is relative; what is 'sound practice' in one context may be manifestly 'bad practice' in another.

Again, these notions of relativity were familiar to occupational psychologists several generations ago. For example, Myers wrote the following when commenting on physicists' unsuccessful attempts to construct a scale of absolute intensity of differently perceived stimuli:

> Here we have a second example of the vain attempt of the physicist to replace the relative by the absolute in psychology. It is perhaps idle to ask whether, if physics had been willing to learn a lesson from psychology, instead of trying to teach it one, its present position would have been sooner reached. We now find Newton's absolute time and space discarded and replaced by concepts of relativity.
>
> (1937: 67)

This relativist position, we suggest, is embedded in the nature of science as espoused by the occupational scientist–practitioner. Contemporary occupational psychology has also engaged in some of the constructionist arguments that other branches of psychology, particularly social psychology, have espoused recently but it is debatable whether they have made much difference to the way occupational scientist–practitioners operate. Applied psychologists have always had to be sensitive to context and the range of social constructions (and beliefs) about the world that they and their clients hold. However, the relative longevity of occupational psychology as a profession and the adoption of a critical realist stance regarding the social world of organizations means that, on the surface, such concerns do not always seem apparent.

Co-existence within multiple realities

The critical realist stance means co-existing within a range of realities; not just the reality of 'traditional' university departments' versions of academic psychology:

> We have known of other worlds for thousands of years . . . not far away but interpenetrating with this one. Here on this deck, millions of other universes exist, unaware of one another . . . there, I have just brushed other worlds, and they knew nothing about it . . . we are as close as a heartbeat.
>
> (Serafina Pekkala's daemon, Philip Pullman, 1995: 187)[1]

When working with leaders in business, industry, the Health Service, education and the military we are, more than ever, aware that an applied psychologist has to co-exist within several worlds at once. We must understand these worlds as far as we can and use language and thinking appropriate to each. We have to be much more pragmatic than textbooks or neat accounts of experiments would have us believe. At the same time, we must be completely ethical and evidence-based in our actions.

A key aspect of being an effective applied psychologist is being able to oper-ate in the world outside psychology yet being able to take into that world both knowledge based on a specific subject area and a way of thinking (and of being) that is fundamentally psychological in orientation. It means being able to act from a position where the boundaries of certainty and uncertainty co-exist and yet a scientific understanding of what is known and what is not known (and therefore of what can legitimately be done and what should not be done) informs our thinking and action.

For example, what might be described as research in applied psychology may often be better depicted as an audit, an evaluation or even a high-level descrip-tion. It is often paramount in an applied context to know whether an intervention has worked or not. Yet, in the real world, neat 2X2 ANOVA designs (or Latin Squares) with random assignation of subjects to conditions are rarely possible or always ethical. Contact with the real world also means that we are exposed to our clients' social constructions of reality (and perhaps even groupthink and related phenomena). We also co-exist within, represent and identify with a professional group and are bound by a code of conduct and ethics which acts as a measure of protection for us and our clients. In a very real way, as soon as one moves beyond one's professional reference group to interact with others who are not members of that profession, it is extraordinarily important to know what you really know, what you thought you knew, what you imagined, where theory is informing or conversely biasing you, and the limits of your understanding.

In many ways, this is directly analogous to the notion of science, and particularly modern notions of physics, hedged about as they are with ideas of uncertainty. (See Chapter 5 for some interesting links between chaos, uncertainty, the 'new science' and psychology.) In fact, the notion of error is now firmly embedded in business, both in obvious arenas such as process control, operations management and decision science, but also in what is often assumed to be a 'hard' area of businesses, such as accountancy. Thus, what may be thought of as a post-modern attitude of questioning what we know, and positing (at the nihilistic extreme) that all is socially constructed has modern day parallels in many areas of business as well as being part of psychology before the war. We do not have space here to develop the story of why a reductionist experimental model came to be ascendant in psychology, and would direct the interested reader to Bunn et al., (2001).

ON BEING AN APPLIED SCIENCE

As Myers observes, 'Applied sciences can only grow by use. Their success must largely depend on the skill with which they are applied' (1920: 104). Applied psychology exists in order to act on the world. We cannot, therefore, conceive of an applied psychology separate from its application. Whilst, on the face of it, this may seem a simple position to take, it belies the fact that the questioning of assumptions is a fact of everyday life for the competent applied psychologist. For example, in negotiating an entry into another organization, the occupational psychologist must necessarily be aware of the culture and values that they bring as well as the culture and values of the organization which they are entering.

The myriad organizational forms faced by contemporary occupational psychologists (who often operate in a consultancy capacity) is arguably one factor that differentiates occupational psychologists from those working in clinical or educational contexts where common frames of reference are more likely to exist. Hence, every entry into an organization is different and one's own position and philosophy must necessarily be critically examined on each of those occasions, otherwise the engagement will simply fail, perhaps even fail to begin.

Beyond post-modern conceptualizations

Postmodernism and deconstructionist approaches seem to us to emphasize the importance of examining and challenging assumptions and texts. They seek to identify and understand deeper levels of meaning and relationships reflected in those texts (Alvesson and Deetz, 2000; Lincoln and Guba, 1985; Symon and Cassell, 1998). We tentatively suggest that, rather ironically, some outside researchers and commentators applying sociological, political, and post-modern approaches to applied psychology may actually fail to fully understand, and sometimes even belittle, the complex understanding that applied psychologists have tacitly, implicitly and deliberately built up of the complex worlds within which they necessarily operate. Whilst an action undertaken may seem simple and 'technical' from the outside, it may actually be a sophisticated response to a complex world and may belie an intricate and multifaceted understanding. It may arise as a result of a great deal of thought and deliberation about what action is the right action for *this* circumstance.

In our work and in our teaching we thus implicitly adopt a more critical realist and pragmatic position. We have to *do something* in order to apply our art. We will not be paid otherwise. But we, as psychologists, are going into these encounters with our eyes open. We understand that organizations are political and that actions can have multiple meanings. There is an aphorism quoted in aikido and other martial arts: 'Beginners make big circles, masters make small circles'. What we have observed in working with many skilled psychologists over the years is that a small and seemingly obvious comment, technique or intervention, expertly applied at just the right moment will produce a much greater impact than agonized, arduous, conspicuous reservations and indecisive (often self-indulgent) fence sitting. As psychologists we need to be very aware of the impact we are having on our clients.

Certainly, what some of the post-modern (and indeed older psychodynamic and existential) approaches have shown us is that it is easy, but not always appropriate, to imagine that things are as they seem. For example, what might seem like a slavish adherence to a mechanistic model of organizations (Morgan, 1986) with an occupational psychologist adopting an expert role, apparently as a 'servant of power', or technician (Hogan, 2001) may actually be a finely judged performance (Goffman, 1959) that allows that actor to fit into a complex drama, and by their presence as a complete participant, influence the direction of the lives of the other actors. Is this a *post hoc* rationalization and have occupational psychologists sold out? We hope not and would wish to examine our position through considering the client and the context as well as providing some examples of practice.

We very much concur with the position of Anderson, *et al.*, (2001) and their optimistic assertion that the multiple stakeholders present in the world of applied psychology are heralding a move from pedantic, puerile and popularist science towards pragmatic science. We would go further and say that this indicates that we have come full circle.

We do not have enough space in this chapter to fully develop this argument but would like to present a number of examples, both historical and current, in order to illustrate the fact that it is possible and essential for the modern scientist–practitioner to operate at many different levels of understanding at the same time.

THE CLIENT AND THE CONTEXT

The role of occupational psychologists is essentially to apply their psychological science to solve practical problems in the organizational world. The role and context may differ from those of the educational or clinical practitioner in terms of the often highly commercial focus, the lack of a structured and legally recognized profession to validate roles, the myriad organizational forms and the complexity of political and power relationships among multiple clients and stakeholders.

Occupational psychologists always have to start, perhaps in a quasi-humanistic way, with an understanding of the client sitting in front of them. This is very reminiscent of Rogers' work in the counselling arena. However, one must also recognize that there is not one but a number of clients within an organizational setting (managers and employees at its simplest, but also owners, investors, shareholders, lenders, regulators, pressure groups) with whom a 'licence to operate' must be sought. They are powerful and, in the most productive organizations, work together rather than in opposition. At a minimum they all have negative power which means they can act as gatekeepers or even blockers to prevent things from happening. At best, their cooperation can produce huge benefits to all. At worst, interventions will fail and advice will be ignored.

We suspect that this is in contrast to educational, forensic and clinical contexts where, by virtue of occupying a particular role, expert and positional power often accrue to psychologists. We accept that there is increased state scrutiny and public mistrust in comparison with former times but the implicit power relationships still exist and arguably, the person referred to a clinical psychologist with panic attacks will not necessarily sit back dispassionately and have to be persuaded of efficacy before the intervention even begins. We caricature this position for the sake of emphasis but what is important to note here is that the professional context for different sorts of psychologists is radically different and this does have consequences.

Credibility

In gaining credibility, the occupational psychologist often does not have a formal role validated by an organizational career structure. Occupational psychologists have always recognized that they operate in a commercial world where their recommendations must have a monetary impact. The occupational scientist–practitioner frequently tries to use a body of knowledge to gain credibility and hence legitimacy. To a large extent this is how many of us were socialized into the mores of psychology. We believed our lecturers because (as well as formal authority and status) they had recourse to 'science'. We suggest that in the real organizational world this is rarely enough.

In our experience in the field of recruitment and selection, for example, senior managers have looked on with bemused fascination as the occupational scientist–practitioner has attempted to demonstrate the value of their recommendations with first, validity coefficients ('a scale that goes from zero to one' – what? Where else do we use such scales?) and second, utility analysis where the projected paybacks of using a more valid (and more expensive) method are presented. The projected benefits are usually enormous. Any manager worth their salt knows that parameters are easily manipulated (Barwise et al., 1985) and, in any case, fantastic future return is usually irrelevant to the manager's current situation. Managers frequently need to control costs (and almost certainly reject long-term investment) in order to achieve the short-term profit targets demanded of them. Third, an attempt to convince via the use of published empirical studies can be attempted, but this is often equally fruitless. These studies are usually seen as insufficiently specific and again often lack credibility (or perhaps more accurately face validity) in that it is hard for the lay person (and sometimes the practitioner) to distinguish spurious from true results particularly when complex correction factors and esoteric transformations are applied to the data. The client is left in what seems like a gloriously hypothetical world of complexity where they become very afraid that they will need to invest significant time to understand what is being said. All they actually want is the satisfying decision, for instance, to quickly and unreproachfully recruit an additional person so that they can raise production and 'make their quarterly numbers'. That is the reality of the client's life which the scientist–practitioner must recognize but which frequently comes as a surprise to psychologists fresh from an MSc Course, especially if that MSc is based in a largely theoretical psychology department with extensive sections of the programme being taught by non-specialists and, alas, non-practitioners.

Influence and evidence

Occupational scientist–practitioners need to recognize that they are in a contest for influence. They can lose out to other purveyors of solutions, some of whom may present sparse credentials when compared to those trained in the rigour of psychological thinking. However, it is important to recognize that evidence can take many forms, not necessarily based on science but nevertheless valid to the giver and recipient. For example, an anecdote about how another client or a more prestigious organization has profitably implemented a proposed solution might constitute much better proof to a client than a description of a complex study in a top journal with attendant multivariate statistics.

The trade press and presentations at conferences may also disproportionately influence organizational clients. The trade press informs but also entertains its readership. It makes its profits through selling advertising space and so, unsurprisingly given the capitalist model within which it operates, tends to favourably profile companies that buy space. Thus, excellent research on the impact of HR policies and psychological interventions on the bottom line co-exist with features on fads and fashions 'placed' by consultancies who are motivated by sales and new products rather than embedding them in proven best practice. The reader is often unaware of the dynamics underlying the production of the articles they read and whose advice they take. Consequently, it is difficult for the organizational decision-maker to discriminate; these outlets are not 'true' disseminators of proven methods or knowledge, yet they are often the only reading a hard-pressed client will access. They are a million miles from the rigorous double-blind refereeing of psychology journals that psychologists are used to hearing about and the instinctively critical response of most psychologists to an unproven new idea.

But again, the idea of an objective 'science' may be a naive view. There are, for example, also strategies that one can employ to publish in top journals, which then confer a degree of credibility on your views in the wider psychological community. For example, one might edit a special edition, befriend the editor or make sure that one quotes the papers of the editorial board (Sternberg, 2000). Thus, once again the political process of influence is present, though in a post-Khunian world a notion of science as logical, apolitical and somehow pure is no longer really tenable.

Who to believe?

It is no wonder that clients do not know who or what to believe; they are making judgements under conditions of uncertainty. They cannot hope to be expert in everything so have to use other means to decide between alternatives. As long as the psychologist is able to co-exist in multiple worlds (Kwiatkowski and Horncastle, 1990) providing symbolic markers of potential efficacy is fine but if that is all there is, then it is simply spin.

So where does this leave us? The issues raised in this chapter start to point to important issues for the future development of scientist–practitioners in occupational psychology. We are operating in a world where academic qualifications and professional status may appear to be relatively easily gained. At the extreme, a few dollars will buy a PhD or MBA from an apparently legitimately registered university over the internet and consultants will list 'letters after their names' that may look impressive but have little authority. Many people do not know which qualifications are legitimate or which universities are 'better' for particular subjects than others. It is difficult for clients to distinguish between proper professional qualifications and dubious ones. A legacy of 1980s Thatcherism in the UK, and Republican suspicion of 'closed shops' in the USA, somehow leaves professions portrayed as 'anti-market' or, in George Bernard Shaw's words, 'a conspiracy against the laity'.

The attributes of a profession are often overlooked. These are: a systematic theory, authority to act in a domain, community sanction and recognition of expertise and the adherence to ethical codes coupled with an internal culture that supports and develops these other characteristics (Kwiatkowski and Horncastle, 1990). Add to these the interpersonal client handling skills and pragmatism of being 'administratively sound, politically acceptable, organizational expedient' and the future is not so new. Perhaps it is time to remember the past and rehabilitate the pioneering work of Myers at the NIIP and Alec Rodger at Birkbeck College.

DOING PSYCHOLOGICAL SCIENCE

It is pointless for occupational scientist–practitioners to bemoan the commercial context in which they operate. This is the reality of the world and hence it is more productive to focus on what the relatively unscientific practitioner may have supplied that the client so values. A recent study by Winter (1997) examined how clients of psychological services made a decision to buy those services. It showed that organizational clients tend to use two equally weighted factors in their decisions to hire an occupational psychologist. 'Expertise' was seen as crucial but so, equally, were the consultant's interpersonal skills and use of empathy.

Advice is an intangible product and successful consultancy is the 'management of impressions' and expectations (Clark, 1995). The question for scientist–practitioners is how they can create a reality for clients that satisfies (our) scientific scrutiny and gives (them) peace of mind.

Whilst we will rely on knowledge and experience, these are actually the vectors through which much research is translated. Even for trained psychologists it is sometimes hard to distinguish spurious from truly important and useful results particularly when correction factors and transformations are applied to the data. We are left with a hypothetical world where, if normal data existed and the sample was huge, this result would appear. As the real world does not conform to this criterion, we must rely on professional judgement, but this is not anti-science. The same situation applies in many other fields, a prime example being medicine.

It is also relevant to point out that we may actually hinder dissemination in presenting our science in an overly complex way. For example, the Myers-Briggs Type Indicator (MBTI) is a superb instrument and clients are increasingly familiar with it. However, on first meeting, many find the number of personality types (16) it measures difficult to remember (a task compounded by them having strange names like ISTP and ESFJ). Assigning the types memorable names gives clients something immediately useful to use and opens the door to further investigation (and can lead on to training and the possibility of becoming MBTI practitioners themselves). This is the difference between 'giving psychology away' (Shimmin and Wallis, 1994) by making science initially palatable or, conversely, clouding oneself in mystery and having no influence (and ultimately, no clients).

OUR SCIENCE

As we have noted above our implicit model of science is fundamentally a realist one. Although we are aware of both modernist and postmodernist notions and various relativistic and constructionist arguments and, whilst we do use aspects of what might be loosely termed grounded theory in our own practice as indicated earlier, we do firmly believe that there is some sort of reality present outside us. Science can be thought of as a 'conversation with nature'. The part of nature with which we, as psychologists, are conversing concerns human beings and particularly their minds and behaviour. Organizations are creations of human beings and so a legitimate arena for us. We function within a critical realist tradition, one which predates postmodernism but which can, in our opinion, be thought of as going a step beyond it.

Our implicit model of science is one which provides useful, workable rules of thumb that are a guide to operating in the world. For example, a type theory such as that measured by the MBTI is often more useful on a day-to-day basis than something much more complex that our clients may not be able to work with. If we can get a manager to become aware that introverted and extroverted employees behave differently and that, by adapting their style of communication they can have a more positive impact, then that is a constructive outcome. We do not necessarily need to explain the controversies surrounding ideas of personality, competing models, arguments about type versus trait, controversies about ipsative tests and their inherent psychometric properties and so forth. If we feel obliged to do all that, and the client doesn't need it, then we are simply pandering to our own anxieties rather than serving the client's needs. It beholds us as the 'professional' in this arena to be able to make the situation less anxiety provoking rather than more. If we feel we have to demonstrate our 'scientific' credentials at every turn we have probably both not understood the nature of the engagement, and more than that probably lack insight into ourselves and our clients' needs.

Finally, let us give some examples of our practice with three short vignettes. We have chosen examples that are on the edge of practice, because they are more interesting.

Some examples of practice

Our first example involves provision of input into an area where unease was felt about the theoretical context. One of us was asked by a long-standing client to provide some training for a board of a major financial institution on 'emotional intelligence'. This was a concept that was then fashionable and, in the way it had been used in that organization, about which we had some reservations. A series of telephone conversations took place during which it emerged that a training event at group level had taken place on 'EQ' and this was to be rolled out to all senior employees before an in-house training programme communicated it to other staff members. We read Goleman's books (1996, 1998) and some criticisms of it in the mainstream psychological literature, and decided that the first level in his model, namely that of 'awareness', was a legitimate and appropriate aspect upon which to concentrate. (There is an ethical issue present here about how much an organization can legitimately demand from people, and if focus on emotions is appropriate for a commercial organization, or whether these aspects of the person actually 'belong' to the individual.) In the case of these senior managers, the focus was clearly on improving their performance and not as some form of back-door therapy.

We therefore communicated with the client, explaining that experiential work could be undertaken on raising awareness of these emotional aspects of work, but that covering the whole model was impractical, and without long-term experiential work, pointless. The client agreed; a day was planned with a variety of inputs to suit different learning styles and personality types, with a range of exercises that called for a certain level of disclosure which was, nevertheless, under the individuals' control. Confidentiality was seen as essential, as, despite their seniority, the exposure of 'emotions' in the workplace was seen as unusual and potentially threatening. Before and after measures were taken and 'awareness' had, by a self-rated measure, increased by the end of the day. This was confirmed in examining self-reports of group work, which had become markedly more people-focused during the day. The client paid promptly, with expressions of interest, but curiosity about emotional intelligence fizzled out in the broader organization, so the training was not repeated nor followed up in detail.

Another example involves making theoretical interventions personal and meaningful to clients. In this case, an aptitude test examining verbal information-processing was included, as a trial, in a selection system. When collecting post-appointment performance data and carrying out simple statistics it became very clear that the aptitude test was the most predictive component. However, it and the validation study had little face validity with the line managers with whom the selection decision rested, so people were employed using other data, primarily the interview. Not all those hired were successful. Subsequently the data were re-presented to the client as a scattergram with named individuals and annotated comments from their managers which showed how the subsequent performance of those selected (including those actually sacked for poor performance) was related to their ability to process complex information at speed and with accuracy. Following that intervention the decision to use the previously suggested aptitude test cut-off was adopted. From our perspective, human misery as well as time and expense could have been saved by early adoption, but 'psychological' evidence was simply not convincing to the client.

A final example involves coaching a consultant who was having trouble with a client relationship and was in danger of being removed from the account before the client moved the business elsewhere. From the first interview when a cognitive-behavioural framework was used, it became clear that the consultant was becoming anxious about the client's actual or perceived comments about his seniority (the consultant was 'young looking' but normally very effective). The consultant responded by 'freezing up' and trying to complete the task as quickly as possible before leaving; this task focus meant that they were not building an enduring relationship with the client.

The intervention was never positioned as 'cognitive-behavioural' or the theoretical basis discussed. ('Come and see the company shrink!' would frighten even the most thick-skinned consultant.) Instead, a set of coaching exercises to recognize automatic negative thoughts, relax and show calm helped the consultant think more creatively and openly, respond to the client in a positive way (rather than as a threat) and over a relatively short period of time, develop a very strong relationship and build the account.

CONCLUSION

The occupational scientist–practitioner has to understand that we operate in a world in which multiple views are held about how the world works and what is important, by multiple stakeholders, and that traditional science is only one of those views. Science and the trappings of science displayed at universities are not sufficient to gain influence to operate in the complex world of organizations. Our science has to be made palatable without being oversimplified to the point of caricature, being distorted to suit political convenience, or simply being 'given away' to those subsequently unable to fully use it. Practice must involve strong interpersonal skills as well as co-existing in the realm of evidence. In the UK many occupational psychologists work 'undercover' in jobs without any mention of psychology in the title, with few colleagues ever realizing their background, only knowing that they are very effective in solving organizational problems. This is actually a return to many of the fundamental beliefs and methods upon which occupational psychology was founded – good scientists acting on the world and gaining credibility by understanding people (e.g. often doing the jobs themselves) and knowing organizations, by being practical, accessible and helpful; all founded on a fundamentally humanistic position backed up with rigorous science expertly rendered relevant to the context.

To return to our title, a philosophical link to our roots, an understanding of relativity in science and practice, embedded in a core of realism, are fundamental to our day-to-day work as occupational psychologist scientist–practitioners.

Note

1 Extract from *Northern Lights* by Philip Pullman. Copyright Philip Pullman, 1995, published by Scholastic Children's Books. All rights reserved. Reproduced by permission of Scholastic Ltd.

Chapter 12

The scientist–practitioner as thinker: a comment on judgement and design

Edward de Bono

At a time of rapid social, economic and political change, there is a high demand for thinking that is optimally constructive, creative and effective. In my book *Parallel Thinking* I argued that this demand applies not only to global issues but also to nations, communities, families and individuals. It applies equally to those who try to support their clients through psychological interventions.

In a previous chapter of this volume (Chapter 2), Lane and Corrie identified some potential frameworks for enhancing the reasoning skills of professional psychologists. In this chapter, I elaborate on some of these ideas by highlighting how the traditional Western thinking system that permeates much of our reasoning represents an inheritance from specific philosophical traditions that cannot inform the operational aspects of effective thinking. By comparing classification, analysis and design-based approaches, as well as arguing for the explicit teaching of thinking as an operational skill and describing the contribution of 'parallel thinking', this chapter aims to contribute to a fuller appreciation of judgement and design and offers ideas on how to harness these skills within the context of professional practice.

I begin this chapter with a story.

Two men are running against each other, one is overweight, the other is not. It is not a formal race. The thinner man always wins.

There are at least three broad approaches to the above situation.

First of all there is the 'classification' approach. We look at the situation to see how we can apply our repertoire of standard boxes, categories and classifications. This is classed 'Aristotelian thinking'.

We tell the overweight man that he falls in to the 'obese' category. Such men do not run fast. Such men should not expect to run fast. The behaviour of obese men is predictable and running slowly is just such predictable behaviour. We might even go further and suggest that being obese was programmed into his genes and there is nothing much that can be done about it. For very practical reasons this approach is much used by psychologists and psychiatrists. This is the diagnosis. There then follows the expectations and the treatment.

The second approach is the 'analysis' approach. We look at the situation and seek to analyse it. What is happening? Why is it happening? What is the explanation?

We seek to understand what is going on. We seek 'the truth'. Once we understand what is going on then we can do something about it. In particular, if there is something wrong we then seek to put it right. This is problem-solving.

So we analyse the performance of the overweight man. He runs slowly. Why? What is the reason? It is probably because he is obese. Previous experience with obesity, and also the laws of physics, suggest that such men do not run fast.

We move on to the next stage of the analysis. Why is the man overweight? A strong possibility is that he eats more than his body needs and the excess is laid down as fat. It may not be that he eats more than other people, but his metabolism puts down more fat than other metabolisms. Now we think we know the cause of the obesity. So what do we do about it? We move on to the remedy. We put the man on a strict diet. We have analysed the situation. We have found the fault. We have taken measures to correct the fault. This must be good science – at least if we adhere to a Newtonian approach to science which prizes studying component parts in order to arrive at an understanding of the whole.

We now come to the third approach, which is very rarely used. This is the 'design' approach.

In the design approach we simply give the overweight man a bicycle. Will he not, instantly, outperform the thinner man who is without a bicycle?

In the design approach we set out to 'design a way forward'. We are not so much concerned with finding the faults and correcting them but with providing a way forward even if the faults remain in place.

We can now examine each of these three approaches in more detail – and then show how the design approach can be applied to the direct teaching of thinking as a skill and the reasoning skills of professional psychologists.

THE CLASSIFICATION APPROACH

The brain is a superb recognition machine. The brain is designed to be non-creative. The purpose of the brain is to make stable patterns for dealing with an unstable world.

To illustrate this point, let me give an example. One day a man gets up in the morning and programmes his computer to work through all the ways of getting dressed with eleven pieces of clothing. The computer works non-stop for 40 hours to go through all the possibilities. This is not surprising because there are 39,916,800 ways of getting dressed. If you were to try one every minute you would need to live to be 76 years old using every minute of your waking life trying a different way of getting dressed.

However, we do not have to do this because the brain allows incoming information to organize itself into patterns. The way the brain does this is described in my book *The Mechanism of Mind* (1969). Once the pattern has been formed then, on future occasions, the brain 'recognizes' the pattern and uses the appropriate behaviour sequence. This is the nature of self-organizing information systems like the human brain.

THE GG3

Much of our mental software is derived directly from the 'GG3'; that is the 'Greek Gang of Three': Plato, Socrates and Aristotle.

Plato was strongly influenced by the mathematician Pythagoras. Plato believed that just as there was an ultimate truth in mathematics, so there should also be an ultimate truth everywhere. That provided the basis for our obsessive search for 'truth' ever since – a search which has, traditionally, contributed to a model of science firmly embedded within an empiricist worldview (see Chapter 5, this volume).

However, this approach to reasoning can lead us astray. For example, imagine a car is driving along a road. The car runs out of petrol. The driver and passengers get out and rejoice. They congratulate themselves that they have reached the destination. Truth is somewhat similar. When we have 'run out' of thinking we call that the truth. We can see this approach to thinking embedded within much of the literature on information-processing approaches to decision-making in which accuracy is prioritized over usefulness and the shortfall between actuarial and professional prediction all too apparent (see Chapter 2).

Socrates was trained as a Sophist. These were people who became very skilled with the use of words in argument. If you paid them enough they could reach any conclusion you wished. Socrates had a reputation for asking questions. He did ask questions – but they were mainly leading questions:

'Would you choose your best athlete by chance?'
'Of course not!'
'Would you choose the best navigator of your ship by chance?'
'Certainly not!'
'Why then do we choose our politicians by chance (in the last round of the elections)?'

The listener is supposed to say: 'That would be just as stupid.' The situations are not similar at all, however. The Society of the time used chance to select their final politicians in order to avoid bribery, factions and corruption which have little to do with athletes or navigators. However, that approach to enquiry was typical Socrates.

Then there was Aristotle. From the past the mind could create boxes, definitions and categories. When you came across something new you looked to see into which existing box the new thing could be fitted. It would need to be within the box or outside the box, but it could never be half in and half out. Once something had been placed in a box we knew all about it. This was the basis for Aristotelian logic.

A child with a rash is brought to a doctor in a clinic. Operating on the basis of Aristotelian logic, the doctor looks at the child and thinks of some possibilities (possible boxes). The doctor then examines the child more thoroughly, looking for Koplik's spots, etc. The doctor takes a careful history from the parents. The doctor may carry out some tests to exclude certain possibilities. The doctor then makes a judgement or diagnosis. If the doctor decides that the child falls into the 'measles' box then the doctor knows the probable course of the illness, the possible complications and the standard treatment. This standard treatment has been derived from the experience of many and even research. This approach makes full use of the brain's natural capacity to make patterns and to use them.

In the early days of medicine, and in traditional approaches to healing today, there is a need to observe the state of the patient very carefully. This careful observation of clusters of symptoms leads to the labelling of standard, recognizable, conditions. For each condition, or ailment, there is then a specific concoction of herbs and other ingredients. So we go from recognition to label to treatment. Thus, today we recognize the standard symptoms of schizophrenia (even though we are not clear about the underlying mechanism) and then apply the label. There then follows the standard treatment of that label, modified by the actual condition of the patient.

This system follows the way the brain works naturally. This system follows the mental software originally designed by the GG3. This may be the only practical way of proceeding. It is therefore not surprising that psychology and psychiatry love the labelling system. How else could they proceed?

THE ANALYSIS APPROACH

Most of science and much of thinking claims to be based on the 'analysis' approach. With analysis we seek to understand what is going on in the situation or system.

If there is a fault in the system, we seek to understand the basis for this malfunction. It took medicine an astonishingly long time to realize that some peptic ulcers were actually due to an infection (with Helicobacter pylori) rather than an excess of acid in the stomach. Until that time treatment was with antacids – to counteract the supposed excess of acid. Or there were special diets – to prevent the release of acid. Or you could lose some or all your stomach in the Billroth operations.

There was an attempt to understand the situation but the understanding was flawed. So the interventions were also flawed. Today you might be offered antibiotics for one week instead of antacids for years – or losing some or all your stomach.

In general, however, the analysis approach is very useful. Most of our successes and advances in science and technology have come from the analysis approach. Seek to understand the situation and then intervene on the basis of that understanding. However limited or partial that understanding is, there can be little doubt that our knowledge of the world has increased exponentially, as Bhaskar (1975, 1979) observed in his reflections on the advances of science.

The analysis approach is particularly useful in problem-solving. You analyse the situation and detect the cause of the problem. You are now in a position to solve that problem. For example, if there is a problem in starting your car, your analytic mind scans through possibilities. It could be the electric system. It could be the fuel supply. It could be the carburettor. You analyse the situation carefully and even perform some tests. Eventually you find that one of the battery leads has become disconnected. You connect the lead and away you go.

However, while analysis is excellent at problem-solving it is not much use at designing the way forward. The engineer who can instantly diagnose what is wrong with the car engine may not be much use at designing a new and better engine.

You can analyse the past but you have to design the future. Fixing problems is not the same as designing a way forward. This is why a modern conceptualization of what it means to be a scientist–practitioner must include attention to skills in design and creativity, as well as skills in analysis and evaluation.

THE DESIGN APPROACH

The design approach will be considered in a particular context. This context is the direct and explicit teaching of thinking as a skill.

The direct and explicit teaching of thinking as a skill

We can now look to see how the three approaches can be applied to the teaching of thinking as a skill.

In the classification approach there are formal labels such as Down's syndrome, Gifted, ADD, etc. Each of these describes a 'box' into which youngsters with the right symptoms can be placed. The emphasis is on 'what is'. What is the condition? What can we then expect?

In addition to the labelled boxes there are spectra such as the IQ test. These are continuous but youngsters at one end or the other are labelled as Gifted or 'slow learners'. There are many 'box system' models such as the Myers–Briggs framework which might label someone as 'intuitive' or 'judgemental', etc.

Tests and boxes are much loved by psychologists because they seem to make tangible, and true, matters which would otherwise be vague and subjective. Measurement is everything. The possibility that many of the tests do not really measure what the label suggests is not important. For example, IQ tests simply test the ability to do IQ tests. If this ability correlates with other activities then the IQ test may be a predictor for these other activities. The label 'IQ' is itself arbitrary. We could call it 'TTI' or Test Type Intelligence. The issue of psychologists' relationship to these types of testing, and the uses to which the data obtained from them are put is discussed from an educational perspective by Miller and Frederickson in Chapter 7. Moreover, the place of numbers and measurement within science has also been questioned by some working within new science frameworks (see Wheatley, 1999).

Using the very simple 'attention directing framework' designed to improve perception, some six-year-old children with Down's syndrome were asked to consider the 'plus points' of a snake having a head at both ends. They pointed out that the snake could more easily see a pursuer. One head could be awake and one asleep. It would be possible to attack with both heads. The very first idea the children had was that if a snake went down a hole then it would not have to turn around to get out of the hole.

I once asked the same question of 500 educators and secondary school pupils in Belfast, Northern Ireland. As far as I could ascertain, none of them came up with the idea of the snake reversing out of holes.

There is a huge difference between measuring 'what is' and designing frameworks to generate 'what can be'. It is the latter that has traditionally been neglected in the scientist–practitioner debate.

The analytical approach to the teaching of thinking sets out to analyse thinking into its various stages, phases or components. It is not so much a matter of discovering these elements but of creating them through description. If we wished, we could describe a walking stick as being made up of five parts: handle, shaft, end bit; and two linking bits between the handle and middle bit and between the middle bit and the end bit. Descriptions are arbitrary.

Having analysed 'thinking' in this way we then seek to teach each of the identified (description-based) elements. But descriptions are not 'operating tools' and the method simply does not work. The philosophical description of method is not the same as the design of operational tools.

Then there is the critical approach. We analyse what can be wrong in thinking and then we teach youngsters to avoid such mistakes. This is the basis of critical thinking. The word 'critical' comes from the Greek work for 'judge'. So critical thinking implies judgement thinking.

Judgement thinking is excellent but not enough. It is not enough to identify standard situations and then to apply the standard answer. Although this may prove effective when faced with clear-cut and uncontentious problems, and indeed has formed the basis of protocols and other manualized approaches, it is not sufficient for the reasoning skills required of us today. Nor is it enough simply to avoid all mistakes in thinking. You could avoid all mistakes in driving a car by leaving the car in the garage. You would not make any mistakes but you would not get anywhere.

The 'design approach' involves designing frameworks for thinking. These designs are based on an understanding of the human brain as a self-organizing information system which makes asymmetric patterns.

Perception

David Perkins at Harvard (see Perkins, 2000; Perkins and Blythe, 1994, and Perkins et al., 1995, for an overview of this work) showed that in ordinary thinking 90 per cent of errors typically made are errors of perception and not of logic. For centuries we have considered that thinking was all about logic. In fact logic plays only a very small part in practical thinking. If your perception is wrong or inadequate then no amount of excellence in logic will put it right. If the perception is defective the outcome will be rubbish even if the logic is faultless, as the following illustrates:

- All donkeys have four legs and a tail.
- My dog has four legs and a tail.
- Therefore, my dog is a donkey.

Goedel's Theorem shows that from within a system it is impossible to prove the starting points. In the same way, it is impossible to prove the validity of the starting perceptions through the use of logic, because logic has to use some starting perceptions. There is no such thing as neutral observation, as the crisis of rationality illustrated all too clearly.

Moreover, perception is influenced by factors entirely unconnected with logic, such as the anticipated advantages and disadvantages of a given behaviour. In Australia a five-year-old boy is offered, by his companions, a choice between a one dollar coin and a two dollar coin. The two dollar coin is much smaller. The boy chooses the larger coin. His companions laugh and giggle at his apparent 'stupidity'. They repeat the offer on various occasions. The boy always chooses the larger coin.

One day, an adult feels sorry for the 'victim' and tells him that the small coin is actually more valuable than the larger coin. 'Yes, I know that,' said the five-year-old. 'But how often would they have offered me the choice if I had taken the smaller coin the first time?'

It is a matter of perception. If you see the offer as a 'one-off' occasion it makes sense to take the more valuable coin. If you know your companions and see the possibility of multiple occasions, then the choice is different.

Because of our philosophical heritage where perceptions are provided as dogmas and maxims, we have paid far too little attention to perception. We have never sought to teach perception explicitly – either in our schools or our professional trainings.

Perception is largely a matter of attention and possibility. Attention is usually drawn to something interesting or familiar. We need to design frameworks for 'directing attention' as we wish.

Directions in space are given by such instructions as: look right, look left, look up and look down. There are also the compass directions: North, South, East and West. We can use these to direct our gaze where we wish or to instruct others to direct their gaze.

The CoRT Programme (Cognitive Research Trust) sets out directions in which we can 'direct our attention'. Thirty Australian schoolboys (about 12 years in age) were asked to consider the idea of paying youngsters to go to school. All 30 decided it was a very good idea.

The boys were then briefly introduced to the PMI (Plus, Minus, Interesting) framework. First they had to direct attention to the Plus or positive points. Then to the Minus or negative points. Finally to the Interesting points: points which were neither positive nor negative but simply worth noting. After using the PMI framework, 29 out of the 30 had completely changed their minds and decided that paying youngsters for going to school was not a good idea at all.

A group of 250 top women executives in Canada were asked to consider the suggestion that women should be paid 15 per cent more than men for doing the same job (extra responsibilities in society, etc.). Eighty-five per cent of those present thought it a good idea – and about time too! They were then introduced to the C&S tool which directs attention to the 'Consequences and Sequels' of an action or choice: immediate, short term, medium term and long term. After using this simple attention-directing tool, the number in favour dropped from 85 per cent to 15 per cent. Yet every one of those executives, if asked whether they considered consequences, would have replied that that was their job as senior executives.

The CoRT Programme is now in use in thousands of schools around the world. These simple tools taught to youngsters on the Government New Deal programme (by the Holst Group) increased employment by 500 per cent.

David Lane at the Islington Guidance Centre (see Chapter 2) referred to teaching these skills to youngsters suspended from normal schools. In a 20-year follow-up, he showed that the rate of actual criminal convictions in those taught 'thinking' was significantly less than those not taught thinking. This is very powerful stuff.

In a platinum mine in South Africa there used to be 210 fights every month between the seven different groups working there. A few of the CoRT tools were taught to the illiterate miners who had never been to school. The number of fights dropped from 210 to just four.

A teacher in New Zealand reported that teaching this sort of thinking to youngsters in prison reduced the rate of return to prison (recidivism) to one-quarter of what it had been.

In combination, what these findings suggest is that this approach works cross-culturally, for people of different ages and with clients in different organizational and social contexts. The tools are given acronyms so that they come to have an existence in the brain and can be used at will. Whilst they are so simple that they often upset traditional educators, they are powerful and work in practice.

TEACHING CREATIVITY

Creativity is usually regarded as a mystical talent which some people have and others do not. This is rubbish at least as far as 'idea creativity' goes, although it may be the case that a highly evolved artistic creativity relies upon a type of aesthetic judgement unique to those gifted in that field.

There is no mystery about 'idea creativity', however. Creativity is the behavioural information in self-organizing systems that make asymmetric patterns. All patterning systems are asymmetric. All self-organizing systems make patterns.

From an understanding of the nature of these asymmetric systems we can design the formal tools of creativity. These include: challenge, concept extraction, provocation, random entry, etc. These are the formal tools of lateral thinking (see Bono, 1973, for a more detailed description of this approach).

All of these tools can be learned and practised until skill in their use is acquired. Everyone can acquire the skill but, as with any skill, some people might be better at the skill than others. Most people can learn to play a reasonable game of tennis. Some will reach Wimbledon and a few will win.

A group of workshops organized by Carol Ferguson for ISCOR in South Africa, used just one of the lateral thinking tools (random entry). That afternoon, participants generated 21,000 ideas. It took nine months just to sort through the ideas generated in one afternoon. This goes far beyond brainstorming or feeling 'uninhibited'.

Some of the processes of lateral thinking are directly contrary to traditional thinking. With traditional thinking you need to be 'right' at every step. However, in lateral thinking, we can use ideas which are deliberately provocative to open up new possibilities. With provocation you can take a step that you know to be incorrect. For example, we can use a deliberately provocative idea, one we 'know' not to be right, such as: 'Po cars should have square wheels.' (We use the term 'Po', Provocative Operation, to signal that a provocation is being used.)

If we attempted to judge this idea we would foreclose our thinking so instead we use methods that enable us to generate movement in our thinking. We can see a new mental operation of 'movement'. This is totally different from judgement.

From the provocation we might come up with the idea of creating some form of 'anticipatory suspension' where the suspension is active and operates ahead of need – to give a very smooth ride.

Although provocation may sound strange to traditional philosophers, it is based directly on an understanding of the brain as a self-organizing system. Mathematicians understand the need for provocation in such systems. Without provocation you get trapped in a 'local equilibrium', an existing way of thinking, which closes down possibilities. Consequently, you never reach a global equilibrium. We can see this in psychology where foundational beliefs trap us in a way of seeing which foreclose possible alternative perspectives. The use of techniques such as provocative operation gets us out of a local equilibrium of limited possibility.

ARGUMENT

For centuries (since the GG3) we have esteemed argument and debate as the best way of exploring a subject. We use the system in parliament. We use the system in the law courts. In fact, argument is an extremely crude, primitive and inefficient way of exploring a subject.

In a court of law if the prosecuting lawyer thinks of a point which would help the defence case, is that lawyer going to put the point forward? Of course not. If the defence lawyer thinks of a point that would help the prosecution, is that lawyer going to put forward the point? Of course not. It is not a matter of 'exploring the subject' but of 'case making'. When it comes to making judgements and decisions in professional practice, clearly we must not confuse the two.

In argument you have to start out with a position or point of view. This may simply be disagreement with the other point of view, or a different point of view. You cannot argue without a position. In exploring a subject you explore first and reach a position at the end, not at the beginning. Having a position at the beginning leads to selective perception and seeing only what we want to see.

In argument all the energy goes into defending or attacking the starting positions. There is no effort to 'design' new possibilities. Argument focuses on winning and losing. It is about 'attack' and 'defense'. Egos and superiority are heavily involved. But what can we do instead of argument? There is 'parallel thinking'. The thrust of this position is as follows (for a fuller description of this approach, see Bono, 1995).

At every moment all parties are thinking in parallel about a particular issue or dilemma and looking in the same direction. In contrast to other approaches which emphasize argument and the quest for truth, the emphasis in parallel thinking is on looking *at* the subject, not at each other's thinking *about* the subject. The directions change so that the subject is explored from all angles.

The direction to be taken at any one time is indicated by the use of one of six coloured hats. The hats are symbolic and indicate temporary behaviour patterns, as each of the different hats is easily put on and taken off.

Under the white hat everyone focuses on information. The types of questions generated when the white hat is in use include: What information do we have? What information do we need? What information is missing? What questions do we want to ask? How are we going to get the information we need?

The red hat is to do with emotions, intuition and feelings as they exist in that moment. The red hat gives permission for these to be expressed without the need to explain or justify them.

The black hat is for caution and critical thinking. It assesses the dangers and what can go wrong as well as whether something is right or wrong or fits existing information. The black hat is for 'negative judgement' which is an essential part of avoiding mistakes that could cause damage to ourselves or others.

The yellow hat focuses on benefits and values. What are the benefits here? What are the positive points? The yellow hat is for 'positive judgement' where effort is directed towards exploring how something can be done. Both the black and yellow hats require an ability to spell out the reasons behind the options presented.

The green hat is for creativity. The green hat covers new ideas, alternatives, possibilities, modifications or an idea. Under the green hat everyone makes a creative effort. 'Possibilities' are a very key part of thinking and so the green hat facilitates speculation and enables vision.

The blue hat is for meta-cognition and the organization of thinking. The blue hat is like the conductor of an orchestra, deciding the focus. The blue hat puts together the outcome of the thinking and sets the sequence of hats to be used.

The method is very simple. It is used by four-year-olds in schools. It is used by senior executives at some of the world's largest corporations. Some of the examples in which it has been successfully applied include:

- MDS, a company in Canada, who did a careful costing and showed that use of the Hats method saved $20 million in the first year.
- ABB in Finland, who used to take up to 30 days on their multi-national project discussions. Using the Hats method they now do it in two days.
- Statoil in Norway, who had a problem with an oil rig that was costing $100,000 a day. After thinking about the problem for some time, the company introduced the Six Hats. In 12 minutes they had a solution which saved them $10 million.

The results are very powerful for a very simple framework that is practical and easy to use. The results come about because everyone is using his or her full thinking capacity, instead of just waiting to attack what someone else says.

How could the Six Hats inform the reasoning skills of the modern scientist–practitioner? In my book *Parallel Thinking*, I argued how Western technical progress can be attributed to engaging the power of possibility rather than the argument system. We could say that this is equally true of many of the advancements within professional psychology practice. To maximize their reasoning skills, psychologists must be well equipped to operate within each of the domains, symbolized in my method by the Six Hats.

The ability to seek and unearth the relevant information ('white hat' thinking) is essential, but so is a recognition and ability to understand and harness emotional and intuitive reactions (red hat). The ability for both 'negative' and 'positive' judgement enables us to weigh up the benefits that enable certain decisions to be reached over others. As both these hats require logical support, we can appreciate how these need to be grounded in specific frameworks of reasoning, as argued cogently in Chapter 2. Creativity (the focus of the green hat) is how innovations in practice emerge, refined and developed through the positive and negative judgement (black and yellow hat thinking). The blue hat's emphasis on meta-cognition relates to frameworks of reflective and reflexive practice in which professional psychologists demonstrate not only an interest in the outcome of the questions they ask, but also a curiosity in the nature of the questions themselves. Through the Six Hats method, the skills of thinking and doing, analysing and designing begin to come together, providing an additional framework through which psychologists can better understand their own thinking and enable those skills in their clients.

Of course, this leaves us with the question of why it has taken 2,400 hundred years to come up with an alternative to argument. In fact, there may indeed be occasions when argument is more suitable than exploration. But where genuine exploration is the intention then parallel thinking is simple, practical and effective.

SUMMARY

Thinking can be taught in a direct and explicit fashion. It is not enough to suppose that teaching specific subject areas in a 'thinking' manner is sufficient. Judgement and analysis are valid but are only a small part of operational thinking.

We need to detach thinking from the search for meaning of traditional philosophy. Thinking is an operational skill. We need to design simple, practical and effective tools for thinking. As argued elsewhere in this book, it is important for scientist–practitioners to have access to tools and frameworks that enable them to develop skills in judgement and design that help them respond optimally to the challenges of practice today and in the future.

Ultimately, the design approach is much more powerful than the classification or analytical approach. With the classification approach, our clients remain in danger of being put into boxes or pigeon-holes with no hope of emerging from them. The design approach is all about 'what can be' rather than an obsession with 'what is'.

All the processes mentioned here have been in use for a number of years across a wide range of ages, abilities and cultures, from four-year-olds to 90-year-olds (see Roosevelt University in Chicago), children with Down's syndrome to Nobel prize laureates, illiterate miners to top executives. They are currently in use in 35 countries including China, Japan, Australia, Malaysia, Russia, North and South America, Europe, Middle East, India and Pakistan. The frameworks are not unlike mathematics. They are neutral and independent and not culture-based. They can be learned and used deliberately.

Nothing is more important than the teaching of thinking. With the ability to think – and confidence in that ability – people can take control of their lives. Instead of being, and feeling, like corks floating down a stream pushed this way and that by the currents, they can see things more clearly and make decisions and choices. This is surely true of our clients, as well as ourselves. Any education system or professional training that does not teach thinking explicitly as a subject is, therefore, badly failing the society it is supposed to serve. It is not enough to teach thinking only to the most gifted. Thinking can be taught to be most disadvantaged and makes a huge difference to their lives and well-being.

To be fair, most people in education do not yet know that thinking is a skill that can be taught explicitly and directly. However, this must now be rectified. The methods for teaching thinking are available, simple, practical and effective and they have stood the test of time.

It should also be added that thinking is a skill that many people enjoy using. For example, young people hugely enjoy thinking. Each idea is an achievement. Youngsters often choose 'thinking' as their favourite subject. Indeed, in one school the punishment for misbehaviour was that you could not go to your thinking lessons!

The implications for the scientist–practitioner should be clear. We need to pay more attention to the principles of parallel thinking and relinquish our notion that criticism and debate are sufficient for a robust approach to reasoning. As I have argued elsewhere, we need ideas as much as we need information. It is time for psychologists to devote more attention to skills in creative thinking and design, to supplement those of analysis and evaluation to which the profession has devoted such considerable attention. Perhaps the introduction of special interest groups within our professional bodies devoted to creativity and design would represent an important initial step in this direction.

Chapter 13

Learning for tomorrow: professional survival in an uncertain world

> Professionals embody the learning dilemma: they are enthusiastic about continuous improvement – and often the biggest obstacle to its success.
>
> (Chris Argyris)
>
> . . . individually and collectively we have the ability to construct our own futures, albeit in circumstances not of our own choosing.
>
> (Stephen Rose)

Science and practice often end up in different worlds (Goldfried and Wolfe, 1996, 1998). For those who have consistently advocated the importance of a reciprocal relationship, this is deeply disappointing. The increasing trend towards evidence-based, or evidence-informed, practice should, therefore, be a source of pleasure to a science-based profession. However, it can become a source of regret and, at least when interpreted in an overly narrow way, lead to a sense of uneasiness that the advancement of our science could be overtaken by 'the unthinking application of scientism' (Salkovskis, 2002: 4).

The trend towards grounding practice in the available evidence is not a trend that can be ignored. However, it is a trend that must be adapted and refined if evidence-based practice is going to be sensitive to different populations and contexts for delivery (Mace and Moorey, 2001).

In considering the impact of scientific evidence on our practice, now and in the future, and how this might relate to the social embeddedness of psychology as a profession (see Chapter 6), we must acknowledge that science is a marketable product. It has an investment value to commercial sponsors who may have an interest in promoting one interpretation of science over another. Sturdee (2001), for example, comments that, when contemplating the nature of evidence, we must be concerned with some key questions including:

- Who decides what counts as evidence?
- What status should an outcome be given?
- What is the best way to use this information?
- Who will be its principal exploiter?

- What is the likely impact of this information?
- Who will benefit most (and least) from it?

The questions Sturdee poses serve as a reminder that we are not dealing with simple questions about best practice but rather that there are likely to be winners and losers, depending on how the constructs of science and evidence are defined and by whom. In reconceptualizing the scientist–practitioner model we need, therefore, to simultaneously understand our investment value to commercial sponsors and recognize whose interests are being served in order that we might maximize our chances of remaining ethically employed in the years to come.

In thinking about the future, we consider the issue of how psychologists might continue to offer unique value to their clients. Specifically, we examine three critical and inter-related areas that we believe can help secure our future as an applied discipline. These are (1) continuing professional development (CPD) and some of the vehicles through which this can be achieved; (2) the place of psychology in a market economy and (3) how these factors relate to the future of the scientist–practitioner. These are considered in turn.

CONTINUING PROFESSIONAL DEVELOPMENT AS A MEANS OF IMPROVING PRACTICE

Where different forms of knowledge are equally valued as appropriate for different purposes, there is the potential for practitioners to engage with their science more collaboratively. The need for new forms of collaboration that respect different modes of knowledge are essential, as highlighted in Chapter 6. The rapid pace of knowledge development and the diverse forms of practice emerging from this underline the importance of collaboration for our CPD.

As Guest (2000) has pointed out, it was once possible to obtain an initial qualification linked with training and be reasonably confident about keeping well-informed. Attending the occasional course or conference and reading appropriate journals was enough and most professional bodies did not require you to commit to formal, ongoing continuing professional development (Lane, 1980/1991). However, the last decade has witnessed the introduction of compulsory re-accreditation emerging in some professions and compulsory CPD in others. The forms of CPD that are recognized have also been widened to acknowledge the value that practitioners gain from engagement with their community of practice (Garnett, 2004).

There is also a growing recognition that our professional integrity and survival are tied to our commitment to remain informed and to be able to justify our practice (Guest, 2000). We witness this trend from a number of sources. First, there is the application of clinical governance whose presence is increasingly being felt in health and social care settings but which, in adapted forms, is also finding its way into other areas of practice. (One example of this is Viner's (2004) research investigating suitable models for use in general veterinary practice. This research led to the development of a community for practice with other vets which has enabled the community to create an applicable governance model to fit the realities of veterinary practice. Arguably, a similar model could be applied to practice within professional psychology.)

Second, is the creation by the British Psychological Society (BPS) of an explicit policy on CPD (2004). During 2000, the BPS membership voted to make CPD mandatory which means that psychologists holding Practising Certificates are required to undertake CPD if they wish to retain their Chartered Status. The policy states that CPD must cover at least some aspect of each of the four roles shared by all chartered psychologists. The four roles are:

- ethics – developing, implementing and maintaining personal and professional standards and ethical practice;
- practice – applying psychological and related methods, concepts, models and knowledge derived from reproducible research findings;
- research and evaluation – researching and developing new and existing psychological methods, concepts, models, theories and instruments in psychology;
- communication – communicating psychological knowledge, principles, methods, needs and policy requirements.

The function and benefits of CPD are outlined in Table 4 below. Implicit within this is, we believe, a commitment to retaining our identity as scientist–practitioners.

Despite the growing emphasis on CPD, it is interesting to note that professional development is still seen principally as a personal process organized around individual models of learning and development. This is perhaps ironic given that in our professional practice, we emphasize interpersonal and systemic models alongside personal ones. Although the model of the individual practitioner providing service to an individual client remains dominant, many aspects of our work no longer take this form. We work, serve and learn in teams within organizations. Our knowledge exists not just as individual intellectual capital but also as social capital.

It follows then, that if our concern is the impact of learning on practice we need to go further than individualized models of professional development. In operationalizing a competence driven and autonomous professional model of development planning (Lane, 1980/1991) and taking account of our debate here, we need to consider ways in which CPD might come to be broadened to include systemic as well as individual frameworks.

Ensuring the impact of our learning through identifying frameworks for CPD

Learning is (or at least should be) a lifelong process. Senge (1990) goes as far as suggesting that to practise a discipline is to be a lifelong learner. This is implicit in the BPS policy, although yet to be formally espoused through official

Table 4 BPS policy on continuing professional development

Introduction

- CPD is defined as 'any process or activity that provides added value to the capability of the professional through the increase in knowledge, skills and personal qualities necessary for the appropriate execution of professional and technical duties, often termed competence' (Professional Associations Research Network).
- Rapid changes in the evidence base, the technology and the skill requirements of the profession make CPD a career long process through which professionals remain up-to date by augmenting and enhancing their competence. It is an extension of the basic principle in the Society's Code of Conduct (Clause 2): 'Psychologists shall endeavour to maintain and develop their professional competence, to recognise and work within its limits, and to identify and ameliorate factors which restrict it'.
- CPD is not new, it is a continuation of what is needed to keep up-to-date, informed and well-trained in order to deliver quality work in which the public can have confidence. Whilst there is clearly an ethical obligation for Psychologists to undertake CPD, there are also many advantages for the individual practitioner.

Why do we need CPD?

CPD provides benefits at several different levels. Public accountability is seen as being increasingly important to Professionals. The knowledge that Chartered Psychologists are required to update and develop their knowledge and skills on an ongoing basis, serves to reassure the public – this has benefits for clients as well as the individual psychologist, their employing organisation and the Society. A robust system of CPD will also be of benefit in preparation for Statutory Regulation.

There are also links to the National Occupational Standards (NOS) for applied psychologists, which set out the *minimum* level of competence required for qualification as a practitioner. The standards provide a useful reference point when planning CPD, particularly in relation to identifying and clarifying development needs.

The benefits include:

For the Individual Psychologist

- Helping to ensure that psychologists are offering the most effective service they can to their clients.
- Improving long-term career prospects and enhancing professional standing.
- Providing documented evidence of an individual psychologist's commitment to their chosen profession and of their continued competence.
- Providing a reference document for use both in updating a CV and in recalling details of topics studied as well as for appraisals and interviews.
- Anticipating change and not being driven by it.
- Ensuring best practice in the current litigious climate.

For the Employer/Business/Organisation

- Ensuring that professionals are capable, competent and well trained will help to contribute to organisational goals and service provision.

For the Society

- Increasingly, professional bodies are being required to demonstrate that their members are taking a systematic approach to CPD – in order to maintain standards of professional practice.

Source: Reproduced with kind permission of the British Psychological Society

re-registration procedures. However, Guest (2000) maintains that professional bodies will be seen to have made real progress with their lifelong learning policies when advertisements appear asking not just for qualifications but for people whose learning is up-to-date and related to the work they will be doing today and in the future. So how can we achieve this?

The principle which underpins lifelong learning is that we can never fully 'arrive' at mastery but spend our careers working towards it. We see as critical to this endeavour any activity that offers a pathway towards mastery in each of the areas covered in this book: namely our skills in reasoning, formulating, creating and critiquing. However, we would also advocate an increased emphasis on approaches to CPD that explicitly work towards mastery of the skills of team learning, team working and systems thinking. Within this context a number of possibilities emerge, including models of science, reflective practice, supervision, work-based learning and models of intellectual capital. These are considered next.

Models of science

In our reformulated vision of the scientist–practitioner model we see CPD as including a commitment to maintaining ourselves as competent scientists. As noted by the BPS (2004) the training of applied psychologists is grounded in the science of psychology which is then applied to human problems. However, this begs the question 'What type of scientist are we?' If it is not sufficient to maintain a commitment to empiricist theories, as we argued in Chapter 5, we must include alternative models and varied modes of knowledge. At the very least, we need to be familiar with alternative theories of science and consider how we will reflect these in our CPD.

For example, if we were to include as CPD the pursuit of an enquiry from a critical knowledge perspective of our service and ourselves, different perspectives and avenues for development might arise. Thus, for educational psychologists concerned with achievement and exclusion within the school system one area of critical knowledge relevant to our CPD might be the field of critical pedagogy. Critiques of education from a Marxist perspective (see McLaren, 1998) a Marxist feminist perspective (see Davies, 1983), the Black Psychology perspective (Jones, 1972) or the cultural perspective (Keise *et al.*, 1993) raise important questions about the purpose of education (to socialize the young into compliance with a capitalist ethic) the process used (the achievement and exclusion agenda) and the perspective employed (a deficit model). These provide a useful counterpoint to the notion that our practice is based on enhancing personal potential based on a person-centred perspective. (There is also an argument that no educational system anywhere has really been driven by a commitment to realizing the potential of all our children, see Eggleston *et al.*, 1986; Ford *et al.*, 1982; Herrick, 1971).

Using a systems framework goes beyond making individual objectives congruent with organizational ones. Specifically, it requires us to look not at the beliefs of individuals (ourselves as practitioners) but the effects of the system (our activity as part of it) on life chances. The interest is not so much in what individual practitioners say, but how their actions form part of a whole which discriminates against certain groups and also against those who refuse to conform to the dominant ideology. From a systems perspective self-reflection and personal development are not enough. Engagement with alternative modes of knowledge (including social action) need to form part of CPD.

Reflective practice

Alongside the central role of the psychologist as scientist–practitioner is increasing recognition of the psychologist as a self-reflective practitioner (BPS, 2005). As reflective practitioners, psychologists must appreciate the critical importance of self-awareness and the need to reflect on their own practice from this perspective. This self-awareness is extended to 'the importance of diversity, the social and cultural context of their work, working within an ethical framework, and the need for continuing professional and personal development' (BPS, 2004: 17). Specifically, the BPS policy requires that psychologists show in their CPD record that they have been able to identify personal development needs, plan appropriate development activities to meet identified needs and reflect upon learning and its application to practice.

Within counselling psychology and psychotherapy practice this goes further and reflects a broader philosophical commitment to intersubjective experience and the use of self-knowledge as part of the shared enterprise with the client. The requirements for continued registration on the BPS Register of Psychologists Specialising in Psychotherapy include just such a commitment to personal development work. However, this register goes further and requires re-registration after a defined period for which evidence of supervision, personal and professional development are necessary. This it shares with other psychotherapy bodies such as the British Association for Behavioural and Cognitive Psychotherapies which has a five-year re-registration process and the European Federation of Psychologists' Associations which similarly includes a re-registration process for its awards.

If use of self is part of the offer we make to our clients, then a commitment to CPD in the field of personal as well as professional development is critical. This tradition is long-standing in the counselling field more generally, but the form that this should take within applied psychology is more contentious. For example, should it involve personal therapy or would life coaching be more appropriate? Should individual psychologists be able to identify their own vehicles for personal development or should choice be circumscribed, with specific guidelines laid down by our professional bodies? What would be the expected 'outputs' of personal development and how do we monitor the impact of more diverse approaches?

Encompassing a broader outlook also raises cultural considerations. Much personal development work, for example, has a distinctly Western slant, as is evident in many forms of therapy and workshops which emphasize overcoming problems (located within the individual) and achieving personal authenticity. In view of the increasing need to ground our practice in context, and to remain respectful of diversity, we need to consider whether these approaches are sufficient or whether we should embed our personal development within frameworks that are more systemically-oriented, multiculturally-aware and politically-informed. At the same time, there is a growing interest in Eastern philosophies, alternative and holistic approaches to personal growth which are pervading our culture in the form of the so-called 'mind, body and spirit' resources. Would any personal development work couched within these approaches be recognized as legitimate CPD or not? Thus, although CPD includes personal as well as the professional development, the forms this might usefully take are yet to be substantively explored.

Supervision

How should the personalization of knowledge and its links with both scientist- and reflective-practitioner models link with supervision? Supervision is one of the most critical and frequently described forms of CPD, providing a formal, independent process of reflection and review which enables practitioners to increase individual self-awareness, develop their competence and critique their work. In exploring the contribution of supervision to coaching psychology, Lane and van Oudtshoorn (cited in Jarvis, 2004) identify a number of benefits that supervision provides. These are adapted here:

- It offers protection to clients. Cases are discussed with trained professionals who are able to identify areas of potential concern and offer advice or referral to specialist support if appropriate.
- It offers practitioners the opportunity to reflect on their work and gain insights to improve their interventions.
- It helps practitioners identify their own personal strengths and weaknesses in order to realistically judge what limitations to set with respect to the type of work they undertake.
- It facilitates learning from peers who have had similar experiences and thus further develops practitioner-related skills.
- It offers the opportunity to keep up-to-date with professional developments in the field and to continually work to increase practitioner-based competencies.

Because of these benefits, many in the various branches of applied psychology believe that supervision is an important part of continuing professional development. There is less agreement, however, about what exactly constitutes 'supervision' and whether it is necessary throughout a career or just while training. Some fields of practice take a much stronger line on supervision than others (Lawton and Feltham, 2000).

In the context of therapy practice Stoltenberg and Delworth (1987), amongst others, have argued for a developmental approach in which supervision is modified according to the stage of professional development. They identify how practitioners' capacity for autonomy and self-awareness and their degree of anxiety and confidence need to be accommodated by the style of supervision and supervisory methods. Thus, didactic supervisory input early on in individuals' careers offers structured advice in a way that is helpful and containing; later stages are increasingly focused on the less tangible aspects of therapy such as case formulation, the therapeutic relationship and process-oriented issues.

Although some have warned against applying stage models too rigidly (see Hawkins and Shohet, 1989), developmental approaches can map on to theories of the stages of professional development more broadly (Eraut, 2000; Skovholt and Rønnestad, 1992) and thus foster practitioner progression more systematically. We would also advocate that supervision provides a key mechanism for promoting a knowledge culture, particularly if we adopt a broader approach which transcends relying on the traditional one-to-one mentor figure. In adopting this broader position, we can begin to incorporate the elements identified by Rajan *et al.* (1999) that underpin a successful knowledge culture, where supervision includes:

- communities of practice – self-organized groups to exchange ideas and thoughts on common practices;
- virtual teams – brought together across locations or divisions (functional and theoretical);
- cross-functional team working – to break up stultified modes of thinking;
- toleration of mistakes – to support a 'no blame' culture which acknowledges that if you innovate mistakes will happen;
- action learning – to arrange work in such a way that it encourages experiential learning.

The notion of supervision as creating distinct knowledge cultures also enables us to consider the contribution of the workplace as a setting through which lifelong learning is achieved.

Work-based learning

An additional framework for thinking about CPD is the rapidly developing discipline of work-based learning. Work-based learning is not about the location of learning (in the sense of the old-style sandwich courses) but rather about forms of learning specific to practice and how they may be developed and applied. Our work can be a source of learning to improve and critically challenge practice. Ongoing experience from organizations such as the National Centre for Work Based Learning Partnerships (Middlesex University) and the Professional Development Foundation has led to the development of ways in which practitioners can share learning and research about learning from analysis of their practice. Particular tools that have added value to the CPD debate include:

- a 'learning review', including a personal knowledge and skills audit in order to establish what knowledge and skills the practitioner has acquired to be applied to future learning;

- programme planning, to create learning that aligns service focus, client and personal need, stakeholder commitment and access to related structural capital;
- work-based research that addresses the forms of analysis applicable to the issues that the practitioner faces in order to capture, use and enhance the structural capital of the organization.

Experience in a number of Centres over many years (for example between the Professional Development Foundation and the National Centre for Work-Based Learning, as well as the various practitioner-led conferences organized within BPS Divisions) together with numerous projects brought together in the annual British Association for Counselling and Psychotherapy Practitioner Research Conference, has pointed to the high quality research that can be generated from practice. Practice Research Networks are an increasing trend (Goldfried and Eubanks-Carter, 2004). Practitioner-led research as CPD is under-reported in the literature but its impact on practice through workshops and conferences can be substantial. (For example, the work of the Nottingham University based Behaviour Support Conference has brought practitioners together over many years to share and develop innovative practices; see Gray *et al.*, 1994.) Specifically, a work-based learning model of CPD represents a commitment to address impacts and enhance the knowledge capital of the organization. It moves closer to the idea of CPD as part of developing a knowledge culture framework of systems, values and behaviours (Lane and Rajan, 2005). It also ensures that the work setting can become a context for lifelong and transformational learning.

Models of intellectual capital

Schön makes the point that our professional artistry needs to be understood in terms of reflection-in-action, and as such it can play a central role in the description of our professional competence. The concept of reflection-in-action has resonance with work in the field of action learning (Revan, 1998), learning conversations (Thomas and Harri-Augstein, 1985), Bono's Parallel Thinking (1995) and intellectual capital models (Burton-Jones, 1999; Lane and Rajan, 2005; Stewart, 1997). Thus, learning within context becomes central to our CPD. This is taken up further in the following section on the changing market for skills. There is also the potential for the university-based world of science and the work-based world of applied practice to collaborate here thus breaking down the science–practice divide. Garnett (2004) has identified key contributions that university/work-based partnerships can make to building intellectual capital within work-based projects:

- focus on organizational objectives to ensure the knowledge it develops has a performative edge and is thus of value to the organization;
- develop strategies for working with tacit knowledge, by focusing reflexive practice to enhance individual knowledge recognition, creation, dissemination and use;

- fully exploit and reinforce the crucial role of structural capital in fostering knowledge recognition, dissemination, creation and use;
- explore the nature and implications of the apparent lineage between work-based learning, knowledge creation, organizational decision-making and bounded rationality.

The partnership between the workplace (practice) and the university (science) provides a powerful resource to overcome the research–practice divide and adds substantial benefits to both at a time when psychology is having to establish its credibility amongst other professions. What is clear, however, is that if our learning is to impact it needs to be part of a process of knowledge creation and exchange. It has to be embedded in a knowledge culture comprising systems, values and behaviours that transcend individual values, and even the values of single organizations (Rajan *et al.*, 2000). This brings us to the place of psychology within a broader market economy.

THE PLACE OF PSYCHOLOGY IN A MARKET ECONOMY

The major changes to the workplace in the UK in the 1990s (in particular the creation of the single European market, the conclusion of the Uruguay Round of trade liberalization and the recession in the UK) gave rise to the novel concept of employability. The end of the job-for-life culture and move towards inter-industry transferable skills generated the need for individuals having to take more responsibility for their own learning and development and for their own marketability. As noted by Gordon Brown, in his capacity as Chancellor of the Exchequer, 'A new employment agenda is vital given the background of intensified global competition and technological advances we all face as the 21st century approaches' (cited in Lane *et al.*, 2000).

Globalization and the rapid pace of technological change have increased awareness that businesses must remain competitive, both nationally and internationally. Western economies need to play the knowledge game. Britain, alongside every other country, needs to differentiate her uniqueness in ways which competitors find hard to imitate. These assets are increasingly in the form of knowledge, skills and creativity. The Government's main aim is for British business to close the performance gap with its competitors in terms of productivity and ability to produce innovative products and create high value service (Lane *et. al.*, 2000).

This aim is echoed internationally. With the expansion of the European Union specifically, and greater competitiveness generally, there is a need to enhance our skills as individuals and organizations. Government and employers are urging individuals to engage with training and lifelong learning to ensure continued employability. As knowledge becomes increasingly internationalized, new players are offering 'psychology-based' intervention packages in schools, health care, prisons, business and coaching. These commoditize psychology and offer supposed guaranteed results with which individual practitioners and established psychology services now compete.

This development is seriously impacting on us as professionals. We are faced with two contradictory trends: rigidity by regulation through state monopoly of credentialing and flexibility in supply, at a time when emerging professions appear to offer similar services to psychologists without the costs of regulation. For example, why would someone spend several years training to become a counselling psychologist when you can become a life coach after just five days and start offering your services to the public on this basis? The results of psychological research can easily be translated into commercially packaged manuals which bypass the practitioner's traditional role of interpreter of research into practice. As a consequence of operating in a knowledge-driven labour market, we need to be clear where the added value lies in employing a psychologist as opposed to any other professional, including those whose competence derives from life experience and limited training.

Knowledge management for added value is also seen as the key for greater competition. Due to the 'more-for-less' culture so prevalent today, companies have to accelerate the pace of product innovation in tandem with lean production and shorter time-to-market methods. Knowledge management becomes the vehicle through which accelerated innovation occurs. As Paul Lynch, ICL's Director in charge of its alliance with Microsoft observed: 'The speed of change in our market place is such that knowledge had a short shelf life. Getting people to understand that helped them to get their heads around why they needed to share' (cited in Rajan et al., 2000). Global competition has, therefore, forced companies to be fast, innovative and flexible. Professions have to respond to this and become commercially smarter while retaining a commitment to knowledge developed over extended periods. It is a difficult balance to maintain.

Whilst there is a burgeoning literature on how organizations can respond to the pressures of global competition, the application of this to the professions is less developed. However, we do feel these pressures and will increasingly do so. We need to understand what would give psychologists a competitive advantage. We believe that the scientist–practitioner model might be part of our unique professional offer to the market place, not in the sense of enabling us to quote research, but through the application of models of enquiry capable of dealing with complexity.

Two areas that might have particular relevance to understanding how a service might add unique value derive from research which looks at competitive advantage (Barney, 2001, using the Resource Based View) and the Dynamic Capability View (Teece et al., 1997) which has particular value in considering corporate strategy. Within these frameworks an organization can be considered as a bundle of resources which represent the potential source of competitive advantage. That advantage is particularly held where the resources are valuable, rare, inimitable, and non-substitutable (Bowman and Ambrosini, 2003). These same questions can be asked of psychology as a resource. What do we offer that meets these conditions? Possibilities include:

- value that is added by delivering service at lower cost or by differentiating a service through added value;
- psychology as a relatively scarce resource that enables an organization (or profession) to generate superior margins against competitors;
- the combination of a valuable and rare resource that arises from the specific knowledge set psychologists bring which is not shared by our competitors.

Two other conditions address the sustainability of our profession:

- The more difficult it is for others to replicate our service the longer-lived will be our advantage. Inimitability results from mechanisms such as information asymmetries and social complexity which protect the resource from imitation. This has particular relevance to the way a psychological service might be constructed and the difficulty that others would have in imitating that construction.
- A resource is non-substitutable if it cannot be easily replaced by another.

These conditions create a series of questions that we can ask and which we can discuss with the stakeholders in our service. For example:

- What does psychology bring that lowers costs or adds value?
- What do you bring that adds value to your client or reduces the cost of service to your client?
- What does the profession bring that is rare and that generates an advantage?
- What do you bring that is rare and adds advantage?
- What information resources within the community of practice would be difficult for others to copy?
- What makes your own practice inimitable?
- What elements of psychological practice cannot easily be replaced by another resource?
- What elements of your service cannot easily be replaced by another professional or service provider?

The scientist–practitioner model, we believe, creates a framework within which we can research, design, build, deliver and evaluate unique solutions in high impact areas. As we see it, this value is not shared by practitioners from other areas who do not combine science with practice. We all, through the long-standing commitment to giving psychology away (Miller, 1969), have contributed to the provision of lower cost services through training others, including our clients, to operate the models we design. Thus, it could be argued that we are often able to find the most cost-effective solution for a client, regardless of whether that client is an individual or organization.

Nonetheless, the need to demonstrate not only that our interventions work, but also that they are efficient and provide value for money, poses critical challenges for the way we organize our service as professionals. We would see these challenges as including:

- the need to challenge conventional thinking about measurement and prediction, as well as looking differently at our current models of the assessment cycle, to ensure that we appreciate how our practice is socially embedded;
- the need to recognize that realizing talent for our clients is about development and includes a key role for understanding the learning journey (see Chapter 6) on which they are embarked;
- the need to understand why initiatives/interventions can fail by recognizing the key role of the client context/environment, its internal workings and culture;
- the need to understand that psychological consulting is itself changing. The task is not one of offering psychological products but rather developing services that reflect what clients want and need and ensuring that different models of consulting meet their requirements.

A service organization has an obligation to maximize leverage on its financial capital or resources. Similarly, as professionals we have a duty to realize the intellectual capital and capability of our clients and ourselves. If we think of this in relation to our client relationships we see each learning journey as an opportunity to enhance talent (human capital), not simply as a way to solve problems. We can consider our role as professionals within an organizational context (our service offer) and examine our potential to leverage that capital.

This potential is expressed where we have the freedom required to innovate through reconceptualizing the service, developing ourselves through the experience and achieving quantum shifts in raising stakeholder value. How the organization enables its stakeholders to recognize the relationship between their own commitments and development and the success of the organization in delivering service more broadly represents the core mechanism for converting intellectual capital into stakeholder value. Where an organization also acts to acknowledge, celebrate and develop all its stakeholder relationships the potential for leverage of human capital is multiplied. We need, therefore, to ask of the structure within which we offer our services to clients: Does the organization have as a core purpose the enhancement of the human capital of all its stakeholders?

THE FUTURE OF THE SCIENTIST–PRACTITIONER

As scientists we must respond to the economic and political requirements for relevance and applicability to social issues. Applied psychology clearly has that responsibility. Psychology as both a science and as an applied discipline must continue working towards effectively breaching some of the barriers that have existed between different branches of our profession. We cannot continue to live in the separate worlds of researcher and practitioner. This requires a balancing of the relationship between the scientific norm of single discipline research groups working on curiosity-led research questions and transdisciplinary, collaborative working aimed at achieving impact on issues of direct relevance to society.

This change in knowledge production mode requires changes in the culture of research organizations, the professional aspirations of researchers, the assessment criteria by which research is judged and the method of allocation of research funding. Thus, the organization of research is critical to the achievement of transdisciplinary knowledge production and the realization of the economic benefits of research. But it also touches crucially on our identity as scientists and the way we are judged.

The public, private and university research sectors have undergone dramatic changes over the last two decades. In the early 1990s the Government White Paper 'Realising Our Potential' (Cm 2250, 1993) sought to maximize value for money from the public investment in science and technology through improved management and closer engagement with industry. Simultaneously the private research establishments were under increasing pressure to focus research on specific goals and serving the customer (Corcoran, 1994). However, by the new millennium it became clear that scientific research was a central hub of the developing knowledge economy. The European Commission identifies both excellence in scientific research and innovation as the key to European industrial competitiveness (2004). Indeed, the New Economy is based upon the development of new creative and knowledge-based industries. Thus, facilitation of the flow of research outputs from the universities and research institutions to the perceived end-users has been a central tenet of government initiatives to develop the UK capability to enter this New Economy. A third role for universities (supplementary to their teaching and research roles) and an explicit role for scientific research institutions has arisen: to engage with industry and end-users directly and focus on production of more relevant outputs capable of providing returns for the investment of public money (Boden et al., 1998). Thus, universities are envisaged as major agents of economic growth with an onus on them as stimulators of technology transfer (Department of Trade and Industry, 2004).

The economic and political drivers outlined above have resulted in a substantial shift in the process of knowledge production. Gibbons et al., (1994), as we argued in Chapter 6, postulated that the mode of knowledge production has moved away from mode 1 (as epitomized by single discipline working isolated from its economic, social and political context) towards mode 2 (identified by transdisciplinary working aimed at specific applications through the collaborative engagement of networks of investigators). Such a research production mode (mode 2) sits at the centre of the European Research Area (ERA) envisaged by the European Commission. These Networks of Excellence and Integrated Projects seek to establish fluid networks of workers contributing to the 'solution' of a single issue of social and political import. These networks engage not only the scientific élite but also other 'actors' such as practitioners and policy-makers. Etzkowitz and

Leydesdorff's (2000) triple helix model describes the resulting dynamic and fluctuating interplay between university–industry–government. We would argue that this needs to go much further and encompass all of the four modes of knowledge outlined in Chapter 6.

Thus, the conventional linear model of innovation where research is seen as the creative first stage in a process leading from science to technology to service or product within the market is no longer seen to apply. As Salter *et al*. (2000) argue such a model is dead. Within this context, our professional aspirations and identity as scientists must also be addressed. We are still often judged by our ability to acquire the traditional rewards for scientific endeavour; that is, professional reputation and access to further resources. Our professional identity as scientists is too often bound by our reputation to publish significant work in peer-reviewed journals.

In their study of scientists' experiences and perceptions of management in science research institutes, Cohen *et al*. (1999) found there to be a perceived tension between the engagement with downstream end-users (clients) and the professional aspirations of the scientific worker with the increasing emphasis on entrepreneurship being experienced as problematic. Mode 1 knowledge production was associated with single discipline 'blue sky' research and creativity resulting in high-impact publications and access to research grants. Mode 2 production was more focused on application, tended to be through commissioned work and resulted in a report to the sponsor. The role of scientific reputation and the intensity of reputational competition has been identified by Whitley (2002) as a determinant of the ability to co-ordinate research to solve problems and the ease by which new intellectual goals and approaches are incorporated within programmes to deal with new kinds of problems. The traditional structures of research assessment tend to inhibit use of these broader modes (3 and 4) of knowledge production, favouring mode 1 while proclaiming mode 2.

This split in perception of the 'quality' of research outputs highlights the paradox lying at the heart of the current assessment process for publicly funded research. Science policy is aiming for integration of commissioned and publicly funded work whilst assessment of and incentive for the individual scientist is dominated by the outputs of mode 1 production. Current assessment exercises in publicly funded research organizations depend upon criteria of 'research excellence' and quality of published outputs. A recent study by Waldron (in press) has shown the assessment criteria of publicly funded research in the UK to be inconsistent with the new roles of the research organizations.

Within this representation the knowledge production cycle assessment process is based upon peer-review of research outputs such as publications and this is the dominant feedback to the research organizations. The feedback from users of the research diminishes the further the research is translated into the provision of goods and services (upper portion of Figure 6). This is mirrored in the wealth-creation cycle (lower portion of Figure 6) where the feedback is diminished as it progresses back to the research provider. Mode 1 knowledge production can be

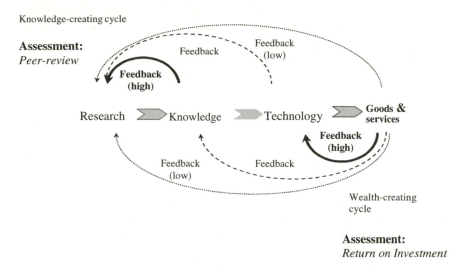

Knowledge-creating cycle

Figure 6 Feedback within knowledge- and wealth- creating cycles

seen as restricted to the left of the diagram with no or little interaction with technology providers or manufacturers, whereas mode 2 seeks to encompass the needs and focus of the right hand of the cycle. We argue that adding mode 3 and 4 to the model could add considerable value between the researcher and the user/provider end. Feedback from all four modes would encourage research that reflects on services as experienced by users, and user and peer consensus, as well as provide a valuable critique of the purpose, perspectives and processes used. However, such expansions in assessment criteria are rare. For the future of society as well as the relationship between science and practice this needs to change.

PSYCHOLOGY AND LEARNING FOR TOMORROW

In thinking about learning for the needs of tomorrow we must hold in mind the question Schön (1987) poses on whether prevailing concepts of professional education can ever create a curriculum which is capable of addressing the complex, unstable, uncertain, and conflictual worlds of practice. There can be little doubt that we are witnessing a new outlook on learning across the lifespan as something that is individually-tailored, organizationally embedded and culturally and politically mindful and that we need to find ways of responding to this in the context of global competition and the internationalizing of knowledge.

Several implications flow from this position. The first is that we must actively prepare for this future and ensure that we have the tools necessary to plan, respond to current pressures, recover from periods of difficulty and mitigate the effect of events outside our control. We would see CPD as critical to achieving this. However, what emerges from the current milieu surrounding CPD is that as learners, we are all different. Consequently, varied purposes may require alternative learning journeys and we will need to tailor our models of CPD accordingly. (A similar position was advocated in Chapter 4, in relation to maximizing creativity in practice.) Through carving out individually-tailored development plans, we can be challenged to consider our core perspectives and allow them to be open to deconstruction and possible reconstruction. Arguably, this could be one of the most critical functions of CPD through which we can prevent intellectual rigor mortis and maintain flexibility and growth.

In order to accommodate the demands of an increasingly competitive world, we need to embrace forms of CPD that encourage transformational rather than accumulative learning. There is now considerable activity in the field of transformational learning. Since its introduction to the literature by Mezirow (1991) it has become possible to conceive of learning as a process by which previous uncritically accepted perspectives become open to challenge and change (Cranton and Roy, 2003; Lane and Donegan, 1993).

Wang and Sarbo (2004) have challenged us to consider a contextually adapted approach to learning philosophies and the situational role we take as adult teachers and learners in generating transformational experiences. In terms of CPD, this may help us focus our attention on the underlying philosophical and psychological models we use and their appropriateness to different learning purposes. For example, Mezirow's (1991) theory of transformative learning focuses on how we can make sense or meaning out of our experiences whilst Knowles' (1989, 1990) notion of andragogy builds on humanistic theory which emphasizes the relationship elements of learning. Elias and Merriam (1995), in contrast, point to the value of behavioural concepts in terms of design of learning environments, liberal philosophical models as frameworks for expertise in the transmission of knowledge, and the contribution of radical models for supporting but not determining directions for learning. These models, amongst others, provide food for thought in how to approach the design of CPD in ways that might enhance our ability to respond to organizational, economic, political and global trends as well as individual needs.

The second implication, as we proposed in Chapter 6, is that we need to think of applied psychology as an identity not a specific set of competencies. Being a scientist–practitioner is about engaging with a psychological view and balancing our commitment to delivering client benefits with our own personal agenda. It is important to encourage openness in that discussion; psychology is an applied discipline in which the self of the practitioner is very present and through which the creative and scientific basis of our work comes to life.

In order to establish and maintain this identity, we also need to ensure that the profession has leaders at all levels who have the skills, values and behaviours consistent with the professional culture we are seeking to develop. Helpful recent trends in this area include the creation by the BPS of a College of Fellows to address future issues in science and practice. We cannot have fine words which talk of inclusion yet marginalize certain client groups or members of the profession.

Similarly, we cannot allow the profession to operate according to the dictates of a dominant ideology that says that science determines practice, rather than representing a mutual exchange. Addressing this issue adequately will involve the courage to eschew concepts and models that promise far more than they can deliver.

We should also acknowledge the role our discipline has played in generating the recognition that valuing, nurturing, and managing our human resources appropriately really is critical to society. New social partnerships are likely to emerge to assist people in pursuit of employability, health, education and quality of life. We have an important role to play in these areas, informing practice through research, and research through practice and this is likely to continue in the future.

Finally, in spite of the best efforts of those of our profession who have committed themselves to promoting diversity within the workforce and the profession, major barriers still exist. While some are flourishing on a range of initiatives, others may lack the opportunity to navigate their way through the professional networks which can dominate practice. There are implications for increasing social exclusion if this dilemma is not addressed. Dominant ideologies have, in the past, been used to exclude some areas of practice and it is only through a combination of active policies and equity initiatives that we will overcome this. As psychologists we are actively involved in researching this area and its impact. We need to ensure that our practice within the profession reflects what we know from research. The professions in general and psychology in particular need to ensure that their initiatives are coherent thereby ensuring that all parties involved come to believe that they are full stakeholders.

Conclusion: The scientist–practitioner model: a new vision

> We must interact with the world in order to see what we might create. Through engagement in the moment, we evoke our futures.
>
> (Margaret Wheatley)
>
> The voyage of discovery is not in seeking new landscapes but in having new eyes.
>
> (Marcel Proust)

In this book, we have argued that an identity as a scientist–practitioner continues to add unique value to our work as psychologists. However, as originally conceived it was but one narrative. Multiple narratives are now possible, each one contributing a different type of rigour and value to our practice. It is up to us, individually and collectively, to identify which narratives serve us best in which situations, including those that might arise in an uncertain future.

Each chapter of this book has attempted to address a different 'strand' of the tension between the worlds of conceptual- and practice-based knowledge. In focusing on reasoning, formulating, creating and evaluating, we do not pretend that these are the only tasks relevant to the modern scientist–practitioner. However, by identifying and exploring at least some of the skills that are fundamental to applied psychology, we hope that this book might contribute to the debate about how to unite different sources of information in the quest for effective and transformational approaches to our clients' dilemmas and hopes for the future.

Specifically, we have attempted to consider ways in which the scientist–practitioner model now needs to be revised and why. Born (at least officially) within the world of 1940s psychology, we can appreciate how the model as originally conceived was a product of its time. We can appreciate the enormity of the task that faced our predecessors and admire their resolve to identify a model that could serve the needs of future generations of psychologists. By considering more contemporary attempts to realign the scientist–practitioner model in the light of social and economic change, we can similarly appreciate the need to embrace more multifaceted interpretations, with all the implications for identity and our place alongside other professions to which this gives rise.

We have presented the argument that, for the modern scientist–practitioner, rigour is not enough. Skills in analysis must be integrated with skills in innovation and design which have traditionally been neglected in the science–practice debate. We need frameworks for developing creative and analytical skills, but the quest for accuracy has sometimes obscured the extent to which we have to invent new maps and tools. The art of telling psychological stories, manifest in formulation, requires an ability to improvise and invent because there are multiple ways through which we can come to know the world. Freeing ourselves from the notion of one ideal way is liberating both for ourselves and our clients and is a challenge that the scientist–practitioner debate has traditionally failed to address.

This does, of course, have major implications for our understanding of ourselves as 'scientists'. There are many ways of being a scientist and we need to engage with the possibilities afforded by different theories about scientific enquiry. To question the nature of science does not diminish its importance, but there is an urgent need to revisit our allegiance to the empiricist model as the epitome of scientific respectability because this does not reflect how science itself is evolving. Moreover, we have argued that our scientific knowledge must be tempered by the wisdom of practitioners who are actually facilitating transformations in their clients' lives and the need to recognize the socially embedded nature of scientific studies. The relationship between science and practice cannot be one-way. Considering the contribution of different scientific stories enables us to grasp this reality more fully, presenting us with the new challenge of how we straddle the tension between the inconsistencies of scientific practices with the definitive pronouncements about truth increasingly demanded of us.

It is inevitable that in the current professional and political climate, we will attempt to manage some of these dilemmas through recourse to an over-arching professional identity. Ideas about who 'owns' knowledge changes over time and is a contentious issue. Do we own it, or give it away? Do we create it or have it imposed upon us? At a time when different professions, stakeholders and even nations vie for power, claiming knowledge through recourse to an over-arching identity facilitates a sense of belonging and safety. It also provides a framework through which we can organize our activities and plan our future learning.

The need to tell new stories, create new maps, improvise and evaluate, are skills illustrated clearly and, we believe, cogently in the chapters from our guest contributors.

As noted in our introduction, it was not our intention to represent all forms of applied practice as there are simply too many to do justice to them all. Moreover, to lay claim to any degree of representativeness would have been problematic as there are increasingly wide variations amongst practitioners within the same discipline. The chapters from our guest contributors are not, therefore, offered as definitive pronouncements about the position of a particular discipline on the scientist–practitioner debate but rather one of many potential responses to what it means to be a professional psychologist. Their diversity is intentional and something that, in this book, we have aimed to capitalize on because it reflects our belief that there are multiple ways in which being a scientist–practitioner might manifest itself.

Different in subject matter, work context and scientific stance, each chapter nonetheless illustrates some central dilemma associated with being a scientist–practitioner – dilemmas with which we are all grappling, in some shape or form, on a daily basis. Andy Miller and Norah Frederickson, for example, highlight the incomplete nature of many theories and research studies for understanding the complexity of issues which face modern educational psychologists and argue the case for 'best guess' interventions. They make the point that we do not become scientist–practitioners simply by carrying out a large number of measurements. Educational psychologists are often perceived by the public and other professions as having a critical role through their skills in testing, but their identity as scientist–practitioners comes from being able to engage with the complex terrains of epistemology, science and practice in the context of multiple social systems (family, school, social, political and so on).

As counselling psychologists, Dennis Bury and Susan Strauss consider some of the challenges of finding a scientific frame that is consistent with the profession's emphasis on the quality of the relationship between practitioner and client. How is it possible to operate in settings where formal psychological testing, diagnosis and standardized interventions are applied, whilst retaining a commitment to a discipline that has consistently questioned assumptions of labelling and pathologizing in favour of the search for more subjective and idiographic meanings? In looking at the scientific aspects of the counselling psychologists' identities, and through returning to fundamental questions relating to 'doing' and 'being', they argue that it is possible to bring together science and practice in ways that are consistent with the humanistic roots of counselling psychology. The scientist–practitioner model, as they conceptualize it, helps define the larger framework in which psychologists practise and assists the task of problem-setting through equipping counselling psychologists with a comprehensive range of tools that can inform a multifaceted approach to knowing.

Val Haarbosch and Ian Newey, in contrast, describe the dilemmas they encountered when attempting to work with young people who have sexually offended. They highlight the particular constraints imposed by society's unwillingness to recognize this client group and the initial absence of theories and research to guide their decision-making and treatment planning. Their attempts to carve out safe, ethical and effective interventions that were underpinned by a scientist–practitioner framework highlight a fact of life for all of us: namely the need to take a leap of faith, to invent, to rely on past experience, or as Miller and Frederickson describe it, 'best guess'.

Michael Cavanagh and Anthony Grant also highlight the dilemmas of working in an area of psychology where there is, as yet, no specific scientific literature. As an emerging discipline, the lack of a substantive knowledge-base poses considerable challenges to the psychology of coaching, not least because of the explosion of interest in coaching in settings as diverse as government, business, community and personal development sectors. Drawing on complexity theory to illustrate a reconstructed understanding of our science, they propose that the scientist–practitioner model enables the profession to differentiate those coaches who practise from a background in professional psychology, and those whose experience is not under-pinned by formal training in the behavioural sciences. Innovations in coaching practice can still be grounded in an evidence base, but one that involves the reflec-tive use of current knowledge to consider how best to deliver coaching rather than ideas about which interventions are most effective or cost-efficient.

In their exposition of how the scientist–practitioner framework might apply to modern occupational psychologists, Richard Kwiatkowski and Barry Winter consider the question of what we actually 'do' with our science. In order to inter-vene effectively, they argue that we must be able to navigate the worlds of indus-try and commerce as our endeavours are embedded within domains that require non-linear thinking and creative solutions. They highlight the need to make our science palatable to our clients without allowing it to become caricatured in the process. The difference between sophistication and impact is paramount, as the most elegant responses drawn from state of the art science/evidence may not have anywhere near as much impact as a simple observation or small intervention that is well timed. In the world of organizational psychology, having recourse to evidence is not enough. We can hinder the 'take-up' of our science by presenting it in an overly complex way.

Finally, Edward de Bono addresses the much-neglected issue of how modern scientist–practitioners develop reasoning skills that are optimally constructive and creative. By comparing classification, analysis and design-based approaches, he makes the compelling case for a broader understanding of what it means to 'think effectively'. The ability to analyse, judge and evaluate, he argues, are an insufficient foundation for the reasoning skills of the modern scientist–practitioner which must also encompass the capacity to design. This will require psychologists to be explicitly trained in the art of thinking as an operational skill. It is this ability which ultimately underpins our capacity to innovate effectively, especially when formal psychological knowledge is absent, as in the case of coaching psychology and working with young people who sexually offend.

Although each chapter emphasizes one particular aspect of what it means to operate as a modern scientist–practitioner each theme will, surely, resonate with all of us. We constantly straddle the different worlds in which we operate: the need to know and the need to be open to what our clients might teach us; the need to be rigorous and the need to be realistic; the need to be theoretically astute and the need to be pragmatic. How multiple stakeholders shape what we offer and how we offer it is vital. This is not a sacrificing of rigour but a call to exist in many worlds simultaneously and an ever-insistent requirement to bring our knowledge of psychology to the outside world.

Despite the diversity of material covered in this book, two central conclusions emerge. The first is that applied psychologists are interested not solely in the 'actioning' of knowledge – of the effective implementation of a particular process, method or tool – but also in the process of enquiry itself. Arguably, more than any other profession, psychologists seek evidence of the value of the questions they ask, not just the outcome of having asked them. This is clear from the way that applied psychology continues to redefine itself, in the ongoing debates about our relationship to knowledge and how we apply this knowledge in our relationships with the stakeholders of our services.

Interpreted in this light, we can define the scientist–practitioner as someone who has embarked upon a never-ending search for new stories that facilitate increasingly elegant and helpful ways of working with clients to make sense of the puzzles that we, and they, are attempting to solve. In addition to identifying these narratives, we search for ways through which they might be validated and refined which are grounded in, although not limited to, the discipline of psychology.

We could summarize a vision of the scientist–practitioner in psychology as a distinct approach to enquiry rather than the undertaking of any specific activity or activities. The scientist–practitioner can no longer be a model in any static sense, but rather a narrative framework in which our discipline is paramount but individualized. Consequently, this identity will be expressed in diverse forms based on the specific choices made within the context in which the encounter with the client takes place, as well as all the other factors (direct and indirect) that have shaped that context.

We believe that in choosing such an identity, the practitioner will be committed to explicitly holding in mind a framework for differentiating ways of knowing and a general set of psychological principles for informing the selection of modes of knowledge to assist with the creation of a systematic approach to professional decision-making. For example, when approaching a particular enquiry, we anticipate that the scientist–practitioner will be explicitly holding in mind a particular style of reasoning, that they will be able to articulate and justify the reasons for using one style of reasoning over another and have some sense of what would be likely to occur if they were to switch reasoning style. Similarly, when investigating their own practice or when reading or conducting research, we would expect the scientist–practitioner to justify (in an informed way) their decision to rely on one model of science rather than another and the implications of doing so. In this way, the scientist–practitioner model becomes a process through which we can both evaluate the limitations of our chosen perspective and be clear about the purposes it can fulfil.

If the above represents a valid reformulation of what it means to be a modern scientist–practitioner, then re-affirming our allegiance to this framework will require an ability to articulate our reactions to the domains of practice outlined in the preceding chapters. One way of supporting this process, which is consistent with the spirit of this book, is to engage with the series of reflective prompts which we have presented below, in the form of specific questions. Engaging with this reflective tool will, we hope, enable you to draw together the key ideas contained within each of the preceding chapters in a way that also helps you articulate or refine the vision of practice that guides your work.

These questions may, on first reading, appear quite simple. However, to engage with them in any meaningful way requires expansive and creative thinking, as well as rigorous and analytical review. There are no right or wrong answers, but there may be answers that are more or less helpful, according to your level of experience, career aspirations, working context and preferred models of practice. Our invitation would be to use each section in a way that feels personally meaningful, to dip in and out of various sections as befits your particular needs and, where necessary, to refer back to each of the main chapters for clarification.

A REFLECTIVE TOOL FOR REFINING YOUR IDENTITY AND WORK AS A SCIENTIST–PRACTITIONER

I Exploring your definition of the scientist–practitioner model

Think about the relationship between science and practice in your own work, identifying any specific examples that feel particularly pertinent as well as more general themes that strike you as relevant. Then consider the following:

A What are some of the different ways in which science has influenced your practice (individually, organizationally and more globally, as well as directly and indirectly)?

- What have been the most satisfactory elements of those experiences?
- What have been the least satisfactory elements of those experiences?
- How has your use of science been influenced by your practice?
- How does current research impact on your practice and what are the modes of interaction between the two communities in your work?

B In relation to your own model of practice, how would you define the scientist–practitioner model? Specifically:

- Do you see it as one model of many possible models? What are the implications of your choice?
- Do you see it primarily as a model or a vision of practice? What are the implications of your choice?
- What would be the range of activities and methods of science and practice that you would see the scientist–practitioner model as encompassing?
- In what way is your definition enabling and constraining for you and your clients?

2 Your practice

Spend some time reflecting on your approach to professional practice until you feel you have developed a clear description of what this entails. Then, using that description, consider:

A What factors impact on your reasoning skills in the workplace?

- What is your preferred reasoning style when it comes to solving the puzzles you encounter in your practice?
- How do you monitor your practice to ensure that your decision-making is not unduly biased by irrelevant or counterproductive influences (such as heuristics, fatigue, service pressures or personal feelings towards your clients)?
- How has your decision-making style evolved over time?
- What are the different reasoning styles to which you have been exposed in different services? How have they shaped your outlook on modes of knowledge and how to apply them?

B What factors influence your ability to formulate effectively?

- How do you decide whether your formulations are (a) accurate and (b) helpful?
- How do you know when you need to revise a formulation? How would you go about doing so?
- How do you adjust your formulation in the light of new information?

C What factors impact on your ability to create novel solutions to practice-related puzzles?

- How do you go about implementing an action plan? Based on your formulation, how do you decide which intervention tool to use, when and how?
- What form does your creativity most often take in your practice?
- What learning preferences underpin your 'inventions' in the workplace?
- Which types of improvisation do you feel comfortable about using in the name of innovative practice? Which types of improvisation would you decline to use? What does this tell you about the assumptions and frameworks that govern the way you work?
- What forms of improvisation would be considered acceptable by the organizations to which you are accountable? What would be considered unacceptably radical?
- In what ways do the explicit and implicit assumptions held by the organization govern the use of your creative skills?
- What type of client is best served by your skills or your service context? With whom would you not work? Where is the margin of that boundary and what factors do you take into account in arriving at judgements of this kind?

3 The 'science' in your scientist–practitioner model

Your approach to evaluation:

- How do you determine the impact of your decision-making, formulating and creativity?

- How do you determine whether you have done a 'good' piece of work?
- How do you determine whether you have done a 'bad' piece of work?
- What types of method (including but not restricted to measurement tools) could you usefully employ to enhance your effectiveness on a day-to-day basis?
- What resources do your draw upon to assist you to reflect on the impact of your work in a systematic way?

Your use of science:

A What is your own definition of science? How does this definition facilitate and inhibit your use of science in the workplace?

B What is the purpose that underpins your use of science? Specifically:

- What are you setting out to achieve (whether defined as outputs, results, processes of change or journey)?
- What is the story about science that underpins your purpose? Do you subscribe to a story that is interested in generalizable findings and universal laws or one that prioritizes the discovery of multiple, equally valid truths?
- What results are expected of you by the wider organizational context in which the work is taking place? How does this shape your ideas about what you are aiming to achieve?

C What are the perspectives (assumptions, values and beliefs) that influence your purpose? Specifically:

- When critiquing your professional practice, which scientific theory do you intuitively tend to favour and why?
- What does your preferred definition of science tell you about the values and beliefs you hold about 'legitimate' knowledge? What implications does this have for your practice?
- Which perspectives does your scientific story lead you to exclude, and with what implications?
- How do you ensure that your clients are able to explore their values and beliefs about 'legitimate' knowledge? How do you manage different worldviews?

D What is the process, filtered by which perspectives, through which you are going to achieve your results? Specifically:

- What implications does your scientific story have for your choice of methodology?
- How might the perspectives of different stakeholders (including their views about legitimate knowledge) influence the types of questions deemed relevant to ask?

- How might the perspectives of different stakeholders influence your choice of investigative technique?
- Which questions (and, therefore, methods) are ruled in and out by your purpose and perspectives? What are the potential implications of this for the enquiry, for your clients and for your understanding of their needs?

E How might you be differentially enabled and constrained in your practice by changing your definition of science?

4 Your identity as a scientist–practitioner

The concept of scientist–practitioner identity, as we have construed it, is one that evolves over the course of your career. It is also integrally linked with individual learning needs and values, the extent to which these 'fit' within the organizational contexts in which you work and the way in which you define and own that identity. In terms of your own journey, consider how you approach:

A Continuing professional development: career review and future planning

- What type of learning journey are you embarked upon at the current time?
- How do you best absorb new ideas? What might this tell you about your learning style and preferences?
- How are you enabled and constrained by the theories, models, technologies and contexts in which you have been immersed? Which theories, ideas or contexts do you need to become more familiar with at the current time?
- How is your learning enabled and constrained by the organizations in which you currently work? What forms of knowledge are preferred and which are marginalized – with what consequences for yourself and your clients?
- To what extent does the available training/development prepare you for your current roles?
- What are the types of environment that most often enable you to generate good ideas?
- When you need inspiration, to which sources do you typically turn? (Do not restrict your answers to psychological theories here, but consider any other resource you regard as relevant.) What are the implications of incorporating these resources into your work with clients and your career development plan?

B Clarifying the parameters of your identity as a scientist–practitioner

- What is the essence of your identity as a scientist–practitioner?
- What were the key influences on your journey to becoming a scientist–practitioner?
- How do you currently see your professional identity – as an individual and as part of a collective body?

- How do you draw the boundaries between yourself and allied professions?
- What is the purpose of your practice of psychology? What is its value-added contribution to organizational or individual effectiveness?
- What values, attitudes, models and theories underpin your practice?
- What processes typify your work? What would others see happening in your practice?
- What are the competencies required for the tasks you are currently undertaking?

5 Positioning yourself as a scientist–practitioner as 'human capital' and seeing yourself within a larger organizational context

Review the organization(s) in which you currently manage and/or are being managed. Then consider:

- How does the organization assess its human capital? How is this linked to development options relevant to personal and service/business growth?
- What are the processes for building the human capital base of the organization and how is that capital leveraged to achieve outstanding results?
- How does the organization prepare individuals for development, apply learning to leverage work in progress, and develop them for future challenges?
- What process does the organization use to (1) experiment with alternative ways of leveraging human capital; (2) reflect on that experience and (3) apply the lessons learned?
- What process does the organization use to align the aspirations of its employees with service/business needs? In particular:
    - o What are the key competitive drivers for the business and how is the human capital marshalled to address these drivers?
    - o What does the 'brand' (of psychology as a profession and your service specifically) stand for – professionally, intellectually, scientifically, in terms of stakeholder inclusion, diversity, equality, ethics and to generate sustainability?
    - o To what extent do you feel that the organization encourages you to share your ideas? To what extent do you have your ideas acknowledged?
    - o How far are different models of knowledge use and production encouraged or are some, particularly critical knowledge, discouraged?
- What attempts are made to understand the aspirations, hopes and needs of all stakeholders and how does the organization capture and leverage these to build and sustain its future?

A FINAL WORD

Just as we have argued that there are many ways of being a scientist–practitioner, so we suggest that there are multiple ways in which this tool can be used. We leave it to you, the reader, to decide how best to apply it to your work but hope, nonetheless, that it is a tool to which you will return, as and when you need it. As Stacey (1992) suggests, the key to success is not one of imitating existing maps, ideas and practices, but rather creating new ones. We offer this tool in the hope that it can support you in creating some new maps, ideas and practices of your own.

As we reflect on the process of writing this book, including the conversations that have fuelled its creation, we realize that there is an invitation woven into its very fabric: namely, the need to personalize the debates, stories and ideas contained within it. We believe that it is up to each of us to make the case for our own scientist–practitioner identity by considering the kind of scientist–practitioner we wish to be and then taking responsibility to convey this to our colleagues and the wider community. This involves, for each of us, an understanding of the contexts in which we offer our services, the developmental transitions we have negotiated (and anticipate in the future), and ultimately the values that are central to who we are and what we do.

Our choices about how we inhabit the worlds of science and practice have critical implications for the type of work we do and how we approach it. Consequently, they cannot be arrived at easily or swiftly. However, this does not mean that they should be arduous. As Williams (1999) suggests, in the context of any enquiry that is worth pursuing, the aim is not so much one of arriving at clear-cut conclusions but more about being willing to entertain the question, to ponder its meaning and implications for our lives. Through the willingness to engage with some of the questions raised in this book, we hope that you will have identified for yourself a number of themes that are interesting, thought-provoking and relevant to your career. At the very least, we hope that its content will have (re-)engaged your enthusiasm for some of the foundations of professional psychology practice in all its glorious complexity.

We wish you an enjoyable, lifelong and ultimately transformational voyage of discovery.

Bibliography

Abrahamson, D.J. and Pearlman, L.A. (1993) 'The need for scientist–practitioner employment settings', *American Psychologist*, **48**: 59–60.

Ainscow, M. and Tweddle, D. (1979) *Preventing Classroom Failure. An Objectives Approach*, Chichester, UK: Wiley.

Ajzen, I. (1991) 'The theory of planned behaviour', *Organizational Behaviour and Human Decision Processes*, **50**: 179–211.

Allen, C. (1985) 'Training for what? Clinical psychologists' perceptions of their roles', unpublished MSc Thesis, University of Newcastle upon Tyne.

Allingham, M. (2002) *Choice Theory: a Very Short Introduction*, Oxford: Oxford University Press.

Alnervik, A. and Svidén, G. (1996) 'On clinical reasoning: patterns of reflection on practice', *The Occupational Therapy Journal of Research*, **16**, 2: 98–110.

Alvesson, M. and Deetz, S. (2000) *Doing Critical Management Research*, Sage: London.

American Psychiatric Association (1994) *Diagnostic and Statistical Manual of Mental Disorders*, 4th edn, Washington, DC: American Psychiatric Association.

Amerio, P. and Ghiglione, R. (1986) Cambiamento sociale, sistemi di rappresentazione e d'identita di attori vs. agenti sociali. *Giornale Italiano di Psicologia*, **13**: 615–36.

Anderson, N., Heriot, P. and Hodgkinson, G.P. (2001) 'The practitioner researcher divide in industrial, work and organizational psychology; where are we now, and where do we go from here?', *The Journal of Occupational and Organizational Psychology*, **34**, 4: 391–412.

Argyris, C. (1999) *On Organisational Learning*, 2nd edn, Oxford: Blackwell.

Ashforth, B.R. and Mael, F. (1989) 'Social identity theory and the organisation', *Academy of Management Review*, **14**: 20–39.

Aspenson, D.O., Gersh, T.L., Perot, A.R., Galassi, J.P., Schroeder, R., Kerick, S., Bulger, J. and Brooks, L. (1993) 'Graduate psychology students' perceptions of the scientist–practitioner model', *Counselling Psychology Quarterly*, **6**, 3: 201–15.

Australian Psychological Society (2004) *Coaching Psychology*. Online. Available <http://www.psychology.org.au/units/interest%5Fgroups/coaching/> (accessed November 15, 2004).

Baillie, A. and Corrie, S. (1996) 'The construction of clients' experience of psychotherapy through narrative, practical action and the multiple streams of consciousness', *Human Relations*, **49**, 3: 295–311.

Baird, D. (2004) *Thing Knowledge: a Philosophy of Scientific Instruments*, Berkeley, CA: University of California Press.

Baker, D.B. and Benjamin, L.T. (2000) 'The affirmation of the scientist–practitioner', *American Psychologist,* **55**, 2: 241–7.

Baker, E.T., Wang, M.C. and Walberg, H J. (1994–1995) 'The effects of inclusion on learning', *Educational Leadership*, **52**, 4: 33–5.

Balchin, N. (1933) 'The psychological difficulties of the Institute's work', *The Human Factor*, **7**, 7: 257–65.

Ban Breathnach, S. (1999) *Something More: Excavating Your Authentic Self*, London: Bantam Books.

Barkham, M. and Mellor-Clark, J. (2000) 'Rigour and relevance: the role of practice-based evidence in the psychological therapies', in N. Rowland and S. Goss (eds) *Evidence-based Counselling and Psychological Therapies: Research and Applications*, London: Routledge.

Barlow, D.H. (1981) 'On the relation of clinical research to clinical practice: current issues, new directions', *Journal of Consulting and Clinical Psychology*, **49**: 147–55.

Barlow, D.H., Hayes, S.C. and Nelson, R.O. (1984) *The Scientist Practitioner: Research and Accountability in Clinical and Educational Settings*, Needham Heights, MA: Allyn & Bacon.

Barney, J.B. (2001) 'Resource-based theories of competitive advantage; a ten year retrospective on the resource-based view', *Journal of Management*, **27**: 643–50.

Barwise, P., Marsh, P.R. and Wensley, R. (1985) *Must Finance and Strategy Clash? The State of Strategy,* Boston, MA: Harvard Business Review Press.

Beck, A.T. (1995) *Cognitive Therapy: Past, Present, and Future*, New York: Springer Publishing.

Beck, A.T., Rush, A., Shaw, B. and Emery, G. (1979) *Cognitive Therapy of Depression*, New York: Guilford Press.

Belar, C.D. and Perry, N.W. (1992) 'National conference on scientist–practitioner education and training for professional practice of psychology', *American Psychologist*, **47**: 71–5.

Belenky, M.F., Clinchy, B.M., Goldberger, N.R. and Tarule, J.M. (1986) *Women's Ways of Knowing*, New York: Basic Books.

Bergan, J.R. and Kratochwill, T.R. (1990) *Behavioural Consultation and Therapy*, New York: Plenum Press.

Bergin, A. and Strupp, H. (1972) *Changing Frontiers in the Science of Psychotherapy*, Chicago, IL: Aldine.

Berliner, D.C. (1992) 'Telling the stories of educational psychology', *Educational Psychologist*, **27**: 143–61.

——(1993) 'The science of psychology and the practice of schooling: the one hundred year journey of educational psychology from interest, to disdain, to respect for practice', in T.K. Fagan and G.R. VandenBog (eds) *Exploring Applied Psychology: Origins and Critical Analysis: Master Lecturers,* Washington, DC: American Psychological Association.

Bertalanffy, L. von (1968) *General Systems Theory*, New York: Brazitter.

Bertollotti, G., Zotti, A.M., Michielin, P., Vidotto, G. and Sanavio, E. (1990) 'A computerized approach to cognitive behavioural assessment: an introduction to CBA-2.0 primary scales', *Journal of Behavior Therapy and Experimental Psychiatry*, **18**: 245–8.

Bettle, S., Frederickson, N. and Sharp, S. (2001) 'Supporting schools in special measures: the contribution of educational psychology', *Educational Psychology in Practice,* **17**, 1: 53–68.

Bevington, S. (1924) 'The analysis of factor "atmosphere"', *The Journal of the National Institute of Industrial Psychology*, **2**, 2: 84–7.

Bhaskar, R. (1975) *A Realist Theory of Science*, Leeds, UK: Leeds Books.

——(1979) *The Possibility of Naturalism: A Philosophical Critique of the Contemporary Human Sciences*, Atlantic Highlands, NJ: Humanities Press.

Bieling, P. and Kuyken, W. (2003) 'Is cognitive case formulation science or science fiction?' *Clinical Psychology: Science and Practice*, **10**, 1: 52–69.

Billig, M. (1987) *Arguing and Thinking: A Rhetorical Approach to Social Psychology*, Cambridge: Cambridge University Press.

Boden R., Gummett, P., Cox, D. and Barker, K. (1998) 'Men in white coats . . . men in grey suits: new public management and the funding of science and technology services to the UK government', *Accounting, Auditing and Accountability Journal*, **11**, 3: 267–91.

Bohm, D. (1980) *Wholeness and the Implicate Order*, London: Routledge & Kegan Paul.

Bond, F.W. (1998) 'Utilising case formulations in manual-based treatments', in M. Bruch and F.W. Bond (eds) *Beyond Diagnosis: Case Formulation Approaches in CBT*, Chichester, UK: Wiley.

Bono, E. de (1969) *The Mechanism of Mind*, London: Jonathan Cape.

——(1973) *Lateral Thinking: Creativity Step by Step*, New York: Harper.

——(1995) *Parallel Thinking*, London: Penguin.

Booker, R., Hart, M., Moreland, D. and Powell, J. (1989) 'Struggling towards better practice: a psychological service team and anti-racism', *Educational Psychology in Practice*, **5**, 3: 123–9.

Bor, R. and du Plessis, P. (1997) 'Counselling psychology research in health care settings', *Counselling Psychology Review*, **12**, 1: 19–22.

Bowen, A.C.L. and John, M.H. (2001) 'Ethical issues encountered in qualitative research: reflections on interviewing adolescent in-patients engaging in self-injurious behaviours', *Counselling Psychology Review*, **16**, 2: 19–23.

Bowman, C. and Ambrosini, V. (2003) 'How the resource-based and the dynamic capability views of the firm inform corporate-level strategy', *British Journal of Management*, **14**: 289–303.

Branwhite, T. (1986) *Designing Special Programmes: a Handbook for Teachers of Children with Learning Difficulties*, London: Methuen.

Breer, W. (1987) *The Adolescent Molester,* Springfield, IL: Charles C. Thomas.

British Psychological Society (1991) *The Future of Psychological Science*, Leicester, UK: British Psychological Society.

——(1999) *Dyslexia, Literacy and Psychological Assessment, Report of a Working Party of the Division of Educational and Child Psychology*, Leicester, UK: British Psychological Society.

——(2003) *Register of Psychologists Specialising in Psychotherapy*, Leicester, UK: British Psychological Society.

——(2004) *Continuing Professional Development*. Leicester: British Psychological Society. Online. Available HTTP: <http://www.bps.org.uk/cpd> (accessed December 15, 2004).

——(2005) *Subject Benchmarks for Applied Psychology*, Leicester, UK: British Psychological Society.

Bruch, M. and Bond, F.W. (1998) *Beyond Diagnosis. Case Formulation Approaches in CBT*, Chichester, UK: Wiley.

Bullock, A., Stallybrass, O. and Trombley, S. (1988) *The Fontana Dictionary of Modern Thought*, London: Fontana Press.

Bunn, G.C. (2001a) 'Introduction', in G.C. Bunn, A.D. Lovie and G.D. Richards (eds) *Psychology in Britain: Historical Essays and Personal Reflections*, Leicester, UK: BPS Books.

——(2001b) 'Charlie and the chocolate factory', *The Psychologist*, **14**, 11: 576–9.

Bunn, G.C., Lovie, A.D. and Richards, G.D. (2001) *Psychology in Britain: Historical Essays and Personal Reflections*, Leicester, UK: BPS Books.

Burden, R. (1973) 'If we throw the tests out of the window what is there left to do?' *Journal of the Association of Educational Psychologists*, **3**, 5: 6–9.

——(1978) 'Schools systems analysis: a project centred approach', in B. Gillham (ed.) *Reconstructing Educational Psychology*, London: Croom Helm.

——(1981) 'Systems theory and its relevance to schools', in B. Gillham (ed.) *Problem Behaviour in the Secondary School: a Systems Approach,* London: Croom Helm.

Burden, R., Green, H. and Pettersen, J. (1982) 'Even trainees can do it! Applying educational psychology in secondary schools', *Association of Educational Psychologists Journal*, **5**, 10: 24–8.

Burr, V. (1995) *An Introduction to Social Constructionism*, London: Routledge.

Burton-Jones, A. (1999) *Knowledge Capitalism*, Oxford: Oxford University Press.

Busch, C.G. and Steinmetz, B. (2002) 'Stress management for executives', *Gruppendynamik*, **33**, 4: 385–401.

Cade, B. and O'Hanlon, W.H. (1993) *A Brief Guide to Brief Therapy*, New York: Norton.

Calder, M.C. (2001) *Juveniles and Children who Sexually Abuse: Frameworks for Assessment*, 2nd edn, Lyme Regis, UK: Russell House Publishing.

——(2002) *Young People who Sexually Abuse*, Lyme Regis, UK: Russell House Publishing.

Cameron, J. (1995) *The Artist's Way,* London: Pan Books.

Caplan, G. (1970) *The Theory and Practice of Mental Health Consultation,* New York: Basic Books.

Capra, F. (1997) *The Web of Life: a New Synthesis of Mind and Matter,* London: Flamingo.

Carkhuf, R.R. and Berenson, B.G. (1967) *Beyond Counselling and Therapy*, New York: Holt, Rinehart & Winston.

Carnes, P. (1983) *Out of the Shadows: Understanding Sexual Addiction*, Minneapolis, MN: CompCare.

Carr, A. (2000) *What Works with Children and Adolescents? A Critical Review of Psychological Interventions with Children, Adolescents and their Families*, London: Routledge.

——(2004) *Positive Psychology: the Science of Happiness and Human Strengths*, Hove, UK: Brunner-Routledge.

Carter, J.A. (2002) 'Integrating science and practice: reclaiming the science in practice', *Journal of Clinical Psychology*, **58**, 10: 1285–90.

Casement, P.J. and Wallerstein, R.S. (2004) *'Learning from the Patient'*, Hove, UK: Guildford Press.

Castonguay, L.G., Goldfried, M.R., Wiser, S., Raue, P.J. and Hayes, A.M. (1996) 'Predicting the effect of cognitive therapy for depression: a study of unique and common factors', *Journal of Consulting and Clinical Psychology*, **64**: 497–504.

Ceci, S.J. (1996) *On Intelligence*, Cambridge, MA: Cambridge University Press.

Chalmers, A.F. (1982) *What is this Thing Called Science?* 2nd edn, Milton Keynes, UK: Open University Press.

Chappell, C., Rhodes, C., Solomon, N., Tennant, M. and Yates, L. (2003) *Reconstructing the Lifelong Learner: Pedagogy and Identity in Individual, Organisational and Social Change*, London: Routledge-Falmer.

Checkland, P. (1981) *Systems Thinking, Systems Practice*, London: Wiley.

——(1999) *Systems Thinking, Systems Practice: a 30 Year Retrospective,* London: Wiley.

Checkland, P. and Holwell, S. (1998) *Information, Systems, and Information Systems*, Chichester, UK: Wiley.

Christie, P., Newsom, E., Newsom, J., and Prevezer, W. (1992) 'An interactive approach to language and communication for non-speaking children', in D.A. Lane and A. Miller (eds) *Child and Adolescent Therapy: a Handbook*, Milton Keynes, UK: Open University Press.

Clark, T. (1995) *Managing Consultants: Consultancy as the Management of Impressions*, Milton Keynes, UK: Open University Press.

Clarke, D.D. (2004) '"Structured judgement methods" – the best of both worlds?', in Z. Todd, B. Nerlich, S. McKeown and D.D. Clarke (eds) *Mixing Methods in Psychology: the Integration of Qualitative and Quantitative Methods in Theory and Practice*, London: Routledge.

Cm 2250 (1993) *Realising Our Potential: a Strategy for Science, Engineering and Technology*, London: HMSO.

Coan, R.W. (1979) *Psychologists: Personal and Theoretical Pathways*, New York: Irvington.

Cohen, L., Duberly, J. and Mcauley, J. (1999) 'The purpose and process of science: contrasting understandings in UK research establishments', *R D Management* **29**, 3: 233–45.

Cohen, R. (1982) *Whose File is it Anyway?* London: National Council for Civil Liberties.

Coleman, B.A. (2001) 'From Hawton and Carr to Pokemon', *Clinical Psychology*, **4**: 14–16.

Conner, M., Knott, S. and Bulman, B. (2003) *Excellence in the Public Sector. Redefining the Patient/User Experience*, Chichester, UK: Kingsham.

Corcoran E. (1994) 'The changing role of UK corporate research labs', *Research Technology Management,* **37**, 4: 14–25.

Corrie, S. and Callanan, M.M. (2000) 'A review of the scientist–practitioner model: reflections on its potential contribution to counselling psychology within the context of current health care trends', *British Journal of Medical Psychology*, **73**: 413–27.

Corrie, S. and Callanan, M.M. (2001) 'Therapists' beliefs about research and the scientist–practitioner model in an evidence-based health care climate: a qualitative study', *British Journal of Medical Psychology*, **74**: 135–49.

Corrie, S. and Supple, S. (2004) 'Seeing is believing: adapting cognitive therapy for visual impairment', *Clinical Psychology*, **44**: 34–7.

Coulby, D. and Harper, T. (1983) *DO5 Schools Support Unit: Evaluation Phase 2*, London: Croom Helm.

Cowie, H. and Glachan, M. (2000) 'Designing and disseminating research in counselling psychology', *Counselling Psychology Review*, **15**, 3: 27–31.

Crabtree, M. (1998) 'Images of reasoning: a literature review', *Australian Occupational Therapy Journal*, **45**: 113–23.

Craig, L.A. (2004) 'Assessing risk in sexual offenders', unpublished PhD Thesis. University of Birmingham, UK.

Craig. L.A., Browne, K.D., Hogue, T.E. and Stringer, I. (2004) 'New directions in assessing risk for sexual offenders', *Issues in Forensic Psychology*, **5**: 81–99.

Crane, D.R. and McArthur Hafen (Jr) (2002) 'Meeting the needs of evidence-based practice in family therapy: developing the scientist–practitioner model', *Journal of Family Therapy*, **24**: 113–24.

Cranton, P. and Roy, M. (2003) 'When the bottom falls out of the bucket: toward a holistic perspective on transformative learning', *Journal of Transformative Education*, **1**: 86–98.

Crawshaw, M. (2000) *Facilitator for Area 1. British Psychological Society Occupational Psychology Search Conference*, Leicester, UK: British Psychological Society.

Crellin, C. (1998) 'Origins and social context of the term "formulation" in psychological case-reports', *Clinical Psychology Forum*, **112**: 18–28.

Critten P. (2002) 'Recognising the Spiritual Potential within Communities of Practice through Appreciative Inquiry', *International Conference on Organisational Spirituality*, University of Surrey, July 22–24, 2002.

Cunningham C. and McFarlane, K. (1991) *When Children Molest Children*, UK: The Safer Society Press, Brandon VT: The Safer Society Press.

(Safer Press books are obtainable through Bookstall Forum Ltd., 86 Abbey Street, Derby, DE22 3SQ UK. (01)-332-368039; www. bookstallforum.co.uk enq@bookstallforum. co.uk)

Davies, C. (1995) *Gender and the Professional Predicament in Nursing*, Philadelphia, PA: Open University Press.

Davies, P. (1983) *God and the New Physics*, London: J.M. Dent & Sons.

Davis, A.S., Mcintoish, D.E., Phelps, L. and Kehle, T.J. (2004) 'Addressing the shortage of school psychologists: a summative overview', *Psychology in the Schools*, **41**, 4: 489–95.

Davison, G.C. and Gann, M.K. (1998) 'The reformulation of panic attacks and a successful cognitive-behavioural treatment of social evaluative anxiety', in M. Bruch and F.W. Bond (eds) *Beyond Diagnosis. Case Formulation Approaches in CBT*, Chichester, UK: Wiley.

Dawes, R.M. (1994) *House of Cards. Psychology and Psychotherapy Built on Myth*, New York: The Free Press.

Dawes, R.M., Faust, D. and Meehl, P.E. (1989) 'Clinical versus actuarial judgement', *Science*, **243**: 1668–74.

Department for Education and Employment (2000) *Educational Psychology Services (England): Current Role, Good Practice and Future Directions*, London: DfEE. Publications.

——(2001) *Special Educational Needs and Disability Act*, London: HMSO.

Department for Education and Skills (2001) Special Educational Needs Code of Practice, London: DfES.

Department of Health (1996) *NHS Psychotherapy Services in England. Review of Strategic Policy*, London: HMSO.

——(1997) *The New NHS: Modern, Dependable*, London: HMSO.

——(1999) *Working Together to Safeguard Children: A Guide to inter-agency Working to Safeguard and Promote the Welfare of Children*, London: HMSO.

——(2001) *Treatment Choice in the Psychological Therapies and Counselling: Evidence Based Clinical Practice Guideline*, Leeds, UK: NHS Executive.

Department of Social Security (1995) *Disability Discrimination Act*, London: HMSO.

Department of Trade and Industry White Paper (2004) *Excellence and opportunity: A Science and Innovation Policy for the 21st century*, London: HMSO.

Division of Educational and Child Psychology, British Psychological Society (1999) 'A Framework for Psychological Assessment and Intervention', *DECP Newsletter*, **89**: 6–9.

Dosier, C. (1947) 'Report of roundtable on internship and training of clinical psychologists', *Journal of Clinical Psychology*, **3**: 184–90.

Douglas, J. (1982) 'A systems perspective to behavioural consultation in schools: a personal view', *Bulletin of the British Psychological Society*, **35**: 195–7.

Dowie, J.A. and Elstein, A.S. (1988) *Professional Judgement: a Reader in Clinical Decision-Making*, Newcastle upon Tyne: Cambridge University Press.

Dowling, E. and Osborne, E. (1994) *The Family and the School: a Joint Systems Approach to Problems with Children*, London: Routledge.

Doyle, L.H. (2003) 'Synthesis through meta-ethnography: paradoxes, enhancements, and possibilities', *Qualitative Research*, **3**, 3: 321–44.

Drabick, D.A.G. and Goldfried, M.R. (2000) 'Training the scientist–practitioner for the 21st century. Putting the bloom back on the rose', *Journal of Clinical Psychology*, **56**, 3: 327–40.

Drewery, W. and Winslade, J. (1997) 'The theoretical story of narrative therapy', in G. Monk, J. Winsdale, K. Croket and D. Epston (eds), *Narrative Therapy in Practice: the Archaeology of Hope*, San Francisco, CA: Jossey–Bass.

Dryden, W. (1991) *A Dialogue with Arnold Lazarus*, Milton Keynes, UK: Open University Press.

Duerzen-Smith, E. van (1990) 'Philosophical underpinnings of counselling psychology', *Counselling Psychology Review*, **5**, 2: 8–12.

Edwards, L. (2002) 'Clinical psychologists' decision-making processes during therapy assessment: a qualitative study', unpublished D.Clin.Psychol Thesis, Canterbury Christchurch University College.

Efran, J.S. and Clarfield, L.E. (1992) 'Constructionist therapy: sense and nonsense', in S. McNamee and K.J. Gergen (eds) *Therapy as Social Construction*, London: Sage.

Eggleston, S., Dunn, D.K. and Anjali, M. (1986) *Education for Some: The Educational and Vocational Experiences of 15–18 Year Olds from Ethnic Minority Groups*, Stoke-on-Trent, UK: Trentham Books.

Elias, J.L. and Merriam, S.B. (1995) *Philosophical Foundations of Adult Education*, Malabar, FL: Krieger Publishing Company.

Elliott, J. (1981) *Action Research Framework for Self-evaluation in Schools*, Schools Council Programme 2, Working Paper No. 1, Cambridge: Institute of Education.

Elliott, M. and Williams, D. (2003) 'The client experience of counselling and psychotherapy', *Counselling Psychology Review*, **18**, 1: 34–40.

Ellis, A. and Harper, R.A. (1961) *A New Guide to Rational Living*, Englewood Cliffs, NJ: Prentice-Hall.

Entwistle, N.J. and Ramsden, P. (1983) *Understanding Student Learning*, London: Croom Helm.

Epstein, S. (1996) *Impure Science: AIDS, Activism, and the Politics of Knowledge*, Berkeley, CA: University of California Press.

Eraut, M. (2000) 'Non-formal learning, implicit learning and tacit knowledge in professional work', in F. Coffield (ed.) *The Necessity of Informal Learning*, Bristol, UK: The Policy Press.

Etzkowitz, H. and Leydesdorff L. (2000) 'The dynamics of innovation: from National Systems and "mode 2" to a triple Helix of university–industry–government relations', *Research Policy*, **29**, 2: 109–23.

European Association for Behavioural and Cognitive Therapies (2004) *XXXIV Annual Congress*, Manchester: September 9–11, 2004.

European Commission [COM 353] (2004) on the future of research in the EU, *Science and Technology, the Key to Europe's Future – Guidelines for Future European Union Policy to Support Research*. Online. Available HTTP: <http://www.europa.eu.int/comm/research/future/pdf/com-2004-353_en.pdf> (accessed December 15, 2004).

European Mentoring and Coaching Conference (2004), Brussels: November 17–19, 2004.

Eysenck, H.J. (1949) 'Training in clinical psychology: an English point of view', *American Psychologist*, **4**: 173–6.

——(1952) 'The effects of psychotherapy: an evaluation', *Journal of Consulting Psychology*, **16**: 319–24.

——(1990) *Rebel with a Cause: the Autobiography of Hans Eysenck*, London: W.H. Allen.

Eysenck, H.J. and Martin, I. (1987) *Theoretical Foundations of Behaviour Therapy*, New York: Pergamon.

Farouk, S. (1999) 'Consulting with teachers', *Educational Psychology In Practice*, **14**, 4: 253–63.

Feather, N.T. and Rauter, K.A. (2004) 'Organizational citizenship behaviours in relation to job status, job insecurity, organizational commitment and identification, job satisfaction and work values', *Journal of Occupational and Organizational Psychology*, **77**: 95–113.

Fehrenbach, P.A., Smith, W., Monastersky, C. and Deisher, R.W. (1986) 'Adolescent sexual offenders; offender and offense characteristics', *American Journal of Orthopsychiatry* **56**: 225–33.

Feist, G.J. (1999) 'The influence of personality on artistic and scientific creativity', in R.J. Sternberg (ed.) *Handbook of Creativity*, Cambridge: Cambridge University Press.

Feyerabend, P.K. (1975) *Against Method: Outline of an Anarchistic Theory of Knowledge*, London: New Left Books.

Figg, J. and Stoker, R. (1990) 'Mental health consultation in education: theory and practice', in C. Aubrey (ed.) *Consultancy in the UK*, London: Falmer Press.

Fillery-Travis, A., Garnett, J. and Lane, D.A. (2005) *Work Based Knowledge: a New Frontier for Professional Development*, London: Professional Development Foundation and Middlesex University.

Finkelhor, D. (1984) *Child Sexual Abuse: New Theory and Research*, New York: The Free Press.

Fleming, N. (2002) *A Guide to Learning Styles*. Online. Available <http://www.vark-learn.com> Copyright Version 4.1 (2002) held by Neil D. Fleming, Christchurch, New Zealand and Charles C. Bonwell, Green Mountain Falls, Colorado 80819, USA (accessed August 15, 2004).

Follette, W.C., Houts, A.C. and Hayes, S.C. (1992) 'Behaviour therapy and the new medical model', *Behavioural Assessment*, **14**: 323–43.

Ford, J., Mongon, D. and Whelan, M. (1982) *Special Education and Social Control: Invisible Disasters*, London: Routledge & Kegan Paul.

Forrester, A. (1993) 'Negotiating the perils of establishing an EPS database: a first attempt to benefit from soft system methdology', *Association of Educational Psychologists Journal*, **9**, (1), 47–52.

Foucault, M. (1983) 'The subject and power', in H. Dreyfus and P. Rabinow (eds) *Michael Foucault: Beyond Structuralism and Hermeneutics*, Chicago, IL: University of Chicago Press.

Fox, T.G, Cole, D.R. and Lieberman, J.A. (1984) 'Three generations of family medicine: a comparison of social identities', *Social Science and Medicine*, **18**: 481–6.

Frank, G. (1984) The Boulder model: history, rationale and critique', *Professional Psychology: Research and Practice*, **15**: 417–35.

Frederickson, N. (1990) 'Systems approaches in educational psychology', *Journal of Applied Systems Analysis*, **17**: 3–20.

—— (1993) 'Using Soft Systems Methodology to rethink special educational needs', in A. Dyson and C. Gains (eds) *Rethinking Special Needs in Mainstream Schools: Towards the Year 2000*, London: David Fulton.

—— (1999) 'The ACID Test: Or is it?', *Educational Psychology in Practice*, **15**, 1: 3–9.

—— (2002) 'Evidence based practice and educational psychology', *Educational and Child Psychology*, **19**, 3: 96–111.

Frederickson, N. and Cline, T. (2002) *Special Educational Needs, Inclusion and Diversity: a Textbook*, Buckingham, UK: Open University Press.

Frederickson, N. and Turner, J. (2003) 'Utilizing the classroom peer group to address children's social needs: an evaluation of the "circle of friends" intervention approach', *Journal of Special Education*, **36**, 4: 234–45.

Freidson, E. (2001) *Professionalism: the Third Logic of the Practice of Knowledge*, Chicago, IL: University of Chicago Press.

Fuller, S. (1993) *Philosophy of Science and its Discontents*, London: Guilford Press.

Gambrill, E. (1993) 'What critical thinking offers to clinicians and clients', *The Behavior Therapist*, **16**: 141–7.

Gardner, H. (1993) *Frames of Mind: the Theory of Multiple Intelligences*, 2nd edn, London: Fontana Press.

Gardner, J. and Tweddle, D. (1979) 'Some guidelines for sequencing objectives', *Journal of the Association of Educational Psychologists*. **5**, 2: 23–30.

Garland, J. (1997) *Phelps v the Mayor and Burgesses of the London Borough of Hillingdon*, London: The Stationery Office.

Garman, A.N., Whiston, D.L. and Zlatoper, K.W. (2000) 'Media perceptions of executive coaching and the formal preparation of coaches', *Consulting Psychology Journal: Practice and Research*, **52**: 203–05.

Garnett, J. (2001) 'Work based learning and the intellectual capital of universities and employers', *The Learning Organisation*, **8**: 78–81.

—— (2004) *The Potential of University Work based Learning to Contribute to the Intellectual Capital of Organisations*, London: National Centre for Work Based Learning Partnerships, Middlesex University.

Gergen, K. (1985) 'The social constructionist movement in modern psychology', *American Psychologist*, **40**: 266–75.

—— (1992) 'Toward a post-modern psychology', in S. Kvale (ed.) *Psychology and Postmodernism*, Beverley Hills, CA: Sage.

Gersch, I., Kelly, C., Cohen, S., Daunt, S. and Frederickson, N. (2001) 'The Chingford Hall School Screening Project', *Educational Psychology in Practice*, **17**, 2: 135–56.

Gibbons, M., Limoges, C., Nowotny, H., Schwartzmann, S., Scott, P. and Trow, M. (1994) *The New Production of Knowledge: the Dynamics of Science and Research in Contemporary Societies*, London: Sage.

Gibbs, G. (1992) *Improving the Quality of Student Learning*, Bristol, UK: Technical and Educational Services.

Gillham, B. (1978) 'The failure of psychometrics', in B. Gillham (ed.) *Reconstructing Educational Psychology,* London: Croom Helm.

Gilligan, C. (2003) *Listening as a Method.* Seminar sponsored by Gender Studies Working Group, Cambridge: Cambridge University Press.

Gladwin, T. (1964) 'Culture and logical process', In W. Goodenough (ed.) *Explorations in Cultural Anthropology. Essays Presented to George Peter Murdoch*, New York: McGraw-Hill.

Glover, J.A., Ronning, R.R. and Reynolds, C.R. (1989) *Handbook of Creativity*, New York: Plenum Press.

Goffman, E. (1959) *The Presentation of Self in Everyday Life*, London: Penguin.

Goldberg, L. (1959) 'The effectiveness of clinicians' judgments: the diagnosis of organic brain damage from the Bender-Gestalt test', *Journal of Consulting Psychology*, **23**: 25–33.

Goldfried, M.R. and Wolfe, B.E. (1996) 'Psychotherapy practice and research: repairing a strained alliance', *American Psychologist*, **51**: 1007–16.

Goldfried, M.R. and Wolfe, B.E. (1998) 'Toward a more clinically valid approach to therapy research', *Journal of Consulting and Clinical Psychology*, **66**: 143–50.

Goldfried, M.R. and Eubanks-Carter, C. (2004) 'On the need for a new psychotherapy research paradigm: comment on Westen, Novotny, and Thompson-Brenner (2004)', *Psychological Bulletin*, **130**: 669–73.

Goleman, D. (1996) *Emotional Intelligence and Why it Can Matter More than IQ*, London: Bloomsbury.

——(1998) *Working with Emotional Intelligence*, London: Bloomsbury.

Golsworthy, R. (2004) 'Counselling psychology and psychiatric classification: clash or co-existence?', *Counselling Psychology Review*, **19**, 3: 23–8.

Goodstone, E. (2003) 'Orgasms for two: the joy of partnership', *Journal of Sex and Marital Therapy*, **29**, 5: 401–2.

Gosling, P. (2001) 'Partnership for change: effective practice in behaviour support', unpublished PhD Thesis, University of London.

Grant, A.M. (2003) 'The impact of life coaching on goal attainment, metacognition and mental health', *Social Behavior & Personality*, **31**, 3: 253–64.

Grant, A.M. and Greene, J. (2001) *Coach Yourself: Make Real Change in Your Life*, London: Momentum Press.

Grant, A.M. and Cavanagh, M.J. (2004) 'Toward a profession of coaching: sixty five years of progress and challenges for the future', *International Journal of Evidence-Based Coaching and Mentoring* (in press).

Grant, P. (2005) *Business Psychology in Practice*, London: Whurr.

Gray, P., Miller, A. and Noakes, J. (1994) *Challenging Behaviour in Schools*, London: Routledge.

Green, F. (1980) 'Becoming a truant: the social administrative process applied to pupils absent from school', unpublished Masters Thesis, Cranfield University.

Greenwood, J.D. (1989) *Explanation and Experiment in Social Psychological Science*, London: Springer-Verlag.

——(1991) *Relations and Representations: an Introduction to the Philosophy of Social Psychological Science*, London: Routledge.

Grof, S. with Bennett, H.Z. (1993) *The Holotropic Mind*, San Francisco, CA: Harper.

Gruber, H.E. and Wallace, D.B. (1999) 'The case study method and evolving systems approach for understanding unique creative people at work', in R.J. Sternberg (ed.) (1999) *Handbook of Creativity*, Cambridge: Cambridge University Press.

Guest, G. (2000) 'Coaching and Mentoring in Learning Organizations', *Conference Paper TEND United Arab Emirates*, April 8–10, 2000.

Guilford, J.P. (1950) 'Creativity', *American Psychologist*, **5**: 444–54.

——(1967) *The Nature of Human Intelligence*, New York: McGraw-Hill.

Gutkin, T.B. (1993) 'Moving from behavioral to ecobehavioral consultation: what's in a name', *Journal of Educational and Psychological Consultation*, **4**: 95–9.

Gutkin, T.B. and Curtis, M.J. (1999) 'School-based consultation: theory and practice', in C.R. Reynolds and T.B. Gutkin (eds) *The Handbook of School Psychology*, 3rd edn, New York: Wiley.

Hackett, S. (2003) 'Evidence-based assessment: a critical evaluation', in M.C. Calder and S. Hackett (eds) *Assessments in Child Care: Using and Developing Frameworks for Practice*, Lyme Regis, UK: Russell House Publishing.

Hacking, I. (1983) *Representing and Intervening*, Cambridge: Cambridge University Press.

Hage, S.M. (2003) 'Reaffirming the unique identity of counseling psychology: opting for the road less traveled by', *The Counseling Psychologist*, **31**, 5: 555–63.

Haines, S. (1998) *The Manager's Pocket Guide to Systems Thinking and Learning*, Amherst, MA: HRD Press.

Haley, J. (1963) *Strategies of Psychotherapy*, New York: Grune & Stratton.

Halgin, R.P. (1999) 'Clinical training: challenges for a new millennium', *Journal of Clinical Psychology*, **55**: 405–9.

Hammond, K.R. (1996) *Human Judgement and Social Policy: Irreducible Uncertainty, Inevitable Error, Unavoidable Justice*, New York: Oxford University Press.

Hargreaves, D. (1996) *Teaching as a Research-based Profession: Possibilities and Prospects,* The Teacher Training Agency Annual Lecture. London: TTA.

Haring, N.G., Lovitt, T.C., Eaton, M.D. and Hansen, C.L. (1978) *The Fourth R – Research in the Classroom,* Columbus, OH: Merrill.

Harris Williams, M. (1998) 'Emotional problems of thinking with literature', *Changes: an International Journal of Psychology and Psychotherapy,* **16**, 3: 201–8.

Hawkins, P. and Shohet, R. (1989) *Supervision in the Helping Professions,* Milton Keynes, UK: Open University Press.

Hayes, N.J. (1991) 'Social identity, social representation and organisational culture', unpublished Doctoral Thesis, University of Huddersfield.

Haynes, S., Lemsky, C. and Sexton-Radek, K. (1987) 'Why clinicians infrequently do research', *Professional Psychology: Research and Practice*, **18**: 515–19.

Head, D. and Harmon, G.A. (1990) 'The scientist–practitioner in practice: a short reply', *Clinical Psychology Forum*, **33**: 33.

Held, B.S. (1995) *Back to Reality: A Critque of Postmodern Theory in Psychotherapy*, New York: Norton.

——(1996) 'Solution-focused therapy and the postmodern: a critical analysis', in S.D. Miller, M.A. Hubble and B.L. Duncan (eds) *Handbook of Solution-Focused Brief Therapy*, San Francisco, CA: Jossey–Bass.

Henwood, K. (1996) 'Qualitative inquiry. Perspectives, methods and psychology', in J.T.E. Richardson (ed.) *Handbook of Qualitative Research Methods for Psychology and the Social Sciences*, Leicester, UK: BPS Books.

Henwood, K. and Pidgeon, N. (1995) 'Grounded theory and psychological research', *The Psychologist*, **8**, 3: 115–18.

Herrick, M.J. (1971) *The Chicago Schools: a Social and Political History*, Beverley Hills, CA: Sage.

Herzlich, C. (1973) *Health and Illness: a Social Psychological Analysis*, London: Academic Press.

Hewstone, M. (1983) *Attribution Theory: Social and Functional Extensions*, Oxford: Blackwell.

Hickey, N. (2004) 'Actuarial risk prediction for future violence amongst mentally disordered offenders', *Issues in Forensic Psychology*, **5**: 50–61.

Hill, W.F. (1971) *Learning: a Survey of Psychological Interpretations,* London: Methuen.

Hogan, D. (2001) 'Has occupational psychology succumbed to managerialism?', *BPS Centenary Conference*, April 2001: Glasgow.

Hogarth, R. (1981) 'Beyond discrete biases: functional and dysfunctional aspect of judgmental heuristics', *Psychological Bulletin*, **90**: 197–217.

Holdsworth, N. (1993) 'Philosophy, wisdom and psychotherapy', *Changes: an International Journal of Psychology and Psychotherapy*, **11**, 2: 139–44.

Hollon, S.D. and Kris, M.R. (1984) 'Cognitive factors in clinical research and practices', *Clinical Psychology Review*, **4**: 35–76.

Home Office (1993) *Criminal Statistics for England and Wales 1992* London: HMSO.

Hopf, C. (2004) 'Research ethics and qualitative research' in U. Flick, E. von Kardorff and I. Steinke (eds) *A Companion to Qualitative Research*, 334–9. London: Sage.

Hoshmand, L.T. and Polkinghorne, D.E. (1992) 'Redefining the science–practice relationship and professional training', *American Psychologist*, **47**: 55–66.

Hume, D. (1739/1985) *A Treatise of Human Nature*, London: Penguin Books.

Ihde, D. (1991) *Instrumental Realism*. Indianapolis IN: Indiana University Press.

—— (2003) 'A phenomenology of technics' in R.C. Scharff and V. Dusek (eds) *Philosophy of Technology: an Anthology*, Oxford: Blackwell.

Imich, A. and Roberts, A. (1990) 'Promoting positive behaviour: an evaluation of a behaviour support project', *Educational Psychology in Practice*, **5**: 201–9.

Intrator, J., Allan, E. and Palmer, M. (1992) 'Decision tree for the management of substance-abusing psychiatric patients', *Journal of Substance Abuse Treatment*, **9**: 215–20.

Ivey, D.C., Scheel, M.J., and Jankowski, P.J. (1999) 'A contextual perspective of clinical judgement in couples and family therapy: is the bridge too far?' *Journal of Family Therapy*, **21**, 4: 339–59.

James, J.E. (1994) 'Health care, psychology and the scientist–practitioner model', *Australian Psychologist*, **29**, 1: 5–11.

James, W. (1899/1958) *Talks to Teachers*, New York: Norton.

Jarvis, J. (2004) *Coaching and Buying Coaching Services*, Wimbledon: Chartered Institute of Personnel Development.

Jenkins, G.M. (1969) 'The systems approach', *Journal of Systems Engineering*, **I**, 3–49.

John, I.D. (1984) 'Science as a justification for psychology as a social institution', *Australian Psychologist*, **19**: 29–37.

—— (1998) 'The scientist–practitioner model: a critical examination', *Australian Psychologist*, **33**, 1: 24–30.

Johnson, G. (1992) 'Managing strategic change: strategy, culture and action', *Long Range Planning*, **25**, 1: 28–36.

Johnson, T.J. (1972) *Professions and Power*, London: Macmillan.

Jones, A. (1998) '"What's the bloody point?" More thoughts on fraudulent identity', *Clinical Psychology Forum*, **112**: 3–9.

Jones, L.W., Sinclair, R.C., Rhodes, R.E. and Courneya, K.S. (2004) 'Promoting exercise behaviour: an integration of persuasion theories and the theory of planned behaviour', *British Journal of Health Psychology*, **9**, 4: 505–21.

Jones, R.L. (1972) *Black Psychology*, New York: Harper Row.

Jordan, J.V. (1999) *Work in Progress: 'Toward Connection and Competence'*, Wellesley, MA: Center for Research on Women, Stone Center, Wellesley College.

Kahneman, D., Slovic, P. and Tversky, A. (eds) (1982) *Judgement under Uncertainty: Heuristics and Biases*, New York: Cambridge University Press.

Kanellakis, P. (2004) 'Introduction to Special Edition on Counselling Psychology and Psychological Testing', *Counselling Psychology Review*, **19**, 4: 4–5.

Kanfer, F.N. and Nay, W.R. (1982) 'Behavioural assessment', in G.T. Wilson and C.M. Franks (eds) *Contemporary Behaviour Therapy,* New York: The Guilford Press.

Kassirer, J.P., Kuipers, B.J. and Gorry, O.A. (1982) 'Toward a theory of clinical expertise', *The American Journal of Medicine*, **73**: 251–9.

Keise, C., Kelly, E., King, O. and Lane, D.A. (1993) 'Culture and child services', in A. Miller and D.A. Lane (eds) *Silent Conspiracies: Scandals and Successes in the Care and Education of Vulnerable Young People,* Stoke-on Trent, UK: Trentham Books.

Keller, E.F. (1995) 'The origin, history, and politics of the subject called gender and science', in S. Jasanoff, G.G.E. Markle, J.C. Petersen and T. Pinch (eds) *Handbook of Science and Technology Studies*, London: Sage.

Kelly, L., Regan, L. and Burton, S. (1991) *An Exploratory Study of the Prevalence of Sexual Abuse in a Sample of 16–21 Year Olds*, London: University of North London Polytechnic: Child Abuse Studies Unit.

Kennedy, P. and Llewelyn, S. (2001) 'Does the future belong to the scientist–practitioner?' *The Psychologist*, **14**, 2: 74–8.

Kilburg, R.R. (2000) *Executive Coaching: Developing Managerial Wisdom in A World of Chaos.* Washington, DC: American Psychological Association.

Kinderman, P. and Lobban, F. (2000) 'Evolving formulations: sharing complex information with clients', *Behavioural and Cognitive Psychotherapy*, **28**, 3: 307–10.

Kiresuk, T.J. and Sherman, R.E. (1968) 'Goal attainment scaling: a general method for evaluating community mental health programmes', *Community Mental Health Journal*, **4**: 443–53.

Knowles, E. (1999) *The Oxford Dictionary of Quotations*, 5th edn, Oxford: Oxford University Press.

Knowles, M. (1989) *The Making of An Adult Educator*, Houston, TX: Gulf Publishing.

——(1990) *The Adult Learner: a Neglected Species*, 4th edn, Houston TX: Gulf Publishing.

Kolb, D.A. (1984) *Experiential Learning*, Englewood Cliffs, NJ: Prentice-Hall.

Korman, M. (1974) 'National conference on levels and patterns of professional training in psychology: the major themes', *American Psychologist*, **29**: 441–9.

Kratochwill, T.R. and Stoiber, K.C. (2000) 'Empirically supported interventions and school psychology: conceptual and practice issues. Part II', *School Psychology Quarterly*, **15**: 233–53.

Krause, E. (1996) *Death of the Guilds: Professions, States and the Advance of Capitalism, 1930 to the Present*, New Haven, CT: Yale University Press.

Kuhn, T.S. (1970) *The Structure of Scientific Revolutions*, Chicago: University of Chicago Press.

Kurtz, P. (1992) *The New Skepticism*, Amherst, NY: Prometheus.

Kwiatkowski, R. and Horncastle, P. (1990) 'On the consumption of the Golden Goose', *Paper presented at the BPS Annual Occupational Psychology Conference*, January, 1990: Windermere, UK.

Lakatos, I. (1970) 'Falsification and the methodology of scientific research', in I. Lakatos and A. Musgrave (eds) *Criticism and the Growth of Knowledge,* Cambridge: Cambridge University Press.

——(1976) *Proofs and Refutations: The Logic of Mathematical Discovery*, Cambridge: Cambridge University Press.

Lalljee, M., Lamb, R., Furnham, A. and Jaspers, J. (1984) 'Explanations and information search: induction and hypothesis-testing approaches to arriving at an explanation', *British Journal of Social Psychology*, **23**: 201–12.

Landy, F.J. and Conte, J.M. (2004) *Work in the 21st Century, An Introduction to Industrial and Organizational Psychology*, Boston, MA, McGraw-Hill.

Lane, D.A. (1973) 'Pathology of communication: a pitfall in community health', *Community Health*, **5**, 3: 157–62.

——(1974) *The Behavioural Analysis of Complex Cases*, Islington, London: Islington Educational Guidance Centre.

——(1975) *The Guidance Centre: a New Approach to Childhood Difficulties*, London: The Kings Fund Centre.

——(1978) *The Impossible Child*, London: Inner London Education Authority.

——(1980/1991) *Personal Development Planning: the Autonomous Professional Model*, London: Professional Development Foundation.

——(1983) *Models for Analysis of Uncertainty*, London: Professional Development Foundation.

——(1990) *The Impossible Child,* Stoke-on-Trent, UK: Trentham Books.

——(1992) 'Antisocial behaviour in children: a long-term follow-up', in F. Lösel, D. Bender and T. Bliesener (eds) *Psychology and Law: International Perspectives*, Berlin: Walter de Gruyter.

——(1993) 'Counseling psychology in organisations', *Revue Européenne de Psychologie Appliquée*, **43**: 41–6.

——(1998) 'Context focused analysis: an experimentally derived model for working with complex problems with children, adolescents and systems', in M. Bruch and F.W. Bond (eds) *Beyond Diagnosis: Case Formulation Approaches in CBT*, Chichester, UK: Wiley.

——(2002) 'The emergent models in coaching', *European Mentoring and Coaching Council*, Cambridge: November 12, 2002.

Lane, D.A. and Green, F. (1990) 'Partnership with pupils', in M. Scherer, I. Gersch and L. Fry (eds) *Meeting Disruptive Behaviour: Assessment, Intervention, Partnership*, Basingstoke, UK: Macmillan.

Lane, D.A. and Miller, A. (1992) *Child and Adolescent Therapy: a Handbook*, Milton Keynes, UK: Open University Press.

Lane, D.A. and Donegan, J. (1993) *Employability: a New Social Contract between Employer and Employee*, London: Professional Development Foundation.

Lane, D.A. and Rajan, A. (2005) 'Business psychology – the key role of learning and human capital', in P. Grant (ed.) *Business Psychology in Practice*, London: Whurr.

Lane, D.A., Puri, A., Cleverly, P., Wylie, R. and Rajan, A. (2000) *Employability: Bridging the Gap Between Rhetoric and Reality: Second Report: Employees' Perspective*. Tonbridge, UK: Create/PDF/CIPD.

Lane, D.A., Jarvis, J. and Fillery-Travis, A. (2005) *Making the Case for Coaching: Does it work?*, Wimbledon, London: Chartered Institute of Personnel and Development.

Larson, M.S. (1977) *The Rise of Professionalism: a Sociological Analysis*, Berkeley, CA: University of California Press.

Lawton, B. and Feltham, C. (2000) *Taking Supervision Forward: Enquiries and Trends in Counselling and Psychotherapy*, London: Sage.

Lawton, R. and Parker, D. (1999) 'Procedures and the professional; the case of the British NHS', *Social Science & Medicine*, **48**: 353–61.

Lazear, D. (1991) *Seven Ways of Knowing. Teaching for Multiple Intelligences*, 2nd edn, Paladine, IL: IRI/Skylight Publishing.

Leadbetter, J. (2000) 'Patterns of service delivery in educational psychology services: some implications for practice', *Educational Psychology in Practice*, **16**, 4: 449–60.

Leary, D.W. (1992) 'William James and the art of human understanding', *American Psychologist*, **47**, 2: 152–60.

Levy, L.H. (1962) 'The skew in clinical psychology', *American Psychologist*, **17**: 244–9.

Lewin, K. (1936) *Principles of Topological Psychology*, New York: McGraw.

——(1951) *Field Theory in Social Science*, Chicago, IL: University of Chicago Press.

Leyden, G. (1978) 'The process of reconstruction: an overview', in B. Gillham (ed.) *Reconstructing Educational Psychology*, London: Croom Helm.

Lincoln, Y.S. and Guba, E.G. (1985) *Naturalistic Inquiry*, Newbury Park, CA: Sage.

Linehan, M. (1993) *Cognitive-Behavioral Treatment of Borderline Personality Disorder*, New York: Guilford Press.

Lo, Ming-cheng M. (2004) 'Professions: prodigal daughter of modernity', in J. Adams, E.S. Clemens and A.S. Orloff (eds) *Remaking Modernity: Politics, Processes and History in Sociology*, Durham, UK: Duke University Press.

Logan, C. (2004) 'Foreword', *Issues in Forensic Psychology*, **5**: 10–12.

Lokke, C., Gersch, I., M'gadzah, H. and Frederickson, N. (1997) 'The resurrection of psychometrics: fact or fiction?', *Educational Psychology in Practice*, **12**, 4: 222–33.

Lord, C., Lepper, M. and Ross, L. (1979) 'Biased assimilation and attitude polarization: the effects of prior theories on subsequently considered evidence', *Journal of Personality and Social Psychology*, **37**: 2098–110.

Lovie, S. (2001) 'Three steps to heaven; how the British Psychological Society attained its place in the sun', in G.C. Bunn, A.D. Lovie and G.D. Richards (eds) *Psychology in Britain. Historical Essays and Personal Reflections*, Leicester: British Psychological Society.

Luborsky, L. and Crits-Cristoph, P. (1990) *Understanding Transference: The Core Conflictual Relationship Themes Method,* New York: Basic Books.

Lunt, I. (1996) 'The role of psychological theory in the training of educational psychologists', Unpublished PhD Thesis, Institute of Education, University of London.

Mace, C. and Moorey, S. (2001) 'Evidence in psychotherapy: a delicate balance', in C. Mace, S. Moorey and B. Roberts (eds) *Evidence in the Psychological Therapies: a Critical Guide for Practitioners*, Hove, UK: Brunner-Routledge.

MacKay, G., McCool, S., Cheseldine, S. and McCartney, E. (1993) 'Goal Attainment Scaling: a technique for evaluating conductive education', *British Journal of* Special Education, **20**, 143–7.

Mackay, N. (2003) 'Psychotherapy and the idea of meaning', *Theory and Psychology*, **13**: 359–86.

McKeown, K. (2000) *What Works in Family Support for Vulnerable Families*, Dublin: Department of Health and Children.

McLaren, P. (1998) *Life in Schools: An Introduction to Critical Pedagogy in the Foundations of Education*, New York: Longman.

McLeod, J. (1994) *Doing Counselling Research*, London: Sage.

Macpherson, G. and Jones, L. (2004) 'Risk Assessment and Management', *Issues in Forensic Psychology*, **5** (Issue Editors).

Madden, N.A. and Slavin, R.E. (1983) 'Mainstreaming students with mild handicaps: academic and social outcomes', *Review of Educational Research*, **52**, 4: 519–69.

Madsen, C.H., Becker, W. C. and Thomas, D.R. (1968) 'Rules, praise and ignoring: elements of elementary classroom control', *Journal of Applied Behavioural Analysis*, **1**, 2: 139–50.

Maguth Nezu, C. and Nezu, A.M. (1995) 'Clinical decision making in everyday practice: the science in the art', *Cognitive and Behavioral Practice*, **2**: 5–25.

Mahrer, A.R. (2000) 'Philosophy of science and the foundations of psychotherapy', *American Psychologist*, **55**, 10: 1117–25.

Maliphant, R. (1974) 'Testing, testing (or will it be fine tomorrow?)', *Bulletin of the British Psychological Society*, **27**: 441–6.

Manafi, E. (2004) 'Counselling Psychologists' Perceptions of the Scientist–Practitioner Identity', unpublished PsychD Thesis, University of Surrey.

Manicas, P.T. and Secord, P.F. (1983) 'Implications for psychology of the new philosophy of science', *American Psychologist*, **38**: 399–413.

Maslow, A.H. (1971) *The Farther Reaches of Human Nature*, New York: Viking.

Maurer, T., Solamon, J. and Troxtel, D. (1998) 'Relationship of coaching with performance in situational employment interviews', *Journal of Applied Psychology*, **83**, 1: 128–36.

Medway, F.J. (1979) 'How effective is school consultation: a review of recent research', *Journal of School Psychology*, **17**: 275–82.

Meehl, P. (1954) *Clinical Versus Statistical Prediction: a Theoretical Analysis and a Review of the Evidence*, Minneapolis, MN: University of Minnesota Press.

——(1957) 'When shall we use our heads instead of the formula?' *Journal of Counselling Psychology*, **4**: 268–73.

——(1986) 'Causes and effects of my disturbing little book', *Journal of Personality Assessment*, **50**: 370–5.

Merrett, F. (1981) 'Studies in behaviour modification in British educational settings', *Educational Psychology*, **1**, 1: 13–38.

Meyer, V. and Liddell, A. (1975) 'Behaviour therapy', in D. Bannister (ed.) *Issues and Trends in Psychological Therapies*, London: Wiley.

Mezirow, J. (1991) *Transformative Dimensions of Adult Learning*, San Francisco, CA: Jossey–Bass.

Michael, M. (1989) 'Attribution and ordinary explanation: cognitivist predilections and pragmatist alternatives', *New Ideas in Psychology*, **7**: 231–43.

Miller, A. (1980) 'Systems theory applied to the work of the educational psychologist', *Journal of the Association of Educational Psychologists*, **5**, 3: 11–15.

——(2003) *Teachers, Parents and Classroom Behaviour: a Psychosocial Approach*, Maidenhead, UK: Open University Press.

Miller, A. and Lane, D.A. (1993) *Silent conspiracies: Scandals and Successes in the Care and Education of Vulnerable Young People*, Stoke-on-Trent, UK: Trentham Books.

Miller, A., Jewell, T., Booth, S. and Robson, D. (1985) 'Delivering educational programmes to slow learners', *Educational Psychology in Practice*, **1**, 3: 99–103.

Miller, A., Robson, D. and Bushell, R. (1986) 'Parental participation in paired reading: a controlled study', *Educational Psychology,* **6**, 3: 277–84.

Miller, E. (1999) 'Positivism and clinical psychology' *Clinical Psychology and Psychotherapy,* **6**: 1–6.

Miller, G.A. (1969) 'Psychology as a means of promoting human welfare', *American Psychologist,* **24**: 1063–75.

Miller, J.B. and Stiver, I.P. (1997) *The Healing Connection: How Women Form Relationships in Therapy and in Life.* Wellesley, MA: Wellesley Centers for Women, Wellesley College.

Miller Mair, J. (1988) 'Psychology as storytelling', *International Journal of Personal Construct Psychology,* **1**: 125–38.

Milne, D., Britton, P. and Wilkinson, I. (1990) 'The scientist–practitioner in practice', *Clinical Psychology Forum,* **30**: 27–30.

Milton, M. and Corrie, S. (2002) 'Exploring the place of technical and implicit knowledge in therapy', *The Journal of Critical Psychology, Counselling and Psychotherapy,* **2**, 3: 188–95.

Mohan, J. (1996) 'Accounts of the NHS reforms: macro- meso- and micro-level perspectives', *Sociology of Health and Illness,* **18**: 675–98.

Monsen, J., Graham, B., Frederickson, N. and Cameron, R.J (1998) 'Problem analysis and professional training in educational psychology: an accountable model of practice', *Educational Psychology in Practice,* **13**, 4: 234–49.

Morgan, G. (1986) *Images of Organization,* Beverly Hills, CA: Sage.

Moscovici, S. and Hewstone, M. (1983) 'Social representations and social explanations: from the "naïve" to the "amateur" scientist', in M. Hewstone (ed.) *Attribution Theory: Social and Functional Extensions,* Oxford: Blackwell.

Mumma, G.H. and Smith, J.L. (2001) 'Cognitive-behavioural-interpersonal scenarios: interformulator reliability and convergent validity', *Journal of Psychopathology and Behavioural Assessment,* **23**: 203–21.

Murphy, G. (1949) *Historical Introduction to Modern Psychology,* 5th edn, London: Routledge & Kegan Paul.

Murphy, J., John, M. and Brown, H. (1984) *Dialogues and Debates in Social Psychology,* Hove, UK: Lawrence Erlbaum Associates.

Myers, C.S. (1920) *Mind and Work: The Psychological Factors in Industry and Commerce,* London: University of London Press.

——(1923a) 'The efficiency engineer and the industrial psychologist', *Journal of the National Institute of Industrial Psychology,* **1**, 5: 168–72.

——(1923b) 'The human side of industry' (broadcast from the London Station of the British Broadcasting Company Ltd, June 21, 1923), *Journal of the National Institute of Industrial Psychology,* **1**, 8: 309–12.

——(1937) *In the Realm of Mind,* Cambridge: Cambridge University Press.

Nathan, P.E. (2000) 'The Boulder model: a dream deferred – or lost?' *American Psychologist,* **55**: 250–2.

National Children's Home (1992) *The Report of the Committee of Enquiry into Children and Young People who Sexually Abuse Other Children,* London: NCH.

Naughton, J. (1979) 'Functionalism and systems research: a comment', *Journal of Applied Systems Analysis,* **6**: 69–73.

Neimeyer, R.A. and Raskin, J.D. (2000) *Constructions of Disorder,* Washington, DC: American Psychological Association.

Newman, F. and Holzman, L. (1999) 'Beyond narrative to performed conversation (In the beginning comes much later)', *Journal of Constructivist Psychology*, **12**, 1: 23–40.

Newnes, C. (2001) 'On evidence', *Clinical Psychology*, **1**: 6–12.

Newsom, E. (1992) 'The barefoot play therapist: adapting skills for a time in need', in D.A. Lane and A. Miller (eds) *Child and Adolescent Therapy: a Handbook*, Milton Keynes: Open University Press.

Norcross, J.C., Prochaska, J.O. and Gallagher, K.M. (1989) 'Clinical psychologists in the 1980s: II. Theory, research and practice', *The Clinical Psychologist*, **42**, 3: 45–53.

Oaker, G. and Brown, R. (1986) 'Intergroup relations in a hospital setting: a further test of social identity theory', *Human Relations*, **39**: 767–78.

O'Connell, B. (1998) *Solution-Focused Therapy*, London: Sage.

O'Connor, I. and McDermott, I. (1997) *The Art of Systems Thinking*, San Francisco CA: Thorsons.

OECD (2000) *Knowledge Management in the Learning Society*, Paris: Centre for Educational Research and Innovation.

Office of Special Education Programs, USA Department of Education (2002) *Specific Learning Disabilities: Finding Common Ground*, Washington, DC: US Department of Education.

O'Gorman, J.G. (2001) 'The scientist–practitioner model and its critics', *Australian Psychologist*, **36**: 164–69.

Oskamp, S. (1965) 'Overconfidence in case-study judgments', *Journal of Consulting Psychology*, **29**: 261–5.

O'Sullivan, J.J. and Quevillon, R.P. (1992) '40 years later. Is the Boulder Model still alive?' *American Psychologist*, **47**, 1: 67–70.

Palazzoli, S.M., Cecchin, G., Prata, G. and Bosolo, L. (1978) *Paradox and Counter Paradox: a New Model of the Family in Schizophrenic Transaction*, London: Jason Aronson.

Parker, I. (1992) *Discourse Dynamics: Critical Analysis for Social and Individual Psychology*, London: Routledge.

Parsloe, E. (1995) *Coaching, Mentoring, and Assessing: a Practical Guide to Developing Competence*, New York: Kogan Page.

Pelling, N. (2000) 'Scientists versus practitioners: a growing dichotomy in need of integration', *Counselling Psychology Review*, **15**, 4: 3–7.

Perkins, D. (2000) *Archimedes' Bathtub*, New York: Norton.

Perkins, D. and Blythe, T. (February, 1994) 'Putting understanding up front', *Educational Leadership*, **51**, 5: 4–7.

Perkins, D., Crismond, D., Simmons, R. and Unger, C. (1995) 'Inside understanding', in D. Perkins, J.L. Schwartz, M. West and M.S. Wiske (eds) *Software Goes to School: Teaching for Understanding with New Technologies*, New York: Oxford University Press.

Perls, F.S. (1969) *Gestalt Therapy Verbatim*, Highland, NY: The Gestalt Journal Press.

Persons, J.B. (1989) *Cognitive Theory in Practice: a Case Formulation Approach*, New York: Norton.

Peterson, D.R. (1991) 'Connection and disconnection of research and practice in the education of professional psychologists', *American Psychologist*, **46**, 4: 422–9.

Phillips, B.N. (1999) 'Strengthening the links between science and practice: reading, evaluating and applying research in school psychology', in C.R. Reynolds and T.B. Gutkin (eds) *The Handbook of School Psychology*, 3rd edn, New York: Wiley.

Phillips, D.C. (1992) *The Social Scientist's Bestiary: A Guide to Fabled Threats to, and Defenses of, Naturalistic Social Enquiry*, New York: Pergamon.

Piaget J. (1966) *The Psychology of the Child*, Paris: Presses Universitaire de France.

Pilgrim, D. and Treacher, A. (1992) *Clinical Psychology Observed*, London: Routledge.

Polster, E. and Polster, M. (1974) *Gestalt Therapy Integrated: Contours of Theory and Practice*, New York: Vintage.

Polyani, M. (1967) *The Tacit Dimension*, New York: Doubleday.

Poortinga, Y.H. and Lunt I. (1997) 'Defining the competence of psychologists with a view to accountability', *European Psychologist*, **2**, 4: 293–300.

Pope, C. and Mays, N. (1995) 'Qualitative research. Reaching the parts other methods cannot reach: an introduction to qualitative methods in health and health services research', *British Medical Journal*, **311**, 6996: 42–5.

Popper, K.R. (1963) *Conjectures and Refutations: the Growth of Scientific Knowledge*, London: Routledge & Kegan Paul.

——(1968) *The Logic of Scientific Discovery*, London: Hutchinson.

Potter, J. and Wetherell, M. (1987) *Discourse and Social Psychology: Beyond Attitude and Behaviour*, London: Sage.

Pottharst, K. (1973) 'A brief history of the professional model of training', in M. Korman (ed.) *Levels and Patterns of Professional Training in Psychology*, Washington, DC: American Psychological Association.

Presbury, J., Echterling, L.G. and McKee, J.E. (1999) 'Supervision for inner vision: solution-focused strategies', *Counselor Education & Supervision*, **39**, 2: 146–55.

Presland, J. (1973) 'Dealing with disturbing children', *Journal of the Association of Educational Psychologist*, **3**, 3: 28–32.

——(1981) 'Modifying behaviour long-term and sideways', *Journal of the Association of Educational Psychologists*, **5**, 6: 27–30.

Prifitera, A. and Dersch, J. (1993) 'Base rates of WISC-III diagnostic subtest patterns among normal, learning disabled and ADHD samples', *Journal of Psychoeducational Assessment, WISC-III Monograph,* 43–55.

Pullman, P. (1995) *Northern Lights*, London: Scholastic Books.

Rachman, S.J. (1971) *The Effects of Psychotherapy*, Oxford: Pergamon.

——(1983) 'Clinical psychology in Britain: retrospect and prospect', in A. Liddell (ed.) *The Practice of Clinical Psychology in Great Britain*, Chichester, UK: Wiley.

Raimy, V.C. (1950) *Training in Clinical Psychology (Boulder Conference)*, New York: Prentice Hall.

Rajan, A., Lank, E. and Chapple, K. (1999) *Good Practices in Knowledge Creation and Exchange*, Tonbridge, UK: Centre for Research in Employment and Technology in Europe.

Rajan, A., Eupen, P. van, Chapple, K. and Lane, D.A. (2000) *Employability: Bridging the Gap Between Rhetoric and Reality: First Report: Employers' Perspective.* Tonbridge, UK: Create/PDF/CIPD.

Ratey, N. (2002) 'Life coaching for adult ADHD', in S. Goldstein and A.T. Ellison (eds) *Clinicians' Guide to Adult ADHD: Assessment and Intervention*, San Diego, CA: Academic Press.

Raybould, E.C. and Solity, J.E. (1982) Teaching with precision, *Special Education/ Forward Trends,* **9**: 9–13.

Reisman, J.M. (1991) *A History of Clinical Psychology*, 2nd edn, New York: Hemisphere Publishing.

Rennie, D.L. (1994) 'Human science and counselling psychology: closing the gap between research and practice', *Counselling Psychology Quarterly*, **7**, 3: 235–51.

Revan, R. (1998) *ABC of Action Learning*, Plymouth, UK: Lemos & Crane.

Rhodes, J. and Ajmal, Y. (1995) *Solution Focused Thinking in Schools*, London: BT Press.

Rich, G.A. (1998) 'Selling and sales management in action: the constructs of sales coaching: supervisory feedback, role modeling and trust', *Journal of Personal Selling & Sales Management*, **18**, 1: 53–63.

Rich, S.A. (1998) 'A developmental approach to the treatment of adolescent sex offenders', *The Irish Journal of Psychology* **19**: 101–18.

Richardson, G. and Graham, F. (1997) 'Relapse prevention', in M.S. Hoghugi, S.R. Bhate and F. Graham (eds) *Working with Sexually Abusive Adolescents*, Thousand Oaks, CA: Sage.

Robertson, N., Baker, R. and Hearnshaw, H. (1996) 'Changing the clinical behaviour of doctors: a psychological framework', *Quality in Health Care*, **5**: 51–4.

Robinson, D.N. (2004) 'The reunification of rational and emotional life', *Theory and Psychology*, **14**, 3: 283–94.

Rock, D.L. (1994) 'Clinical judgment survey of mental health professionals: I. An assessment of opinions, ratings, and knowledge', *Journal of Clinical Psychology*, **50**, 6: 941–50.

Roethlisberger, F. J. and Dickson, W. J. (1939) *Management and the Worker: An Account of a Research Program conducted by the Western Electric Company, Hawthorne Works, Chicago* (7th printing, 1946 edn), Cambridge, MA: Harvard University Press.

Rogers, C.R. (1961) *On Becoming a Person*, Boston, MA: Houghton Mifflin.

Rose, H. (1994) *Love, Power and Knowledge: Towards a Feminist Transformation of the Sciences*, Cambridge: Polity Press.

Rose, S. (2001) 'Moving on from old dichotomies: beyond nature–nurture towards a lifeline perspective', *British Journal of Psychiatry, Supplement 40, 178*: S3–S7.

Ross, R.R. and Hilborn, J. (2005) *Time to Think Again: A Prosocial Competence Approach to the Prevention and Rehabilitation of Anti-social Behaviour*, Springfield, IL: C.C. Thomas.

Roth, A. and Fonagy, P. (1996) *What Works for Whom*, New York: Guilford Press.

Ryan, G. (2000) 'Childhood sexuality: a decade of study. Part I – research and curriculum development', *Child Abuse & Neglect*, **24**, 1: 33–48.

Ryan, G. and Lane, S. (1997) *Juvenile Sexual Offending: Causes, Consequences and Corrections*, 2nd edn, San Francisco, CA: Jossey–Bass.

Ryan, S. (1998) 'The relevance of early life experiences to the behaviour of sexually abusive youth', *The Irish Journal of Psychology* **19**: 32–48.

Sackett, D.L., Haynes, R.B., Guyatt, G.H., and Tugwell, P. (1996) 'Evidenced based medicine: what it is and what it isn't', *British Medical Journal*, **13**: 71–2.

Salkovskis, P.M. (2002) 'Empirically grounded clinical interventions: cognitive-behavioural therapy progresses through a multi-dimensional approach to clinical science', *Behavioural and Cognitive Psychotherapy*, **30**: 3–9.

——(2004) 'Editorial. A NICE year for CBT and a CBT year for NICE', *Behavioural and Cognitive Psychotherapy*, **32**: 129–30.

Salter, A., D'Este, P., Pavitt, K., Scott, A., Martin, B., Geuna, A., Nightingale. P. and Patel, P. (2000) *Talent, not technology: the impact of publicly funded research on innovation in the UK*, Science and Technology Policy Research Unit: University of Sussex, UK.

Scandura, T.A. (1992) 'Mentorship and career mobility: an empirical investigation', *Journal of Organizational Behavior*, **13**, 2: 169–74.

Scaturo, D.J. and McPeak, W.R. (1998) 'Clinical dilemmas I. Contemporary psychotherapy: the search for clinical wisdom', *Psychotherapy*, **35**, 1: 1–12.

Schein, E.H. (1969) *Process Consultation: its Role in Organisational Development,* Reading, MA: Addison-Wesley.

Scherer, M., Gersch, I. and Fry, L. (1990) *Meeting Disruptive Behaviour: Assessment, Intervention and Partnership,* London: Macmillan.

Schiffmann, R and Wagner, U. (1985) 'Wie gehen benachteiligte Gruppen miteinander um?' *Gruppendynamik,* **16**: 43–52.

Schön, D.A. (1987) *Educating the Reflective Practitioner,* San Francisco, CA: Jossey–Bass.

Scott, D., Brown, A.J., Lunt, I. and Thorne, L. (2004) *Professional Doctorates: Integrating Academic and Professional Knowledge,* Buckingham, UK: Open University Press.

Sebba, J. (2004) in G. Thomas and R. Pring (eds) *Evidence-Based Practice in Education,* Maidenhead, UK: Open University Press/McGraw-Hill Education.

Secord, P. (1984) 'Determinism, free will, and self-intervention: a psychological perspective', *New Ideas in Psychology,* **2**: 25–33.

Segal, Z.V., Williams, J.M.G. and Teasdale, J.D. (2002) *Mindfulness-Based Cognitive Therapy for Depression: a New Approach to Preventing Relapse,* New York: Guilford Press.

Seidenstücker, G. and Roth, W.L. (1998) 'Treatment decisions: types, models and schools', *European Journal of Psychological Assessment,* **14**, 1: 2–13.

Seligman, M. (2002) *Authentic Happiness: Using the New Positive Psychology to Realize Your Potential for Lasting Happiness,* New York: Free Press.

Senge, P.M. (1990) *The Fifth Discipline: the Art and Practice of the Learning Organization,* London: Century Business.

Sequeira, H. and van Scoyoc, S. (2004) 'Discussion paper: psychological testing', *Counselling Psychology Review,* **19**, 2: 37–40.

Shakow, D., Hilgard, E.R., Kelly, E.L., Luckey, B., Sanford, R.N. and Shaffer, L.F. (1947) 'Recommended graduate training program in clinical psychology', *American Psychologist,* **2**, 539–58.

Shapiro, M.B. (1955) 'Training of clinical psychologists at the Institute of Psychiatry', *Bulletin of the British Psychological Society,* **8**: 1–6.

——(1957) 'Experimental methods in the psychological description of the individual psychiatric patient', *International Journal of Social Psychiatry,* **111**: 89–102.

Shapiro, M.B. and Nelson, E.H. (1955) 'An investigation of an abnormality of cognitive function in a cooperative young psychotic: an example of the application of the experimental method to the single case', *Journal of Clinical Psychology,* **11**: 344–51.

Shazer, S. de (1988) *Clues: Investigating Solutions in Brief Therapy,* New York: Norton.

——(1994) *Words were Originally Magic,* New York: Norton.

Shazer, S. de and Lipchik, E. (1984) 'Frames and reframing', *Family Therapy Collections,* **11**: 88–97.

Sheehan, P.W. (1994) 'Psychology as a science and as a profession: an Australian perspective', *Australian Psychologist,* **29**: 174–7.

Sheridan, S.M., Welsh, M. and Orme, S.F. (1996) 'Is consultation effective? A review of outcome research', *Remedial and Special Education,* **17**: 341–54.

Shimmin, S. and Wallis, D. (1994) *Fifty years of Occupational Psychology in Britain,* Leicester, UK: British Psychological Society.

Siegert, R.J. (1999) 'Some thoughts about reasoning in clinical neuropsychology', *Behaviour Change,* **16**, 1: 37–48.

Sigston, A. (1993) 'Research and practice – worlds apart?', in A. Sigston, P. Curran, A.

Labram and S. Wolfendale (eds) *Psychology in Practice with Young People, Families and Schools,* London: David Fulton.

Simonton, D.K. (1999) 'Creativity and genius', in L. Pervin and O. John (eds) *Handbook of Personality Theory and Research*, 2nd edn, New York: Guilford.

——(2002) 'Creativity', in C.R. Snyder and S.J. Lopez (eds) *Handbook of Positive Psychology*, New York: Oxford University Press.

Singer, J.L. (1980) 'The scientific basis of psychotherapeutic practice: a question of values and ethics', *Psychotherapy. Theory, Research and Practice*, **17**, 372–83.

Siporin, M. (1984) 'Have you heard the one about social work humour?', *Social Casework*, **65**: 459–64.

Skovholt, T.M. and Rønnestad, M.H. (1992) *The Evolving Professional Self. Stages and Themes in Therapist and Counselor Development,* Chichester, UK: Wiley.

Skuse, D., Bentovim, A., Hodges, J., New, M.J.C., Williams, B.T.R. and McMillan, D. (1998) 'Risk factors for the development of sexually abusive behaviour in sexually victimised males', *British Medical Journal*, **317**: 175–9.

Sladeczek, I.E., Elliott, S.N., Kratochwill, T.R., Robertson-Mjaanes, S. and Stoiber, K.C. (2001) 'Application of goal attainment scaling to a conjoint behavioral consultation case', *Journal of Educational and Psychological Consultation,* **12**: 45–58.

Snow, R.E. (1981) 'On the future of educational psychology', *Newsletter for Educational Psychologists*, Division 15, American Psychological Association, **5**, 1: 1.

Sobell, M.B. and Sobell, L.C. (2000) 'Stepped care as a heuristic approach to the treatment of alcohol problems', *Journal of Consulting and Clinical Psychology*, **68**, 4: 573–9.

Sommers, M.R. and Gibson, G.D. (1994) 'Reclaiming the epistemological other: narrative and the social constitution of identity', in C. Calhoun (ed.) *Social Theory and the Politics of Identity,* Oxford: Blackwell.

Song, X–Y. and Lee, S–Y (2004) 'Bayesian analysis of two-level nonlinear structural equation models with continuous and polytomous data', *British Journal of Mathematical and Statistical Psychology*, **57**: 29–52.

Spinelli, E. (2001) 'Turning the obvious into the problematic: the issue of evidence from a human science perspective', *Invited Talk to UKCP NHS Forum Conference, Psychotherapy and Evidence-based Practice for the NHS*, July 11, 2001.

Stacey, R.D. (1992) *Managing the Unknowable Strategic Boundaries Between Order and Chaos in Organizations*, San Francisco, CA: Jossey–Bass.

——(2000) *Strategic Management and Organisational Dynamics: The Challenge of Complexity*, 3rd edn, Harlow, UK: Prentice Hall.

Stage, S.A., Abbott, R.D., Jenkins, J.R. and Berninger, V.W. (2003) 'Predicting response to early reading intervention from verbal IQ, reading-related language abilities, attention ratings and verbal IQ-word reading discrepancy: failure to validate discrepancy method', *Journal of Learning Disabilities*, **36**, 1: 24–33.

Steadman, L. and Rutter, D.R. (2004) 'Belief importance and the theory of planned behaviour: comparing modal and ranked modal beliefs in predicting attendance at breast screening', *British Journal of Health Psychology*, **9**, 4: 447–63.

Sterman, J.D. (1994) 'Learning in and about complex systems', *Systems Dynamics Review*, **10**, 2/3: 291–330.

——(2002) 'All models are wrong: reflections on becoming a systems scientist', *Systems Dynamics Review*, **18**, 4: 501–31.

Stern, E., Lane, D.A. and McDevitt, G. (1994) *Europe in Change: The Contribution of Counselling*, Rugby, UK: European Association for Counselling.

Sternberg, R.J. (1999) *Handbook of Creativity*, Cambridge: Cambridge University Press.

——(2000) *Guide to Publishing in Psychology Journals*, Cambridge: Cambridge University Press.

Sternberg, R.J. and Lubart, T.I. (1999) 'The concept of creativity: prospects and paradigms', in R.J. Sternberg (ed.) *Handbook of Creativity*, Cambridge: Cambridge University Press.

Stewart, T. (1997) *Intellectual Capital: The New Wealth of Nations*, London: Brealey.

Stoker, R. and Figg, J. (1998) 'Action research: redefining the term scientist practitioner', *Educational and Child Psychology*, **15**, 3: 55–64.

Stoltenberg, C.D. and Delworth, U. (1987) *Supervising Counselors and Therapists: a Developmental Approach*, San Francisco, CA: Jossey–Bass.

Stoltenberg, C.D., Pace, T.M. and Kashubeck-West, S. (2000) 'Counselling psychology and the scientist–practitioner model: an identity and logical match, not an option', in C.D. Stoltenberg, T.M. Pace, S. Kashubeck-West, J.L. Biever, T. Patterson and I.D. Welch. 'Training models in counseling psychology: scientist–practitioner versus practitioner-scholar', *The Counseling Psychologist*, **28**, 5: 622–40.

Strawbridge, S. and Woolfe, R. (1996) 'Counselling psychology: a sociological perspective' in R. Woolfe and W. Dryden (eds) *Handbook of Counselling Psychology*, London: Sage.

Strawbridge, S. and Woolfe, R. (2004) 'Counselling psychology in context', in R. Woolfe, W. Dryden and S. Strawbridge (eds) *Handbook of Counselling Psychology*, 2nd edn, London: Sage.

Stricker, G. (1992) 'The relationship of research to clinical practice', *American Psychologist*, **47**, 4: 543–9.

Sturdee, P. (2001) 'Evidence, influence or evaluation? Fact and value in clinical science', in C. Mace, S. Moorey and B. Roberts (eds) *Evidence in the Psychological Therapies: a Critical Guide for Practitioners*, Hove, UK: Brunner-Routledge.

Suchman, L.A. (1987) *Plans and Situated Actions: the Problem of Human-Machine Communication*, Cambridge: Cambridge University Press.

Sue, D.W. (2001) 'Multidimensional Facets of Cultural Competence', *The Counseling Psychologist*, **29**: 790–821.

Swain, R. (2000) 'Awareness and decision making in professional ethics: the new code of the Psychological Society of Ireland', *European Psychologist*, **5**, 1: 19–27.

Symington, N. (1993) *Narcissism: a New Theory,* London: Karnac.

Symon, G. and Cassell, C. (1998) *Qualitative Methods and Analysis in Organizational Research*, London: Sage.

Tarrier, N. and Calam, R. (2002) 'New developments in cognitive-behavioural case formulation. Epidemiological, systemic and social context: an integrative approach', *Behavioural and Cognitive Psychotherapy*, **30**: 311–28.

Teasdale, J.D. and Barnard, P.J. (1993) *Affect, Cognition and Change: Remodelling Depressive Thought*, Hove, UK: Erlbaum.

Teece, D.J., Pisano, G. and Shuen, S. (1997) 'Dynamic capabilities and strategic management', *Strategic Management Journal*, **18**, 7: 509–33.

Thomas, G. and Pring, R. (2004) *Evidence-based Practice in Education,* Maidenhead, UK: Open University Press/McGraw-Hill Education.

Thomas, G. and Vaughan, M. (2004) *Inclusive Education: Readings and Reflections,* Maidenhead, UK: Open University Press.

Thomas, L.F. and Harri-Augstein, E.S. (1985) *Self-Organised Learning: Foundations of a Conversational Science for Psychology*, London: Routledge & Kegan Paul.

Tizard, B. (1990) 'Research and policy: is there a link?', *The Psychologist*, **3**: 435–40.
Tizard, J. (1973) 'Maladjusted Children and the Child Guidance Service', *London Educational Review*, **2**: 22–37.
Tomlinson, S. (1978) *A Sociology of Special Education*, London: Routledge.
Trierweiler, S.J. and Stricker, G. (1992) 'The research and evaluation competency: training the local clinical scientist', in R.L. Peterson, J. McHolland, R.J. Bent, E. Davis-Russell, G.E. Edwall, E. Magidson, K. Polite, D.L. Singer and G. Stricker (eds) *The Core Curriculum in Professional Psychology*, 103–113 Washington, DC: American Psychological Association.
Trierweiler, S.J. and Stricker, G. (1998) *The Scientific Practice of Professional Psychology*, New York: Plenum Press.
Turk, D.C. and Salovey, P. (1985) 'Cognitive structures, cognitive processes, and cognitive-behaviour modification: II. Judgments and inferences of the clinician', *Cognitive Therapy and Research*, **9**, 1: 19–33.
Turkat, I.D. (1985) *Behavioural Case Formulation*, New York. Plenum Press.
Turpin, G. (2001) 'Single case methodology and psychotherapy evaluation: from research to practice', in C. Mace, S. Moorey and B. Roberts (eds) *Evidence in the Psychological Therapies: a Critical Guide for Practitioners*, Hove, UK: Brunner-Routledge.
Tversky, A. and Kahneman, D. (1973) 'Availability: a heuristic for judging frequency and probability', *Cognitive Psychology*, **5**: 207–32.
Tversky, A. and Kahneman, D. (1974) 'Judgment under uncertainty: heuristics and biases', *Science*, **185**: 1124–31.
Tversky, A. and Kahneman, D. (1980) 'Causal schemata in judgments under uncertainty', in M. Fishbein (ed.) *Progress in Social Psychology*, Hillside, NJ: Erlbaum.
Twamley, E.W., Jeste, D.V. and Bellack, A.S. (2003) 'A review of cognitive training in schizophrenia', *Schizophrenia Bulletin*, **29**, 2: 359–82.
Ussher, J.M. (1991) 'Positivistic psychology and social policy: a contradiction in terms?' *Educational and Child Psychology*, **8**, 1: 23–35.
Vacc, N.A. and Loesch, L.C. (1994) *A Professional Orientation to Counselling*, Muncie, IN: Accelerated Development.
Vera, E.M. and Speight, S.L. (2003) 'Multicultural competence, social justice, and counseling psychology: expanding our roles'. *The Counseling Psychologist*, **31**: 253–72.
Vignoles, V.L. Chryssochoou, X. and Breakwell, G.M. (2004) 'Combining individuality and relatedness: representations of the person among Anglican clergy', *British Journal of Social Psychology*, **43**: 113–32.
Viner, B. (2004) 'Clinical audit in veterinary general practice – the story so far', *In Practice* (in press). Online. Available http://www.vetgp.co.uk> (accessed December 20, 2004).
——(2005) 'Clinical audit in veterinary general practice – the story so far', *In Practice*, **27**: 215–18.
Wagner, P. (1995) *School Consultation: a Handbook for Practising Educational Psychologists,* London: Kensington and Chelsea EPCS.
——(2000) 'Consultation: developing a comprehensive approach to service delivery', *Educational Psychology in Practice*, **16**, 1: 9–18.
Wakefield, J.C. and Kirk, S.A. (1996) 'Unscientific thinking about scientific practice: evaluating the scientist–practitioner model', *Social Work Research*, **20**, 2: 83–96.
Waldron, K.W. 'Plant Residues', in K.W. Waldron, C.B. Faulds and A.C. Smith (eds) *Total Food*, Norwich, UK: Institute of Food Research (in press).

Walter, J.L. and Peller, J.E. (1996) 'Rethinking our assumptions: assuming anew in a postmodern world', in S.C. Miller, M.A. Hubble and B.L. Duncan (eds) *Handbook of Solution-Focused Brief Therapy*, San Francisco, CA: Jossey–Bass.

Wang, V.C.X. and Sarbo, L. (2004) 'Philosophy, role of adult educators and learning', *Journal of Transformative Education*, 2: 204–14.

Ward, J. (1976) 'Behaviour modification in education: an overview and model for programme implementation', *Bulletin of the British Psychological Society*, 29: 257–68.

Ward, T., Vertue, F.M. and Haig, B.D. (1999) 'Abductive method and clinical assessment in practice', *Behaviour Change*, 16, 1: 49–63.

Wason, P. and Johnson Laird, P. (1972) *Psychology of Reasoning: Structure and Content*, Cambridge, MA: Harvard University Press.

Wasserman, J. and Kappel, S. (1985) *Morbidity and Mortality Weekly Report*, December 13, 1985, 34, 49: 738–41.

Watkins, B. and Bentovim, A. (1992) 'The sexual abuse of male children and adolescents: a review of current research', *Journal of Child Psychology and Psychiatry* 33, 1: 197–248.

Watson, S. and Winter, D.A. (2000) 'What works for whom but shouldn't and what doesn't work for whom but should?', *European Journal of Psychotherapy, Counselling and Health*, 3, 2: 245–61.

Wehner, L., Csikszentmihalyi, M. and Magyari-Beck, I. (1991) 'Current approaches used in studying creativity: an exploratory investigation', *Creativity Research Journal*, 4, 3: 261–71.

Wellcome Trust (2001) *Booklet on Sciart: Guidance Notes*, London: Wellcome Trust.

Westen, D., Novotny, C.M. and Thompson-Brenner, H. (2004) 'The empirical status of empirically supported psychotherapists: assumptions, findings and reporting in controlled clinical trials', *Psychological Bulletin*, 130: 631–63.

Wetchler, J.L. (1990) 'Solution-focused supervision', *Family Therapy*, 17, 2: 129–38.

Wheatley, M. (1999) *Leadership and the New Science. Discovering Order in a Chaotic World*, San Francisco, CA: Berrett-Koehler Publishers.

Wheldall, K. (1987) *The Behaviourist in the Classroom*, London: Allen & Unwin.

White, M. (1993) 'Deconstruction and therapy', in S.G.E. Gilligan and R.E. Price (eds) *Therapeutic Conversations*, New York: Norton.

Whitley, R. (2002) 'Competition and pluralism in the public sciences: the impact of institutional frameworks on the organisation of academic science', *Research Policy* 32, 6: 1015–29.

Whitmore, J. (1992) *Coaching for Performance*, London: Brealey.

Wilkinson, J.D. (2004) Personal communication, December 19, 2004.

Williams, D.I. and Irving, J.A. (1996) 'Counselling psychology: a conflation of paradigms', *Counselling Psychology Review*, 11, 2: 4–6.

Williams, H. and Muncey, J. (1982) 'Precision teaching before behavioural objectives', *Journal of the Association of Educational Psychologists*, 5, 8: 40–2.

Williams, J.L. (1995) 'What makes a profession a profession?', *Professional Safety*, 43, 1: 18.

Williams, N. (1999) *The Work We Were Born to Do*, London: Element.

Wilson, G.T. (1978) 'Cognitive behaviour therapy: paradigm shift or passing phase', in J. Foreyt and D. Rathjen (eds) *Cognitive Behaviour Therapy*, New York: Plenum Press.

——(1996) 'Manual based treatments: the clinical application of research findings', *Behaviour Research and Therapy,* 34: 295–314.

Windsor, Behaviour Support Group (1997) *Windsor Behaviour Support Group; Essential Components of Behaviour Support,* Professional Development Foundation, Submitted to the Consultation on National Standards for SEN Specialist Teachers, Teacher Training Agency, December, 1998.

Winter, B.C. (1997) *Buying Occupational Psychology: Implications for Marketing Consultancy Services,* BPS Occupational Psychology Conference: Warwick, UK: January 1997.

Winter, D.A. and Watson, S. (1999) 'Personal construct psychotherapy and the cognitive therapies: different in theory but can they be differentiated in practice?', *Journal of Constructivist Psychology,* **12**, 1: 1–22.

Witherspoon, R. and White, R. P. (1996) 'Executive coaching: a continuum of roles', *Consulting Psychology Journal: Practice and Research,* **48**, 2: 124–33.

Witteman, C.L.M. and Kunst, H. (1999) 'Select Care: in aid of psychotherapists' treatment decisions', *Computers in Human Behaviour,* **15**, 2: 143–59.

Wollersheim, J.P. (1985) 'The name and the game – let's keep them both!', *Professional Psychology: Research and Practice,* **16**: 167–71.

Woolfe, R. and Dryden, W. (1996) *Handbook of Counselling Psychology,* London: Sage.

Woolfson, L., Whaling, R., Stewart, A. and Monsen, J. (2003) 'An integrated framework to guide educational psychology practice', *Educational Psychology in Practice,* **19**, 4: 283–302.

Wyld, B. (2001) 'Expert push', *Sydney Morning Herald,* August 4, 2001: 4.

Yalom (1975) *The Delivery and Practice of Group Psychotherapy,* 4th edn, New York: Basic Books, Perseus Book Group.

Young, J.E. (1990/1994) *Cognitive Therapy for Personality Disorders: a Schema Focused Approach,* Sarasota, FL: Professional Resource Exchange.

Zachar, P. and Leong, F. (2000) 'A 10-year longitudinal study of scientist and practitioner interests in psychology: assessing the Boulder Model', *Professional Psychology: Research and Practice,* **31**, 575–80.

Zander, R.S. and Zander, B. (2000) *The Art of Possibility: Transforming Professional and Personal Life,* Boston, MA: Harvard Business School Press.

Zani, B. (1987) 'The psychiatric nurse: a social psychological study of a profession facing institutional changes', *Social Behaviour,* **2**: 87–98.

Author index

Subject index

self 126, 127
self-awareness 191, 192, 193
self-help 67
self-organizing systems 85, 86, 174, 178, 180, 181
service planning initiatives 2
sexual abuse 34, 130–45, 206
sexual experimentation 130, 131
Sexually Appropriate Youngsters (SAY) project 132–3, 135, 138, 139
simulations 37–8
situated action 58
Six Hats method 182–3
skills 2–3, 60, 100, 177, 205; applied psychology 17; coaching 147–8, 150, 155–6; continuing professional development 190; counselling psychology 124, 127; creativity 57, 65, 68, 181; design approach 174; employability 195; formulation 42; learning review 193; practice-based 15; thinking 173, 177–8, 183, 184, 185, 207; young sex offenders 144; see also reasoning skills
social capital 188
social care perspective 136–7
social constructionism 80–3, 93; counselling psychology 121; educational psychology 113, 114; occupational psychology 162, 163, 169
social context: counselling psychology 120; critical realism 121; encounter with client 95; professional identity 91–4
social learning theory 114
social psychology 38, 162
Social Services 133, 134, 139
Soft Systems Methodology (SSM) 112–13, 117, 118
solution-focused brief therapy 115, 150, 151–2, 153
special educational needs 67, 103, 112
spirituality 57, 60
SSM see Soft Systems Methodology
stakeholder value 198
standardization 29, 30, 73, 120; see also manualized approaches
state licensing 92, 93
stigma 145
supervision 121, 142, 192–3
symbolic interactionism 51
systemic family therapy 112, 136
Systems Analysis 112
systems approaches: complexity theory

154–5; continuing professional development 190–1; educational psychology 111–13, 114, 117; shared decision-making 47

Tavistock Institute 112
technical rationality 97
technology 113
theory 47, 51, 72, 74, 126
therapeutic relationship 121, 123, 124, 135, 193
therapy: brief solution-focused 115, 150, 151–2, 153; decision-making 28; Eysenck 13, 14; navigation analogy 59; outcome research 17–18; postmodernist perspective 153; social constructionism 83; supervision 192–3; see also counselling psychology; psychotherapy
thinking 177–8, 184–5, 207; analytical modes of 32; convergent 59, 60; critical 124, 178, 182; divergent 59, 62, 75; lateral 181; parallel 33, 173, 182–3, 184, 194; see also reasoning skills
trade press 167
training: clinical psychology 12, 15, 16; coaching psychology 149, 156; creativity 66; decision-making skills 25, 27, 40; developmental stages of 98–9; educational psychologists 103, 117; formulation 42; modes of knowledge 96
transdisciplinary knowledge 96, 97, 199
transparency 29, 39
truth 88, 124, 153; empiricism 72, 74, 87; Plato 175; social constructionism 80

uncertainty 86, 163, 168
universities 199
unpredictability 155, 156
utility analysis 166

Vail conference (1973) 15, 149
validity 32, 33, 72, 117, 123, 127, 166
value, adding 196, 197
VARK model 63
Veterans Administration 12
violence 132
Voltaire 23

Wellcome Trust 61
women 126, 127

YOT see Youth Offending Team
young sex offenders 130–45, 206
Youth Offending Team (YOT) 132–3, 137, 138